Harmony and
Voice Leading

HARPERCOLLINS COLLEGE OUTLINE

Harmony and Voice Leading

Edgar W. Williams, Jr., Ph.D.
The College of William and Mary

HarperPerennial
A Division of HarperCollins*Publishers*

For Mom

An American BookWorks Corporation Production
Project Manager: Judith A. V. Harlan
Editor: Robert A. Weinstein

Library of Congress Catalog Card Number: 91-58280
ISBN: 0-06-467148-8

92 93 94 95 96 ABW/RRD 10 9 8 7 6 5 4 3 2 1

Contents

Preface

I have sought to make a useful text—one that explains how tonal music is possible, *not* how to formulate a theory for it. I have sought to write a text that is both complete and concise. As a result, this text is thrifty in its prose and profligate in its musical examples; it is concrete in its presentation but general in its scope. Modern harmony texts often do not agree on generalities, and seldom on particulars. I have sought to find points of general agreement and make them particular. This text, then, is not so much a summary of tonal theory (a field too diffuse and varied for summary) as it is a concise presentation of what I take to be tonal harmony's essential concepts and techniques.

It will supplement most modern tonal harmony texts (each chapter is cross-referenced to the major harmony texts) and most first courses in tonal harmony. It should provide an ideal review tool as well, providing the more experienced student an inexpensive, single, and complete source for basic information. At the same time, it should serve as a self-study tool.

All this I intended. Any success achieved will be due in large part to those who made this project possible.

ACKNOWLEDGMENTS

Thanks are hardly enough for Judith A. V. Harlan. Her expert technical advice, encouragement, and—above all—patience guided me throughout this project. I thank my copy editor, Barbara Curialle Gerr, and my reader,

Robert A. Weinstein, as well. Both contributed invaluable suggestions and cogent criticisms.

Everything of musical value in this text arose from making music— often on my own, but just as often with students or colleagues or under the guidance of teachers. There have been several teachers, many colleagues, and uncounted students over the years. Many offered more than I was capable of receiving; none can be held responsible for what follows. Still, I thank them all: in particular, my teachers Paul Earls and Iain Hamilton (Duke University), Jacques Monod (Columbia University), and Jim Randall (Princeton University); and my colleagues and former colleagues Jeff Hall, Conrad Pope, Steve Mackey, Richard Swift, and Charles Wolterink. Conversations with composer-conductor Joel Suben have influenced many aspects of this text; for that, and other things besides, I am grateful. But most of all I thank Edgar Warren Williams (Senior)—"Jack" Williams, teacher, colleague, friend, and father. He gave me my first music lessons, trying to teach me not only where my fingers went and why, but where the music *really* lay. This book (for all its faults) is for Jack.

The contributions of my wife, pianist Christine Anderson Williams, are on every page of this text. Her critical readings have made this text both more useful and more readable. She, along with our children, Joel and Ann, have not only helped make this book possible but a joy for me to write. All three know not only where the music really lies, but how to get there— even when Dad seems to have forgotten. Thanks to you all.

Introduction

THE SUBJECT

This is a text on tonal harmony and voice leading. Although it deals with the music of dead composers, it treats the music as a living language. Is it alive? Is it a language? Scholars disagree. These issues, although important, are beyond the modest scope of this text. For us, here, tonality is alive, vital, and an eloquent musical language.

A Very Brief History of Western Tonality

Tonality (or the "tonal system," or "functional tonality"—all names for the same thing) arose in seventeenth-century Europe, in a distillation of the diffuse styles and techniques that characterized European composition in the fifteenth and sixteenth centuries. By the beginning of the eighteenth century and throughout the nineteenth (the so-called common-practice period), tonality became a Western style. By the end of the nineteenth century, the language had begun to fall apart under the weight of its own devices. Now, at the end of the twentieth century, common-practice tonality—to the extent that it survives at all—is the provenance of some jazz, folk, and popular music styles.

A Tonal Theory

Since the eighteenth century, many musicians have sought to explain tonality, to give it a theoretical grounding. They succeeded in giving tonality *many* theoretical groundings, each incomplete.

Today, music theory is a separate field of study, a large and active one. Most modern texts on tonal theory are not written by composers (or, for that matter, active musicians), but by scholars—music theorists. As a result, these texts aim not so much to teach the student how to write tonal music (or how it was written) as how to understand it. There are as many ways to understand—that is, theories of—tonal music as there are theorists (or alternatively, as there are pieces of tonal music to describe). Still, we can generalize. At one extreme of the music theory spectrum are the chord grammarians; at the other the adherents of the theories of Heinrich Schenker (German music theorist and sometime composer, 1868–1935). The former concentrate on chords, and the ways in which chords may be strung together. The latter concentrate on linear structure, on how the particular expresses the general.

This text borrows freely from both ends of this spectrum, for each has something to offer. It assumes that (a) tonality is too rich and complex to yield to a single explanation and that (b) understanding (not the sort that leads to theory texts, but that leads to enhanced enjoyment and continued enrichment of musical experience) must come from several perspectives—sometimes entertained simultaneously.

This text provides little theory, only some ways in which we might understand the goings-on in tonal works, some ways in which we might go about making some simple tonal music, and some ways in which the techniques of tonal music make possible that rich experience which we associate with the tonal repertoire.

Why Tonal Theory?

Why study tonal theory in the first place? The simplest answer: to learn one way in which we might organize the materials of music. Is tonality the *only* way? Certainly not. There are many others, before and since, East and West. Is tonality the *best* way? That would depend on your goal. So why *this* way? Because it is a tried and true way, a way that has delivered the musical goods—bountifully, for at least three, maybe four, centuries. And what goods they are, whether they come by way of Johann Sebastian Bach or Thelonious Monk.

THE TEXT

This text begins at the beginning—with notation and the nature of sound. From there, it fans out, attempting to touch on as many of the techniques and concepts of common-practice tonality as space (and my ability) allows.

As a Course Supplement

If you are coming to tonal harmony for the first time—either using this text as a supplement to a course or studying it on your own—I recommend that you purchase a copy of Bach's 371 Chorales. (See "Bach's 371 Chorales," page xi, for suggested editions.) Follow up on each excerpt given in the examples. Check the context of each: How is the excerpted progression or technique set up? Where is it going? Use the index to find different harmonizations of the same chorale tune. Does Bach handle the excerpted passage the same way every time? Why? Why not?

By the time you reach the discussion of Mozart's piano sonatas, you may want to buy a copy of those as well. (See "Mozart Piano Sonatas," page xiii.) This may not be necessary, however, since the Mozart examples are longer and, in general, more complete than those from the Bach Chorales.

For Review

If you are using this text to review the subject, I urge you to read the entire text in sequence. Each chapter relies on ideas developed in the previous ones. Despite the large number of examples, the text itself is relatively short. What you lose by having to review familiar material will be repaid with a deeper understanding of its connection to the unfamiliar.

The Examples

With only a few exceptions, I have drawn the examples for this book from two sources: the chorales of Bach and the piano sonatas of Mozart. Both sources are rich and easily available through libraries or music stores. When the text is included in the figure, the translation accompanies it.

THE BACH CHORALES

Traditionally, the student begins a study of tonal harmony with the Bach chorales. I hold to tradition here for two reasons. First, the Bach chorales are compositions—in some cases, quite extraordinary ones. They are not models for students, but the complete expressions of a highly developed, if circumscribed, art. They force the student to deal with larger compositional issues immediately. Second, the severe constraints of chorale style allow the student to focus on specific and well-defined voice-leading techniques. Chorale style allows both student and teacher to put off other issues (such as motivic structure, instrumental textures, and the thematic forms).

History. Chorales are four-voice settings of simple, sometimes folk-like religious hymns called *chorale tunes*. The Reformation of the Catholic church in seventeenth-century Germany sought a simpler, more direct liturgy. Congregational group singing formed a major part of this reformed liturgy. Composers wrote new melodies and adapted old ones to new texts, providing a large repertoire of simple, attractive chorale tunes for this group singing.

Bach's 371 Chorales. Having spent most of his life in the service of the Lutheran church, Johann Sebastian Bach (1685–1750) left hundreds of four-voice settings of chorale tunes. In the nineteenth century, scholars collected many of these in the so-called 371 Chorales. To this collection was added a smaller collection of 69 *figured chorales*— chorale tunes set with a blocked-out accompaniment consisting of bass and figures but no written-out inner voices. (Many of these figured chorales, however, can only be attributed to J. S. Bach.)

The Numbering. The original numbering of the 371 Chorales is the standard today, and the one followed in this text. Albert Riemenschneider's *371 Harmonized Chorales and 69 Chorale Melodies with Figured Bass* (New York: G. Schirmer, 1941) is still the least expensive and most complete collection of the Bach chorales in print. Donald Martino's *178 Chorale Harmonizations of Joh. Seb. Bach* (Newton, MA: Dantalian, 1984) is incomplete but provides a more useful arrangement, grouping different harmonizations of the same tune together and placing all in the same key. However, many of the chorales used in this text are not present in the Martino edition. I recommend, therefore, that you use the Riemenschneider (or another edition of the complete 371 Chorales) to supplement this text.

The Chorale Excerpts in This Text. Limitations of space make it necessary for me to present chorale excerpts (rather than complete chorales) as examples. This has several disadvantages. First, although a measure or two of a chorale might serve to illustrate a particular point, it does not place that point in a larger context. This text attempts to get around this limitation by dealing first with specific voice-leading concerns (as illustrated by chorale excerpts), and then with general context, referring to other examples from different contexts. In spite of their disadvantages, excerpts provide the maximum number of contexts and variations of the various voice-leading techniques discussed within the space allowed.

On occasion, the use of excerpts produces some notational anomalies. Bach's chorale settings are, after all, compositions—which is to say, a Bach chorale is more than a sum of its parts. Excerpts that illustrate one point often arise in the middle of more complex musical motions. This cannot be helped. So rather than leave, say, a dangling nonharmonic note in the last harmony of an excerpt, I leave off with the last note *that makes sense within the context of the excerpt*. As a result, one voice or another may be missing the final half of the duration of its final note. Don't let that bother you. (If it does, look up the complete chorale in your 371 Chorales.)

The key signature given for each excerpt is Bach's. In minor keys, however, Bach's key signatures do not always follow modern convention. Even in major keys, when the excerpt comes from the middle of a chorale setting, the key of the *excerpt* does not always match the key signature. The analysis of each excerpt will always tell you the key.

The Texts. The texts of the chorales are not included in the examples. Text setting, word painting, and related issues are at the heart of the Bach chorales but, unfortunately, beyond the scope of this book. We will discuss the text only when Bach's voice-leading choices seem to be derived directly *from* the text. (This is a common occurrence in the 371 Chorales, but rare in the examples included here.)

THE MOZART PIANO SONATAS

I have drawn most of the excerpts not in chorale style from Mozart's Piano Sonatas. Where I do not specify measure numbers, the excerpt comes from the beginning of the indicated movement. There are two inexpensive and easily obtainable editions of the Mozart sonatas: *Sonatas and Fantasies for the Piano* (Mineola, NY: Dover Publications, Inc.) and *Sonatas and Three Fantasias* in the Kalmus Piano Series (Melville, NY: Belwin Mills). The Dover edition is a modern edition, slightly more accurate than the Kalmus. Each is inexpensive and easily ordered from any bookstore.

Selected Readings

Bamberger, Jeanne Shapiro, and Howard Brofsky. *The Art of Listening: Developing Music Perception*. 5th ed. New York: Harper & Row, 1988. Chapter 1.

Christ, William, et al. *Materials and Structure of Music*. 3d ed. Vol. I. Englewood Cliffs, NJ: Prentice-Hall, 1980. Chapter 1, Introduction.

Kostka, Stefan, and Dorothy Payne. *Tonal Harmony*. 2d ed. New York: Alfred A. Knopf, 1989. "To the Student."

Salzer, Felix. *Structural Hearing*. New York: Dover, 1962. Chapter 1.

Schoenberg, Arnold. *Structural Functions of Harmony*. Rev. ed. Leonard Stein, editor. New York: Norton, 1969. Chapters I–II.

Westergaard, Peter. *An Introduction to Tonal Theory*. New York: Norton, 1975. Chapter 1.

1

Sound and Its Notation

Music is, by a common definition, organized sound. Music notation records this organization. However, sound has many aspects—too many for us to record easily in a written notation. As a result, musical notations record only those aspects of the sound most rigidly organized by the composer, or those of most interest to the performer.

SOUND

The mechanical vibration of any physical body creates slight changes in atmospheric pressure. The delicate workings of the ear detect these changes and create the auditory sensation we call *sound*. Traditionally, in the West, we distinguish among and notate three parts of a sound: *pitch, duration,* and *timbre.*

Pitch

We call the auditory sensation of relative highness or lowness *pitch.* (Frequently, a musical sound is referred to as a "note" or "tone." However, *pitch* is the correct term and the term that we will use in this book.) A violin string vibrating at 440 cycles per second creates the sensation of a particular pitch. We call the rate of vibration of a sound its *frequency.* The sensation of pitch is directly related to a sound's frequency. The sensation of highness corresponds to higher frequencies. The sensation of lowness corresponds to lower frequencies. Thus, a violin string vibrating at 880 cycles per second sounds higher than one vibrating at 440 cycles per second.

Duration

Any musical sound has a definite duration—a beginning and an end. A duration can be relative (longer than or shorter than), or it can be absolute. When we say that one duration is exactly twice as long as another, we describe an absolute duration. The durations that concern us here are absolute durations.

A succession of durations, whether relative or absolute, creates a *rhythm* (see chapter 4).

Timbre

Even though sounds produced by an electric guitar and a flute might have the same pitch and the same duration, we can easily tell one from the other. We call that quality of sound that distinguishes one instrument from another its *timbre* or tone color. Timbral differences result from complex acoustical phenomena that are beyond the scope of this text.

NOTATION

The most important element of Western musical notation is the *note*. A note is the written symbol that represents a sound. A note may have three parts. The body of a note is a small ellipse, either hollow or filled in, called the *note head*. We call the vertical line that either ascends or descends from the note head the *stem*. Often, a *flag* is attached to the stem.

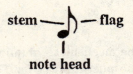

Figure 1.1   The Note

Pitch Notation

The placement of the note head on the staff depicts relative pitch.

THE STAFF

To show relative pitch (that is, relative highness or lowness), we place note heads on a fixed series of five horizontal lines called the *staff* or, rarely, a *stave* (pl. *staves*). We can place a note head on a line or in between two lines—that is, in a space.

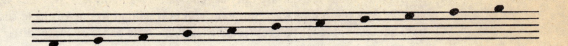

Figure 1.2   The Staff

Intervals. The distance between two note heads is an *interval*. Two note heads written on an adjacent line and space are *adjacent*; two note heads separated by one or more lines or spaces are *nonadjacent*. The interval between *adjacent* note heads is a *step*. The interval between *nonadjacent* note heads is a *skip*.

steps

skips

Figure 1.3   Steps and Skips

Ledger Lines. We can extend the staff indefinitely in either direction. To write a note above the space on top of the staff or below the space at the bottom of the staff, we use *ledger lines* (sometimes spelled *leger* lines). We can add as many ledger lines as we need.

Figure 1.4   Ledger Lines

Pitch Classes. Although the staff system allows us to notate an infinite number of pitches, there are only seven basic note names: *A, B, C, D, E, F,* and *G.* Any pitch that we can notate will correspond to one of these seven note names. Since we can represent each basic note name by many different pitches, we refer to these note names as *pitch-classes.* (See Appendix A for a table of English and foreign pitch and pitch class names.)

THE KEYBOARD

The arrangement of white and black *keys* on a piano or similar instrument is the *keyboard.* The white keys of the keyboard bear the seven note names mentioned above.

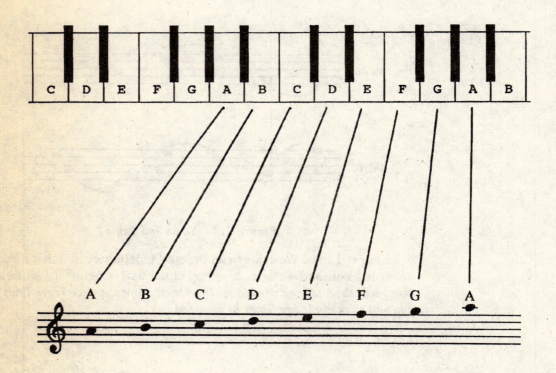

Figure 1.5   The Keyboard

The Octave. The interval between two successive members of the same pitch class (two A's, for example) is an *octave*. *Octave* means "eight," and two successive A's are eight white keys apart. Notice that adjacent white notes are notated as steps.

Half Steps and Whole Steps. Technicians tune the piano so that the twelve white and black keys within the octave—any octave—divide the octave into twelve equal parts.

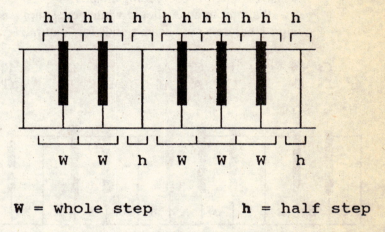

Figure 1.6   Half Steps and Whole Steps

Figure 1.6 shows that two different-sized steps separate adjacent white keys. The distance between any two adjoining keys—that is, any two keys, black or white, with no key between—is a *half step* (or semitone). The distance between any two keys separated by one other key (black or white) is a *whole step*. Sometimes both half steps and whole steps are referred to simply as *steps*.

The White Keys. Any seven successive white keys run through all seven letter names. *A* is the name of the class of white keys found between the two upper (that is, farthest right) members of the cluster of three black keys. Going to the right of A—that is, "upward" or to pitches of higher frequency—we come successively to B, C, D, E, F, and G. Then the cycle repeats itself with the next A, and so on.

The Black Keys. Note the arrangement of the black keys: two black keys, then three, then two again. Two intervening white keys separate each group of black keys from the next. This pattern repeats itself in each succeeding octave. Thus any key, black or white, has exactly the same position within the black-white pattern immediately surrounding it as does that key an octave above it or below it.

The black keys do not have simple letter names, but are considered altered versions of the white keys that they adjoin. Thus we can refer to the black key between A and B as either A♯ (pronounced "A-sharp") or B♭ (pronounced "B-flat"). The *sharp* raises the pitch by a half step. The *flat* lowers the pitch by a half step.

Context determines which of the two terms or *spellings* we use. In general, if the pitch pulls up toward B, we call it A-sharp. If it pulls down toward A, we call it B-flat. (We will consider the factors that provide this sense of "pull" in succeeding chapters.)

We refer to an unaltered white note simply as "A" or "A-natural." The sign ♮ before a note head, stands for "natural."

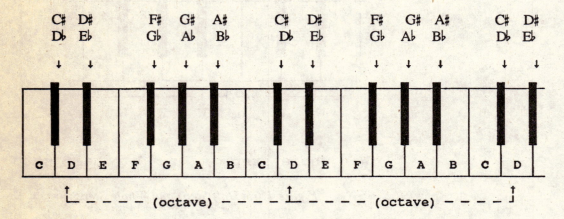

Figure 1.7   Pitch Classes

Enharmonic Equivalents. As we saw above, each black key has two different names. We can think of the black key between C and D, for instance, as C-sharp (C *raised* by a half step) or D-flat (D *lowered* by a half step).

* "E-natural"— that is, the unaltered white key

Figure 1.8   Enharmonic Equivalents

C-sharp and D-flat stand for the same pitch (that is, are produced by the same key on the keyboard). Any two notes that we spell differently but that stand for the same pitch are *enharmonically equivalent*.

CLEFS

To know which pitch class a note head on the staff represents, we must first order the staff. A *clef* (French for "key") placed at the left of each staff shows which pitches are represented by which lines and which spaces. There are three commonly used clefs: the *treble clef* (G clef), the *bass clef* (F clef), and the *C clef*.

Middle C. We call that C found in the middle of the piano keyboard (usually beneath the piano maker's name) middle C. Each clef orders the staff in relation to middle C.

The Treble Clef. The treble clef tells us that the second line from the bottom of the staff is the G above middle C (see Figure 1.9a). For this reason, we sometimes call it the "G clef." When we add this clef to a staff, we call the staff the *treble staff*. Traditionally, students learn the treble staff by remembering the sentence

Every Good Boy Does Fine.

The first letters of the words give the letter names of the *lines*, bottom to top, of the treble staff—E, G, B, D, F.

The Bass Clef. The bass clef tells us that the second line from the top of the staff (the line between the two dots) is the F below middle C (see Figure 1.9b). We sometimes call it the "F clef." When we add the bass clef to a staff we create a *bass staff*. The first letter of each word in the following sentence recalls the *spaces*, bottom to top, of the bass staff—A, C, E, G.

All Cows Eat Grass.

The C Clefs. The several C clefs simply tell us where middle C is. The *alto clef* places middle C at the center line (Figure 1.9c), and the *tenor* clef places middle C at the second line from the top (Figure 1.9d). Of these two surviving C clefs, the alto clef is the most common.

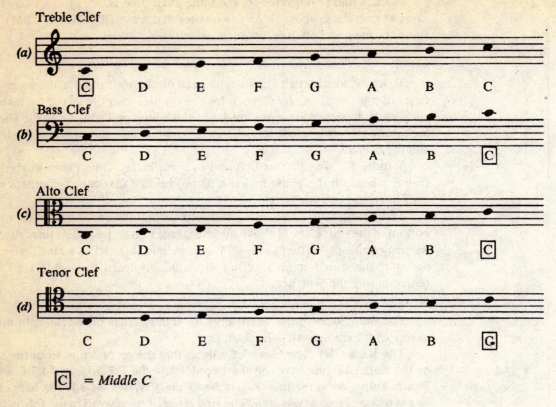

Figure 1.9   The Clefs

THE GRAND STAFF

Often we join the treble staff and bass staff with a brace. We write middle C on the treble staff as the note one ledger line *below* the staff. We write middle C on the bass staff as the note one ledger line *above* the staff. These joined staves are called the *grand staff*.

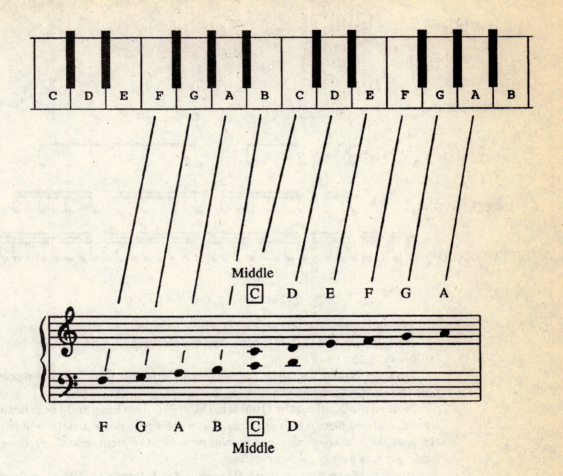

Figure 1.10 The Grand Staff

Rhythmic Notation

The type of note head (hollow or solid), along with the presence or absence of a stem with or without one or more flags, depicts relative duration.

THE NOTE TREE

The basic note value is the *whole note*. Each successively smaller note value is one half the duration of the previous one. Note names reflect this. A *half note* is one-half the duration of a whole note. A *quarter note* is one-half the duration of a half note, and so on.

Figure 1.11   The Note Tree

Whole Notes. The whole note is a hollow note head without a stem.

Half Notes. The half note (one-half the duration of a whole note) has a hollow note head and a stem.

Quarter Notes. The quarter note (one-quarter the duration of a whole note) has a solid note head and a stem.

Notes Smaller than the Quarter. The *eighth note* has a solid note head, a stem, and one *flag*. A *sixteenth note* has a solid note head, a stem, and two flags. A *thirty-second note* has a solid note head, a stem, and three flags. *Adding a flag halves the note value*.

Beams. When two or more flagged notes follow each other, we can replace the flags with *beams* that connect the stems. The number of beams, just like the number of flags, tells us the relative duration of the note (see Figure 1.11).

THE REST TREE

Each note value has a corresponding *rest*. The rest represents a pause or silence of the same duration as the equivalent note value.

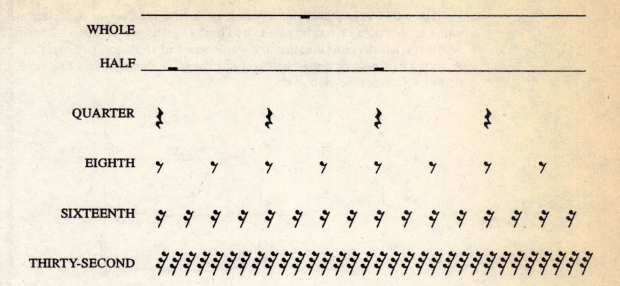

WHOLE				
HALF				
QUARTER				
EIGHTH				
SIXTEENTH				
THIRTY-SECOND				

Figure 1.12   The Rest Tree

Appendix B gives American and foreign note and rest names.

TIES

We can construct more complex durations by connecting two note heads with a curved line called a *tie*. When a tie connects the note heads of two separate durations, the two durations combine to form one duration.

Do not confuse a tie *with a slur or phrasing marking*. A tie connects two note heads *of the same pitch*.

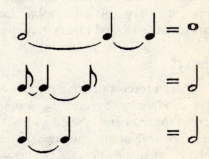

Figure 1.13   The Tie

DOTTED NOTES AND RESTS

The addition of a dot *after* any note head or rest increases the relative value of that note or rest by one-half. Thus, a dotted whole note or dotted whole rest has the same duration as a whole note and a half note tied together. A dotted half note or dotted half rest has the same duration as a half note tied to a quarter note, and so on.

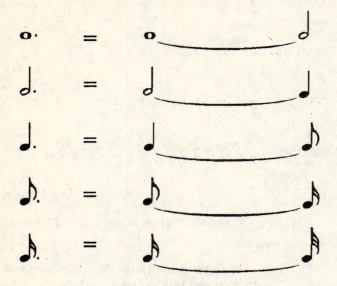

Figure 1.14   Dotted Notes and Rests

Do not confuse a dot *after* a note head, which increases that note's duration by one-half, with the dot *above* or *below* the note head, which represents a type of articulation mark called *staccato* (see "Articulation Marks," page 15; and Figure 1.16, page 14).

TUPLETS

We can force a division of note values into thirds, fifths, sixths, or any other subdivision by creating a *tuplet*. For example, three eighth notes beamed together and labeled with a *3* direct us to divide a quarter note into three (rather than the usual two) equal parts (Figure 1.15a). This particular tuplet is called a *triplet*. We can create tuplets of five subdivisions (quintuplets, Figure 1.15b), six subdivisions (sextuplets, Figure 1.15c), or any other number of subdivisions in the same way.

Figure 1.15   Tuplets

THE HORIZONTAL AND THE VERTICAL

Simultaneously sounding pitches are written one on top of the other, or vertically, on the staff. As a rule, we call two pitches sounding together an *interval*. However, when more than two pitches sound together we use the term *chord* or *sonority* (or, less frequently, *simultaneity*). When dealing with chords, or the *vertical* aspect of music, we are dealing with *harmony*.

Pitches that sound in succession are written one after the other from left to right, or horizontally, along the staff. We call such a succession a *melody* or *tune*—or, more abstractly, a *line* or *voice*. When dealing with melody, we are dealing with the *linear, melodic,* or *horizontal* aspect of music.

As we shall repeatedly discover, Western music binds the vertical and the horizontal tightly together. Although it is possible to concentrate on one or the other from time to time, we cannot meaningfully separate the two.

Timbral Notation

Traditionally, Western musicians notate (and seek to control) three aspects of timbre. First, we represent the sound source by providing each instrument its own staff. Second, we represent the relative loudness or softness of a sound using *dynamic marks*. Third, we control how individual notes are played with *articulation marks*.

THE SCORE

When the individual staves of music for different instruments are joined together by a *brace*, a *score* is created (see Figure 1.16).

Other determinants of timbre are notated less precisely.

Figure 1.16   Franz Liszt, A Faust Symphony; *first movement*

DYNAMICS

The relative loudness or softness of a sound is its *dynamic*. The words, letters, and symbols that depict relative dynamics are *dynamic marks*.

Basic Dynamic Marks. The Italian terms *piano* (soft, abbreviated *p*) and *forte* (strong or loud, abbreviated *f*) are the basic dynamic values. Most others derive from these two. For example, *pianissimo* (*pp*) means "very soft, softer than piano." *Fortissimo* (*ff*) means "very loud, louder than forte."

Other Dynamic Marks. *Crescendo* (abbreviated *cresc.*) tells us to get gradually louder. *Decrescendo* or *diminuendo* (abbreviated *decresc.* and *dim.*) tells us to get gradually softer. We represent a crescendo or decrescendo graphically with what is popularly called a *hairpin*:

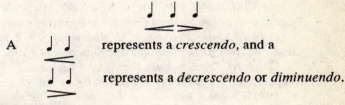

A   represents a *crescendo,* and a

    represents a *decrescendo* or *diminuendo.*

ARTICULATION

Articulation marks tell the performer how to begin a note, how to sustain it, and how to connect it to other notes. Articulation is suggested in three ways.

Articulation Marks. Articulation marks (for example,) affect the way in which the performer is to attack and sustain a note.

Phrasing Marks. A dependent division of a melody is called a *phrase*. It is like a clause in prose. Phrasing marks demarcate these divisions and instruct the performer how to connect one note to another.

Descriptive words. Finally, composers use descriptive words—such as *legato* (smoothly connected), *espressivo* (expressively), or *tenuto* (held, sustained)—to suggest a general manner of articulation and performance.

Figure 1.16 uses and explicates many of these symbols. Appendix C provides definitions of common articulation marks.

A musical sound has three qualities: pitch, duration, and timbre. Western musical notation precisely records all three. The primary symbol is the note. A note can have three parts: a note head, a stem, and a flag.

The placement of the note head on a five-line staff depicts relative pitch. The clef orders the staff, allowing a note to specify a particular pitch. We join the treble staff and bass staff to form the grand staff.

The type of note head (hollow or filled in) and the presence or absence of a stem, flag or flags represent the relative duration of a note.

We accord every instrument its own staff. Articulation marks tell us how to begin, sustain, and connect notes to one another.

Selected Readings

Bamberger, Jeanne Shapiro, and Howard Brofsky. *The Art of Listening: Developing Music Perception*. 5th ed. New York: Harper & Row, 1988. Chapter 1.

Benjamin, Thomas, Michael Horvit, and Robert Nelson. *Techniques and Materials of Tonal Music*. Belmont, CA: Wadsworth, 1992. Part I, section 1.

Christ, William, et al. *Materials and Structure of Music*. 3d ed. Vol. I. Englewood Cliffs, NJ: Prentice-Hall, Inc. 1980. Chapter 1.

Cooper, Paul. *Perspectives in Music Theory*. 2d ed. New York: Harper & Row, 1981. Chapters 1–2.

Kostka, Stefan, and Dorothy Payne. *Tonal Harmony*. 2d ed. New York: Alfred A. Knopf, 1989. Chapter 1.

Mitchell, William J. *Elementary Harmony*. 2d ed. Englewood Cliffs, NJ: Prentice-Hall, 1948. Chapter 1.

Ottman, Robert W. *Elementary Harmony*. 4th ed. Englewood Cliffs, NJ: Prentice-Hall, 1989. Chapter 1.

Piston, Walter. *Harmony*. 5th ed. Revised and expanded by Mark DeVoto. New York: Norton, 1987. Chapter 1.

Westergaard, Peter. *An Introduction to Tonal Theory*. New York: Norton, 1975. Chapters 1–2.

2

Intervals

As we saw in chapter 1, music has both vertical and horizontal dimensions. It consists of both pitches sounded simultaneously (harmony) and pitches sounded in series (melody). The intervals that separate pitches (harmonically or melodically) provide those pitches with either a sense of stability or instability.

The study of harmony is the study of these two states and of the imaginative and dramatic control of the relationship between them. We begin that study by identifying and classifying the different aspects of each.

MEASUREMENT OF INTERVALS

An *interval* is the distance between two notes. We calculate that distance by counting the lines and spaces that separate the two notes on the staff. Alternatively, we can calculate the distance by counting the number of half steps that separate the notes on the keyboard. The former measurement of an interval is its *ordinal* or *diatonic size*. The latter measurement is its *absolute size*. The absolute size of an interval determines that interval's *quality*. We refer to an interval by both its diatonic name and its quality.

The Ordinal or Diatonic Size

We determine the ordinal size of an interval by counting, *inclusively*, the number of lines and spaces that separate the two notes involved. This, in effect, measures the number of white keys that make up the interval.

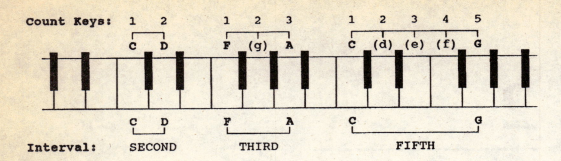

Figure 2.1   *Diatonic Intervals*

The white keys of the piano form what we call a *diatonic collection*. Thus, we frequently call the ordinal size of an interval its *diatonic size*. (The diatonic collection is discussed in detail in chapter 3 and Appendix K.)

The Absolute Size

We measure the absolute size of an interval by counting the number of half steps between the bottom and top notes.

> *Remember:* When you calculate the absolute size of an interval, count the distances *between* successive piano keys, not the keys themselves.

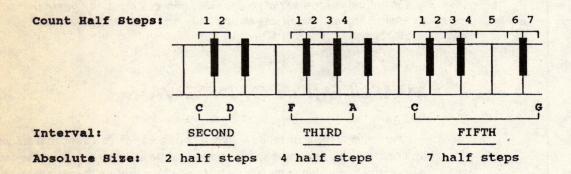

Figure 2.2   *Absolute Intervals*

Remember that the absolute size of an interval determines that interval's *quality*.

THE DIATONIC QUALITIES

Within a diatonic collection (the white keys of the piano, for instance), each diatonic interval smaller than an octave comes in two (absolute) sizes. For instance, of the seven thirds found between white keys, three are large (four half steps) and four are small (three half steps).

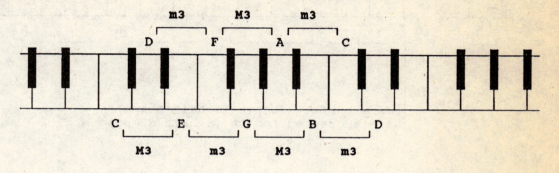

```
M3 = major third (4 half steps)
m3 = minor third (3 half steps)
```

Figure 2.3 Diatonic Thirds

The larger thirds are called *major* thirds. The smaller thirds are called *minor* thirds.

With one exception, diatonic fourths (and fifths) come in a single size—five half steps (fourths) and seven half steps (fifths). These are called *perfect* fourths and fifths.

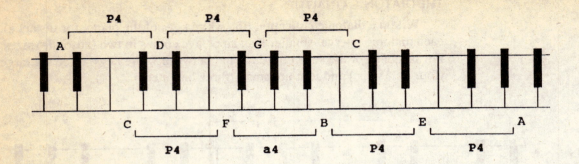

P4 = perfect fourth (5 half steps)
a4 = augmented fourth (6 half steps)

Figure 2.4   Diatonic Fourths

A diatonic interval can be of a type that is major or minor *or* of a type that is perfect. It cannot be of both types.

THE CHROMATIC QUALITIES

One diatonic fourth (F–B) and one diatonic fifth (B–F) are *not* perfect. Six half steps span the fourth F–B, but a perfect fourth is only five half steps. A fourth that is one half step larger than a perfect fourth is an *augmented* fourth.

The fifth B–F spans six half steps as well, but a perfect *fifth* is seven half steps. This B–F fifth, then, is a half step *smaller* than perfect. Such a fifth is called a *diminished fifth*. The interval of six half steps (however it is called) is a *tritone*.

Diminished Intervals. If the absolute size of a diatonic interval is one half step *less* than the minor or perfect interval of that diatonic type, we call it diminished. If it is *two* half steps less, we call it *doubly diminished*.

Augmented Intervals. If the absolute size of a diatonic interval is one half step *more* than a major or perfect interval of that diatonic type, we call it augmented. If it is *two* half steps more, we call it *doubly augmented*.

Appendix E catalogues interval names, qualities, and sizes.

SIMPLE AND COMPOUND INTERVALS

Intervals of an octave or less are *simple intervals*. Intervals that exceed the octave are *compound intervals*. A compound second (that is, the interval of an octave plus a second) is a *ninth*. A compound *minor* second is a *minor ninth*, a compound *major* second is a *major ninth*, and so on.

Inverting Intervals

To *invert* an interval we take the lower pitch of the interval and make it the higher one. Alternatively, we can take the higher pitch of the interval and make it the lower one. To invert an interval, follow these steps *in this order*.

First, find the *inverted diatonic name* by subtracting the original interval's diatonic size from nine. Second, find the *inverted quality* by converting the original quality as follows:

A minor interval inverts into a major interval (and vice versa).

A perfect interval inverts into another perfect interval.

A diminished interval inverts into an augmented interval (and vice versa).

Third, find the *inverted absolute size* by subtracting the absolute size of the original interval from twelve.

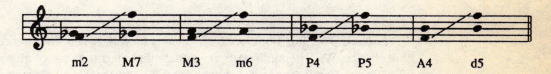

Figure 2.5   Interval Inversion

Remember: You must first find the diatonic size of the inverted interval. For example, a third *always* inverts into some kind of sixth, no matter what the absolute size.

Appendix F illustrates these inversional relationships.

The Acoustic Foundations of Consonance and Dissonance

When we hear a note played by some instrument, we hear not only that primary pitch, or *fundamental*, but a series of other pitches as well. We call these subsidiary pitches *overtones*. Their frequencies are whole-number multiples of the fundamental frequency. (That is, the first overtone is twice the frequency of the fundamental, the second is three times that of the fundamental, and so on.) As the overtones ascend above the fundamental, the interval between successive overtones gets smaller as the ratio between their frequencies becomes more complex.

Informally, musicians sometimes call overtones *harmonics* or *partials*. This is not quite right. When these terms are used properly, the first overtone refers to the *second* harmonic or partial. That is, the first harmonic is the fundamental itself (see Figure 2.6).

Figure 2.6   The Fundamental and Its Overtones

The fundamental and the first five overtones above it form what is sometimes called the *chord of nature*. In what sense this object is "natural" is open to question. However, we do find in it the prototype for each of the traditionally consonant intervals.

CONSONANCE AND DISSONANCE

In large part, this book concerns the relation between dissonance and consonance. We will continually reevaluate these terms as we go along. For now, think of consonance as a state of stability and rest, and dissonance as a state of instability or motion. Disregard the colloquial usage that associates consonance with acoustic pleasure and dissonance with acoustic pain.

Consonance

We call *consonant* all perfect intervals, as well as all major and minor intervals *that do not contain adjacent pitch classes*. Of the consonant intervals, we call those with the least complex interval ratios *perfect* consonances. We call the remainder *imperfect* consonances. (Later, we will discuss in what sense one consonance is more "perfect" than another.)

THE PERFECT CONSONANCES

The perfect unison, the perfect fourth, the perfect fifth, and the perfect octave are all perfect intervals. They are also perfect consonances.

THE IMPERFECT CONSONANCES

Major and minor thirds and sixths are imperfect consonances. (Major and minor seconds and sevenths, since they contain adjacent pitch classes, are not consonant at all, but dissonant.)

THE TRIAD

If you combine any three pitch classes so that none is a step from another, you have created a *triad. A triad contains no adjacent pitch classes.*

Origin. Many theorists derive the triad from the "chord of nature." Many others question the adequacy and others the accuracy of this derivation.

Structure. The triad consists of three pitch classes: the *root, third*, and *fifth*. The *root* of a triad is that pitch class standing respectively a third and a fifth below the other two pitch classes of the triad. The *third* of a triad is that pitch class standing a third above the root of the triad. The *fifth* of a triad is that pitch class standing a fifth above the root of the triad.

Thus, with the root at the bottom of a triad, the other two pitch classes stand a third and a fifth above that root. The kinds of thirds and fifths that make up the triad determine the *quality* of the triad.

Qualities. A triad can be either *major, minor, diminished,* or *augmented.* A *major triad* has a *major third* between the root and third and a perfect fifth between root and fifth. A *minor triad* has a *minor* third between the root and the third. A perfect fifth spans the distance from root to fifth.

A *diminished triad* has a minor third between the root and third and a *diminished* fifth between root and fifth. An *augmented triad* has a major third between the root and third. An *augmented* fifth spans the distance between root and fifth.

Figure 2.7   The Four Triad Types

Appendix G provides a graphic synopsis of triad structure.

DISSONANCE AND CONSONANCE

Major and minor triads are consonant since they contain only consonant intervals. Diminished and augmented triads, however, contain fifths that are not consonant (that is, not perfect). Accordingly, augmented and diminished triads are dissonant.

Dissonance

All sevenths and diminished and augmented intervals are considered *dissonant*. Whether we play the pitches of a seventh or an augmented or diminished interval simultaneously (harmonically) or successively (melodically), they remain unstable.

Major and minor seconds are, however, more ambiguous. If we express their pitches harmonically, they are dissonant; but if we express them melodically they are consonant.

HARMONIC AND LINEAR DISSONANCE

Because triads contain only nonadjacent pitch classes, the distance between any two notes of a triad is always some kind of skip. Melodies, however, move mainly by step between adjacent pitch classes. Thus, in a harmonic context, major and minor seconds behave as dissonances. In a melodic context, they behave as consonances.

ENHARMONIC EQUIVALENCE

Two intervals of the same absolute size but of two *different* diatonic sizes are *enharmonically equivalent*.

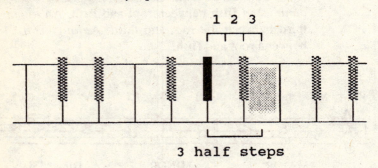

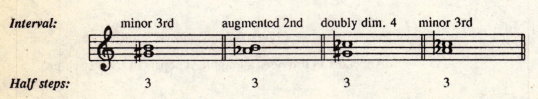

Figure 2.8   Enharmonically Equivalent Intervals

G-sharp–B spans a minor third, an interval of three half steps. Although A-flat–B spans an augmented second, the absolute size is the same three half steps. The distinction is not trivial, however. By the definitions given above, that third is an imperfect consonance and the augmented second is a dissonance, *even though each is the same absolute size.*

DISSONANCE RELATED TO THE TRIAD

Major and minor triads contain only consonant intervals. A major or minor triad contains no dissonant intervals—that is, no augmented or diminished intervals and no adjacent pitch classes (seconds or sevenths). We can define harmonic "dissonance" circularly, then, as *any interval not present in either a major or a minor triad.*

DISSONANCE COMPELLED TO MOTION

Major and minor triads shape and control the harmonic or vertical aspect of music. These triads are consonant—that is, stable. What characterizes the music we love, however, is a sense of motion, of dramatic arrivals and departures. Dissonance provides this sense of motion and drama.

THE PASSING NATURE OF DISSONANCE

Consonance is both a point of departure and a goal. Dissonance is neither; it is unstable. Dissonance takes us from one place (consonance) to another. In fact, "good" harmony is nothing more (or less) than the imaginative and dramatic use of dissonance.

*I*ntervals *have both a diatonic name and a quality. To identify an interval fully, we need both designations. We can invert an interval by placing the bottom pitch on top or the top pitch on the bottom. Intervals are either consonant or dissonant. Acoustics suggests an origin for the consonant intervals.*

Three pitch classes chosen so that none is adjacent to another make up a triad. We call the pitch classes of a triad the root, the third, and the fifth. We consider those triads with perfect fifths consonant and all others dissonant.

Any interval not contained in a consonant triad is a harmonic dissonance. Major and minor seconds, though harmonically dissonant, are melodically consonant.

*Selected
Readings*

Aldwell, Edward, and Carl Schachter. *Harmony and Voice Leading*. 2d ed. 2 vols. New York: Harcourt Brace Jovanovich, 1989. Chapters 1–2.

Bamberger, Jeanne Shapiro, and Howard Brofsky. *The Art of Listening: Developing Music Perception*. 5th ed. New York: Harper & Row, 1988. Chapters 1–3.

Benjamin, Thomas, Michael Horvit, and Robert Nelson. *Techniques and Materials of Tonal Music*. Belmont, CA: Wadsworth, 1992. Part I, Sections 2–3.

Christ, William, et al. *Materials and Structure of Music*. 3d ed. Vol. I. Englewood Cliffs, NJ: Prentice-Hall, 1980. Chapter 1.

Fux, Johann Joseph. *The Study of Counterpoint from Johann Fux's "Gradus ad Parnassum."* Translated and edited by Alfred Mann. New York: Norton, 1965. Chapter 1.

Hall, Donald E. *Musical Acoustics*. 2d ed. Pacific Grove, CA: Brooks/Cole, 1991. Chapter 1.

Kostka, Stefan, and Dorothy Payne. *Tonal Harmony*. 2d ed. New York: Alfred A. Knopf, 1989. Chapter 1.

Mitchell, William J. *Elementary Harmony*. 2d ed. Englewood Cliffs, NJ: Prentice-Hall, 1948. Chapter 1.

Ottman, Robert W. *Elementary Harmony*. 4th ed. Englewood Cliffs, NJ: Prentice-Hall, 1989. Chapter 1.

Piston, Walter. *Harmony*. 5th ed. Revised and expanded by Mark DeVoto. New York: Norton, 1987. Chapter 1.

Schenker, Heinrich. *Harmony*. Edited by Oswald Jonas. Translated by Elisabeth Mann Borgese. Chicago: University of Chicago Press, 1954. Division I.

Schoenberg, Arnold. *Theory of Harmony*. Translated by Roy E. Carter. Berkeley: University of California Press, 1983. Chapter 1.

Westergaard, Peter. *An Introduction to Tonal Theory*. New York: Norton, 1975. Chapter 1.

3

Tonality

The pitch organization of a musical work is its tonality. A tonality based on the major/minor system described below is one type of tonality. There are many others. Yet in the West, the major/minor system is so prevalent that we refer to it simply as the tonal system or, more formally, functional tonality. (We will discover what is "functional" about it in later chapters.)

COLLECTIONS, MODES, AND SCALES

We distinguish among three levels of pitch class organization: *collections*, *modes*, and *scales*. Each reflects an increasingly complex level of organization.

Collections

An unordered group of pitch classes in which each member pitch class is an *equal* member is called a *collection*. For example, we often refer to the twelve pitch classes that span the octave as the "chromatic scale." This is *not* a scale, however, but a collection. Why? Because we have not ordered it. Every member is an equal member. We can begin on any pitch class and end on any pitch class without changing the "scale." Without some hierarchical organization a group of pitch classes cannot be a scale, only a collection.

Modes

Consider the white keys of the piano. When we think of them merely as a group of keys associated by color, we think of them as a *collection*. However, when we think of them as arranged from low to high with a definite beginning and ending point, we think of them as a *mode*. The ancient Church modes are of this type.

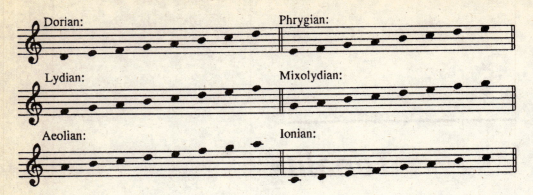

Figure 3.1   *Church Modes*

Each of the Church modes represents a different ordering of the same collection, the white keys.

Scales

A *scale*, on the other hand, is a hierarchical ordering of a pitch-class collection. As a result, each member pitch class has a unique position within that scale. We call the individual pitch classes of a scale *scale degrees*.

In ordering a scale we do more than simply place the pitch classes in order (low to high, high to low). We give certain pitch classes priority over others. In a C scale, for instance, we "begin" on C—that is, C is the first scale degree. By definition, that gives it priority over all other scale degrees. *Each* scale degree has a similarly unique position within that scale. (You will learn more about these scale degrees and their functions later in the chapter.)

The major or minor scale on which we base a composition is its *key*.

MAJOR KEYS

Structure of the Major Scale

If we begin on C, we call the succession of white keys up to the C an octave higher (or down to the C an octave lower) the *C major scale*. We call the first note of this succession the *tonic* of the scale. A scale has only one tonic. The tonic of this white-key scale (beginning on C) is C.

The sequence of whole and half steps going upward from C to C in the C major scale characterizes *any* major scale. To get this sequence of whole and half steps from the collection of white keys, we *must* begin on C.

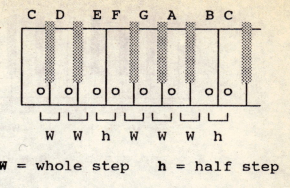

W = whole step   h = half step

Figure 3.2   C major Scale

If we began on any other white key, we would have some other sequence of intervals. Thus, if we want to construct a major scale on any other white key than C, we must replace some white keys with black keys. In this way we get the correct sequence of whole and half steps. For instance, the F major scale requires that B-flat replace B.

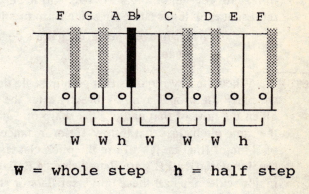

W = whole step   h = half step

Figure 3.3   F major Scale

F is the tonic of this scale. It occupies the same position within the sequence of intervals that makes up the major scale as C did in Figure 3.2.

We can build the major scale on black keys as well. Notice that, although the pitch classes differ, the intervals above the tonic of each of these major keys are in the same order.

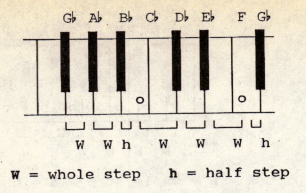

W = whole step   h = half step

Figure 3.4   G-flat major Scale

In every scale, whether major or minor (see Figure 3.5) and no matter where it begins, each letter name is represented exactly once. In the G-flat major scale above, we might inadvertently spell the D-flat as C-sharp. (A glance at the keyboard shows that we use the same black key for either D-flat or C-sharp.) However, if we use the C-sharp spelling, two versions of C result—that is, two versions of the fourth scale degree. We have no D, no *fifth* scale degree, of any sort. This will never be the case; we will always represent each letter name (in some form or another) exactly once.

> *Rule:* In every scale, each scale degree must have a unique letter name.

Key Signatures

When the key requires that certain scale degrees be flatted or sharped, we place the proper symbol directly after the clef in a space or on a line given the note of that name. This sharp or flat will then affect all notes of the same pitch class that follow. If, for instance, a composition is in the key of F major (that is, it will use the pitch classes of the F major scale for its tonal material), all B's are flatted since a B-flat is necessary to create the F major scale. We call these universal flats or sharps placed after the clef a *key signature*. Figure 3.5a gives the key signature for F major.

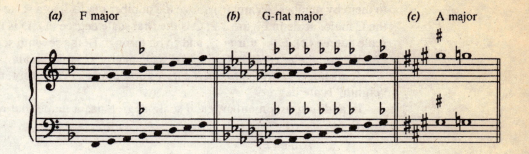

(a) F major   (b) G-flat major   (c) A major

Figure 3.5   Key Signatures

The key of G-flat major requires, for instance, that we flat all G's, as in Figure 3.5b.

SHARP KEYS

The key signature in Figure 3.5c, above, has three sharps. The last sharp farthest to the right is G-sharp. A minor second above G-sharp is A, the major tonic of this key signature.

> *Rule:* Given a major key with a key signature in sharps, *the pitch class a minor second above the last sharp is the tonic.*

FLAT KEYS

The key signature in Figure 3.5b, above, has six flats. The next-to-last flat is G-flat, the tonic of this major key.

> *Rule:* Given a major key with a key signature in flats, *the second-to-last flat in the key signature gives the pitch class of the tonic.* (F major, with one flat, is the single exception to this rule. See Figure 3.5a.)

OVERRIDING THE KEY SIGNATURE

We can override a key signature by using accidentals. For example, the key signature for A major requires that we sharp all G's. We can make the second G of Figure 3.5c a G-natural, however, simply by providing the natural sign. As a rule, accidentals last for the entire measure unless canceled by another accidental. In the following measure, however, the key signature reasserts itself. An accidental attached to the first of two tied notes affects the second as well.

See Appendix H for a table of key signatures.

Scale Degrees

We call the successive pitch classes of a scale *scale degrees* and refer to them by number. A caret (^) above the number marks it as a scale degree. In the C major scale in Figure 3.2, C is the first scale degree ($\hat{1}$). D is the second scale degree ($\hat{2}$), E the third ($\hat{3}$), and so on through B, the seventh scale degree ($\hat{7}$). We call the next pitch, C, the first scale degree ($\hat{1}$) once again.

Scale degrees attach to pitch classes, not pitches. Therefore, there is no "eighth" scale degree.

In addition to a number, each scale degree has a name that reflects its function.

> Tonic ($\hat{1}$)
> Supertonic ($\hat{2}$)
> Mediant ($\hat{3}$)
> Subdominant ($\hat{4}$)
> Dominant ($\hat{5}$)
> Submediant ($\hat{6}$)
> Leading tone ($\hat{7}$)

THE PRINCIPAL SCALE DEGREES

The tonic ($\hat{1}$), mediant ($\hat{3}$), and dominant ($\hat{5}$) are the principal scale degrees. These three scale degrees form a triad whose root is the tonic.

DEPENDENT SCALE DEGREES

All the other scale degrees are dependent. They function in relation to the stable scale degrees $\hat{1}$, $\hat{3}$, and $\hat{5}$ either as *passing notes* or as *neighboring notes*.

Passing Notes. When two stable scale degrees are a third apart, that scale degree which separates them sometimes appears as a *passing note*. A melody can pass from one stable degree through this unstable degree to the next stable degree.

Most passing notes connect stable degrees a third apart. Occasionally, however, a pair of passing notes may span the perfect fourth from $\hat{5}$ up to $\hat{1}$.

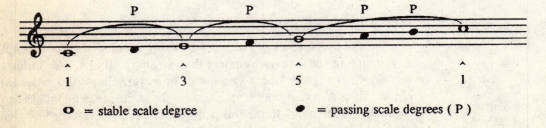

Figure 3.6   Passing Notes

Neighboring Notes. When we repeat a single stable note, we can embellish that repetition with a *neighboring note*. A neighboring note (or, simply, *neighbor note*) must be adjacent to (that is, a step away from) the principal scale degree. A repeated principal scale degree can be embellished with either an *upper-neighbor note* or a *lower-neighbor note*.

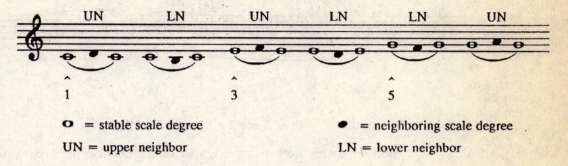

o = stable scale degree   ● = neighboring scale degree

UN = upper neighbor   LN = lower neighbor

Figure 3.7   Neighboring Notes

SCALE DEGREES IN MELODIES

We create tonal melodies by *prolonging* stable scale degrees in time. We do this in two stages—unfolding and embellishing.

Unfolding. First, we can *unfold* a scale degree in time in two ways. We can prolong a stable scale degree by simply repeating or *rearticulating* it. We can prolong two or more stable scale degrees in time by moving from one stable scale degree to another. We call this process *arpeggiation*.

Embellishing. We can embellish a rearticulated stable scale degree with a neighbor note. We can embellish an arpeggiation with one (or more) passing notes. The introduction of such dissonant (unstable) notes makes dramatic the unfolding of the stable degrees. Simple tunes illustrate this principle directly.

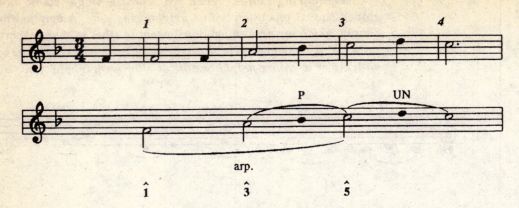

Figure 3.8   In dulci jubilo

Both a passing note and a neighbor note embellish the *arpeggiation*
$\hat{1}$–$\hat{3}$–$\hat{5}$. The *passing note* fills in the $\hat{3}$–$\hat{5}$ arpeggiation (measures 2–3) and
an upper neighbor note prolongs the *rearticulation* of $\hat{5}$ (measures 3–4).

As the unfolding and embellishment of the principal degrees become
more complex, so do the melodies that result.

Figure 3.9   Mozart, Piano Sonata, K. 545; first movement

Here the initial arpeggiation of $\hat{1}$, $\hat{3}$, and $\hat{5}$ divides into two voices as
shown on the lower staff. The bottom voice (shown with downward stems)
rearticulates the initial $\hat{1}$ in measure 2, but first embellishes that rearticulation with a lower neighbor ($\hat{7}$, measure 2). The top voice rearticulates the
$\hat{5}$ of measure 1 in measure 3, but first embellishes that rearticulation with
an upper neighbor ($\hat{6}$) in measure 3. It arpeggiates down to $\hat{3}$ in measure 4,
embellishing that arpeggiation with a passing note ($\hat{4}$).

The sixteenth notes of measures 2 and 4 create, at another level, rearticulations of $\hat{1}$ and $\hat{3}$. An upper neighbor embellishes each (see Figure 3.10).

Figure 3.10   Mozart, Piano Sonata, K. 545; first movement, measures 1–4

Consonant Support. Passing and neighboring notes can be stabilized if they are made consonant. We do this by providing them with *consonant support*. (Such support involves harmonic concerns discussed in later chapters.) Once these notes are stabilized, we can treat these formerly dependent scale degrees as if they were stable, embellishing them in turn.

ACTIVE INTERVALS

All dissonances are active, that is, unstable. Whether they are intervals or chords, all dissonances require *resolution*—an explanation in terms of consonance. Certain augmented and diminished dissonances play an important role in functional tonality. As a rule, diminished intervals resolve inwards. As a rule, augmented intervals resolve outwards.

Figure 3.11   Active Intervals

Diminished Fifth. The naturally occurring diminished fifth (from $\hat{7}$ up to $\hat{4}$) resolves inwards with $\hat{7}$ resolving up to $\hat{1}$ and $\hat{4}$ resolving down to $\hat{3}$ (see Figure 3.11a).

Augmented Fourth. The inversion of that interval (the augmented fourth from $\hat{4}$ up to $\hat{7}$) resolves outwards, with $\hat{7}$ resolving up to $\hat{1}$ and $\hat{4}$ resolving down to $\hat{3}$ (see Figure 3.11b).

Augmented Second. The augmented second that arises in the minor (see "Harmonic Minor," page 39) between $\hat{6}$ and raised $\hat{7}$ also resolves to the outside, with $\hat{7}$ resolving up to $\hat{1}$, and $\hat{6}$ resolving down to $\hat{5}$ (see Figure 3.11c).

SCALE-DEGREE TRIADS

As we have seen, the three primary scale degrees form a triad, with $\hat{1}$ as the root of that triad, $\hat{3}$ the third, and $\hat{5}$ the fifth. A triad can be formed on any scale-degree with that scale degree as the root. We name a triad after its root and we abbreviate that name with a roman numeral that corresponds to the scale degree number of its root. In C major, then, the triad $\hat{1}–\hat{3}–\hat{5}$ is the *tonic triad* or, simply, *I*. The triad built upon the second scale degree ($\hat{2}–\hat{4}–\hat{6}$) is the *supertonic triad* or *ii* (see below).

Figure 3.12   The Triads Built on the Scale Degrees of C major

The Qualities of Scale-Degree Triads

In the major mode, the tonic triad (or *I*) is a major triad, as are the triads built upon *IV* and *V*. On the other hand, *ii, iii,* and *vi* are minor triads. We suggest the quality of a triad by using upper-case roman numerals for major and augmented triads and lower-case roman numerals for minor and diminished triads. However, this usage (illustrated in Figure 3.12) is not standard. We will often see upper-case roman numerals used for *all* scale-degree triads regardless of their qualities.

Figure 3.13   The Quality of Scale-Degree Triads in C major

Scale-degree triads have the same quality in every major scale. Thus the mediant triad (iii) is minor in every major key, the leading-tone triad (vii) is diminished in every major key, and so forth.

Appendix I lists triad qualities in both major and minor.

Inversions

A triad can be arranged in one of three possible vertical positions. We can place the root at the bottom, the third at the bottom, or the fifth at the bottom. When we notate a triad so that the third or the fifth of the triad is the lowest note, that triad is *inverted*. When the root is the lowest note, the triad is in *root position*. When the third is the lowest note, the triad is in *first inversion*. When the fifth is the lowest note, the triad is in *second inversion*.

Figured Bass

A triad's position depends entirely on which member of the triad is the lowest note. The lowest-*sounding* note is the *bass*. By providing a bass note and designating a position, we define a triad. Seventeenth-century musicians developed a system for notating the position of triads called *figured bass*.

THE BASS

The *root* of a triad and the *bass* of a triad are not necessarily the same note, but can be two separate things. *Only in root position is the root of the triad the bass as well.* In first inversion, the third (as the lowest note) is the bass; in second inversion, the fifth is the bass.

In Figure 3.14, the bass of the first triad is the root—that is, the first triad is in *root position*. The bass of the second triad is that triad's third; the second triad is in *first inversion*. The bass of the third triad is that triad's fifth; the third triad is in *second inversion*. The fourth triad is again in root position.

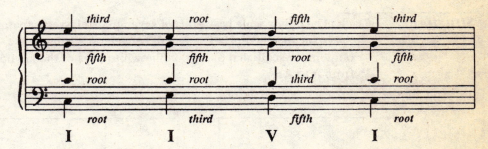

Figure 3.14   Root Position and Inversions

THE FIGURES

Figure 3.15 portrays the same succession of triads and positions as in Figure 3.14. Here we show the positions by arabic numerals below a single line of notes. That line of notes is the bass. The figures tell us what triads to build on those bass notes.

Figure 3.15   Figured Bass

The arabic numerals show diatonic intervals above the bass. Thus, if a bass note is the lowest note of a first inversion triad (that is, if the third of that triad is in the bass), then the root is the pitch class a sixth above it. Similarly, the fifth is the pitch class a third above. The figures we need, then, are $\frac{6}{3}$. If the bass is the fifth of a (second inversion) triad, then we need the figures $\frac{6}{4}$. (The root is a fourth above the bass and the third a sixth above.) For root position, we need $\frac{5}{3}$.

Appendix J explains figured bass practice in more detail.

MINOR SCALES

The minor scale is complex. The basic structure, like that of the major scale, is unambiguous. How composers use the minor scale is not. The major scale is the basic structure of the tonal system. The minor scale works within this system only to the degree that it mimics the major.

Structure

The minor scale is a series of seven pitch classes, separated by seconds, that span an octave. Half steps fall between scale degrees $\hat{2}$–$\hat{3}$ and $\hat{5}$–$\hat{6}$. The only minor scale that occurs on the white keys of the keyboard is the scale from A to A.

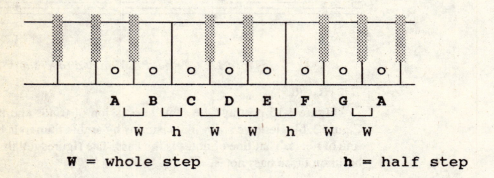

Figure 3.16   The A minor Scale

Note that the A minor scale is nothing more than the notes of the C major scale rotated to begin on A rather than C. That is, A, the sixth scale degree ($\hat{6}$) in the C major scale, becomes the first scale degree ($\hat{1}$) in the A minor scale. This seemingly trivial distinction between C major and A minor in fact has vast consequences.

Natural Minor

We call the original, unaltered version of a minor key the *natural* or *pure* minor. But, from one point of view, the adjective *natural* is misleading. The natural minor does not work "naturally." We must bend and shape the natural minor in order to make it behave tonally.

Harmonic Minor

For example, in minor, the distance between $\hat{7}$ and $\hat{1}$ is a whole step. In major, however, the same distance is a half step. As you will see below, this half-step distance between $\hat{7}$ and $\hat{1}$ is essential to the tonal system. (In fact, we refer to the seventh scale degree as the "leading tone" because of its tendency to leap this tiny gap to the first scale degree.) Now, to create the necessary half step between $\hat{7}$ and $\hat{1}$ in A minor, we must raise $\hat{7}$, that is, change G to G-sharp. This reestablishes the essential half step between $\hat{7}$ and $\hat{1}$. We call this altered version of the minor the *harmonic minor*.

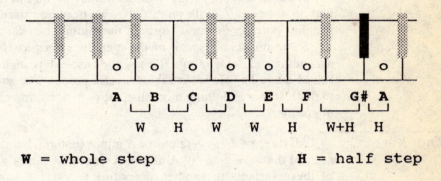

Figure 3.17   A minor Scale, Harmonic

Melodic Minor

Though the distance between raised $\hat{7}$ and $\hat{1}$ is now a half step, the interval between $\hat{6}$ and raised $\hat{7}$ is now the equivalent of a whole step *plus* a half step—an *augmented second*. Thus, motion by "step" between adjacent sale degrees (between $\hat{6}$ and raised $\hat{7}$) sounds rather like a skip. That is, the expected distance of a half or whole step between adjacent scale degrees becomes that of a whole *plus* a half step. The interval sounds more familiar to us as a third and so we hear it more like a skip than a step.

To reestablish the conventional distance between $\hat{6}$ and $\hat{7}$ we must now adjust $\hat{6}$ by raising *it*. (That is, F becomes F-sharp, or raised $\hat{6}$.) Since melodic considerations cause this change, we call this version of the minor the *melodic minor*.

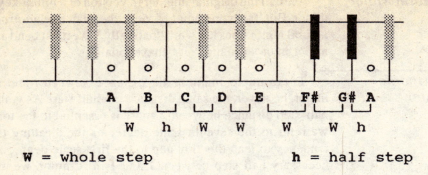

W = whole step   **h** = half step

Figure 3.18   A minor Scale, Melodic

When *descending* from $\hat{1}$ in the minor, we do not need a leading tone and do not raise $\hat{7}$. With no raised $\hat{7}$, we need no raised $\hat{6}$. As a result, we use the "pure" or "natural" form of the minor when descending from $\hat{1}$.

Some musicians speak of the melodic minor as if it had two forms, ascending and descending. The so-called ascending melodic minor requires raised $\hat{6}$ and $\hat{7}$. This is the melodic form proper. The so-called descending melodic minor is nothing more than the pure or natural minor. It requires no alteration.

Minor Keys

All three of these versions of A minor (natural, harmonic, and melodic) are just that—*versions* of A minor. A work in A minor will move from one of these variants to another, according to varying harmonic or melodic contexts, but it remains *in A minor*.

Affect of the Minor

As we have seen, the minor is much more complex than the major. This is why major keys sometimes seem "happy" or "bright," and minor keys "sad" or "dark." These descriptions are metaphors for a systemic relationship. They arise from a subconscious correlation between musical structure and familiar psychological states. We call the subjective emotional or psychological state created by music its *affect*. Affect is, for the most part, culturally determined. It varies from culture to culture and age to age.

THE RELATIONSHIP BETWEEN MAJOR AND MINOR KEYS

Major and minor scales use the same key signatures and are built on the same collection of seven pitch classes. However, the major and minor scales that share the same key signature do *not* share the same tonic. Conversely, the major and minor keys that share the same tonic do *not* share the same key signatures.

The Relative Relation

The minor key that shares the same *key signature* with a major key is that major key's *relative minor*. Thus, A minor is the relative minor of C major. Conversely, C major is the *relative major* of A minor.

> *Rule:* The sixth scale degree of the major is the tonic of its relative minor. The third scale degree of the minor is the tonic of its relative major. Remember: *The key signature remains the same, but the tonic changes.*

The Parallel Relation

We call the minor key that shares the same *tonic* with a major key that major key's *parallel minor*. G minor is the parallel minor of G major. Conversely, G major is the *parallel major* of G minor.

> *Rule:* The key signature of the parallel minor is the key signature of that minor key's relative major. Remember: *The tonic remains the same, but the key signature changes.*

For more about the relationship between major and minor, see Appendix K.

A collection is an unordered group of pitch classes. In a collection, all pitch classes that are members of the collection are equal members. A scale is an ordering of pitch classes such that each pitch class has a unique position within that ordering. We call the pitch class members of a scale scale degrees. In a scale, one and only one pitch class is appointed as the first (second, third, etc.) scale degree.

Scale degrees are either stable or unstable. The principal (stable) scale degrees are $\hat{1}$, $\hat{3}$, and $\hat{5}$. All other scale degrees are dependent. They function as passing notes or neighbor notes in relation to these principal scale degrees. We can momentarily stabilize dependent scale degrees by consonant support.

Each scale degree is the potential root of a triad. We label scale-degree triads with roman numerals that correspond to the root scale degree of that triad.

The minor is complex: its structure changes with the musical context. All these changes, however, reflect the primacy of the major.

Selected Readings

Aldwell, Edward, and Carl Schachter. *Harmony and Voice Leading*. 2 vols. New York: Harcourt Brace Jovanovich, 1979. Chapters 1–2.

Bamberger, Jeanne Shapiro, and Howard Brofsky. *The Art of Listening: Developing Music Perception*. 5th ed. New York: Harper & Row, 1988. Chapter 1.

Benjamin, Thomas, Michael Horvit, and Robert Nelson. *Techniques and Materials of Tonal Music*. Belmont, CA: Wadsworth, 1992. Part I, Sections 4–5.

Christ, William, et al. *Materials and Structure of Music*. 3d ed. Vol. I. Englewood Cliffs, NJ: Prentice-Hall, 1980. Chapters 1–3.

Cooper, Paul. *Perspectives in Music Theory*. 2d ed. New York: Harper & Row, 1981. Chapters 1–4.

Fux, Johann Joseph. *The Study of Counterpoint from Johann Fux's "Gradus ad Parnassum."* Translated and edited by Alfred Mann. New York: Norton, 1965. Chapter 1.

Jonas, Oswald. *Introduction to the Theory of Heinrich Schenker*. Translated and edited by John Rothgeb. New York: Longman, 1982. Chapters 1–2.

Kostka, Stefan, and Dorothy Payne. *Tonal Harmony*. 2d ed. New York: Alfred A. Knopf, 1989. Chapter 1.

Mitchell, William J. *Elementary Harmony*. 2d ed. Englewood Cliffs, NJ: Prentice-Hall, 1948. Chapters 1–2.

Ottman, Robert W. *Elementary Harmony*. 4th ed. Englewood Cliffs, NJ: Prentice-Hall, 1989. Chapter 1.

Piston, Walter. *Harmony*. 5th ed. Revised and expanded by Mark DeVoto. New York: Norton, 1987. Chapters 1–2.

Salzer, Felix. *Structural Hearing*. New York: Dover, 1962. Chapter 1.

Schenker, Heinrich. *Harmony*. Edited by Oswald Jonas. Translated by Elisabeth Mann Borgese. Chicago: University of Chicago Press, 1954. Division I, Sections I–III.

Schoenberg, Arnold. *Theory of Harmony*. Translated by Roy E. Carter. Berkeley: University of California Press, 1983. Chapters 1–5.

Westergaard, Peter. *An Introduction to Tonal Theory*. New York: Norton, 1975. Chapters 1–3.

4

Rhythm and Meter

The durations of tonal music are divisible by the pulse. Pulses are organized into measures. Measures are organized by patterns of accents.

Accents result from both rhythmic placement and harmonic content. The stability of consonance implies strong metrical placement. The embellishing character of dissonance implies relatively weak metrical placement. Techniques of syncopation, however, may displace a strong beat to a weak one by reversing these implicit associations.

The affect of tonal music arises in large part from this interplay of pitch and rhythm. Consonance and dissonance, metrical uniformity and irregularity, all conspire to create dramatic patterns of expectations met, frustrated, and finally resolved.

Rhythmic Organization

Informally, we call the temporal aspect of music its *rhythm*. How tonal music unfolds in time, however, is quite complex, and the relative duration of successive events, their *rhythm*, is only one part of temporal organization. There are four, altogether: *pulse, tempo, rhythm,* and *meter*.

Pulse

Tonal music unfolds in time against a regular grid of stressed beats called *pulses*. The regular beat that we keep with our foot while listening to music reflects this pulse. These pulses result from the interplay of harmony and melody.

Tempo

Our perception of how fast or slow the pulse moves provides us with a sense of *tempo*. When we discuss the tempo of a musical work, we discuss the relative speed of its pulse. A composer controls the tempo of a work by placing descriptive terms at the beginning of the composition. These tempo marks hold until others are introduced that contradict them.

Appendix D lists common tempo markings.

Rhythm

A succession of durations is a *rhythm*. There are three basic types of musical rhythm: free, multimetric, and isometric. A *free rhythm* is one in which we perceive only the relative length of successive notes. A *multimetric rhythm* is one in which every duration is a whole-number multiple of some smaller unit of duration. An *isometric rhythm* is a multimetric rhythm in which the resulting durations group themselves into larger units of equal duration called *measures*.

As a rule, the rhythms of functional tonality are isometric. Isometric rhythm has three components: *rhythm, pulse,* and *meter*.

Meter

The interplay of harmony and melody organizes pulses into groups. We call the arrangement of pulses into groups *meter*. We call the pulse groupings themselves *measures* or *bars*. The division between measures is shown with a vertical line through the staff called the *bar line*. We specify the meter of a musical work with a *meter signature* or *time signature*.

METER SIGNATURES

The meter signature appears after the key signature at the beginning of a musical work. A meter signature has two parts.

The Numerator. The top number gives the number of pulses in a measure.

The Denominator. The bottom number gives the note value that corresponds to the pulse.

For example, $\frac{3}{4}$ indicates a meter in which there are three pulses to the measure, with each pulse having the value of a quarter note. The meter signature $\frac{4}{8}$ indicates a meter in which there are four beats to the measure, with the eighth note acting as pulse. Like other meters of the type, $\frac{3}{4}$ and $\frac{4}{8}$ are called *simple meters*. For simple meters, these simple relations hold. But there is another type of meter called *compound*. For compound meters, the meter signature provides more ambiguous information.

THE TYPES OF METER

Tonal music presents us with two types of meter: *simple meter* and *compound meter*. The pulse of each differs.

Simple Meters. A simple meter has a simple pulse. A simple pulse divides into *pairs* of smaller note values. The numerator of a simple meter signature gives the number of pulses in a measure. The denominator gives the note value that corresponds to the pulse. As a rule, *the numerator of a simple meter will be less than six.*

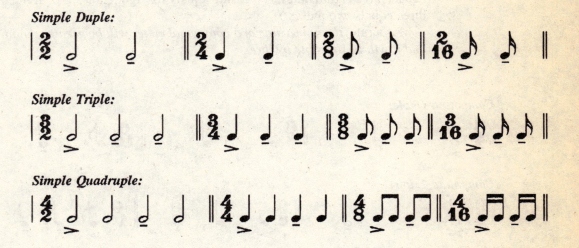

> = *primary accent*   - = *secondary accent*

Figure 4.1   Simple Meters

Musicians sometimes refer to $\frac{4}{4}$ as *common time*. The symbol **c** often replaces the meter signature and stands for common time or $\frac{4}{4}$. Similarly, musicians often call $\frac{2}{2}$ *cut time* (or, more formally, *alla breve*). The symbol ¢ replaces the meter signature and stands for cut time or $\frac{2}{2}$.

Compound Meters. Compound meters have *compound pulses*. A compound pulse divides into *three* equal parts. Since all our note values divide naturally in half, we must represent a compound pulse with a dotted note value. It is impossible to represent a dotted note value with a simple integer, though. As a result, the denominator of a compound meter does not show the note value of the pulse. Rather it shows the note value of the largest equal subdivision of the pulse.

To interpret a compound meter signature then, we must first divide the numerator by three. This gives us the number of pulses in the compound measure. Then, we must group together three of the note values given by the denominator. The combined duration of these three values gives the duration of the pulse.

For example, $\frac{6}{8}$ is a compound meter (see Figure 4.2). The 8 represents the largest equal subdivision of the pulse. Three of these subdivisions make up the pulse, so three eighth notes equal one pulse. Our pulse, then, is three eighth notes long, or the duration of a dotted quarter note. There are six eighth notes in the measure, so there are two pulses to the measure. (A pulse equals three eighth notes. A measure equals six eighth notes. Six divided by three equals two pulses.)

As a rule, *the numerator of a compound meter will be greater than five, and it will be divisible by three.*

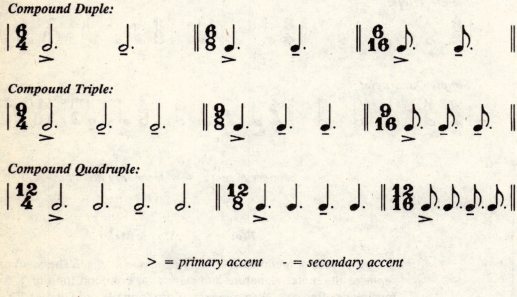

> = *primary accent*   - = *secondary accent*

Figure 4.2   Compound Meters

RHYTHM, METER, AND TONALITY

Pitch and rhythmic organization combine to create a regular pattern of stresses and releases. We call these stresses *accents* and, informally, associate certain patterns of stress with certain meters.

Accents

We observe three types of accents in tonal music: *tonic, agogic,* and *dynamic*. A *tonic accent* results from a harmonic or metrical emphasis. An *agogic accent* results from a greater relative duration. The first two types derive from the interaction of rhythm, meter, and tonality. However, *dynamic accents* result from a momentary increase in relative loudness.

TONIC ACCENTS

The temporal regularity of tonal music creates several layers of tonic accents.

Tonic Accent of the Pulse. Musical events that occur on the pulse sound stressed in comparison with those that occur between pulses.

Metrical Tonic Accents. The regular grouping of pulses into measures of equal length creates a tonic accent on the first pulse of each measure. If a measure is readily divisible into two equal parts, the first pulse of the subdivision receives a stress. Thus, in a quadruple measure ($\frac{4}{4}$ or $\frac{12}{8}$, for instance), the first and the third pulses of the measure receive a tonic accent. The first receives more emphasis than the third. (The accent symbols in Figures 4.1 and 4.2 show these patterns of tonic accent.)

AGOGIC ACCENTS, DYNAMIC ACCENTS, AND SYNCOPATION

Metrical organization, then, creates several layers of tonic accents resulting in an alternating pattern of strong and weak beats. We can contradict this pattern with dramatic effect by emphasizing a weak beat. We call such an emphasis a *syncopation*. We see four sorts of syncopation in tonal music: syncopation resulting from the absence of the (usually) strong beat; syncopation resulting from a dynamic accent; syncopation resulting from an agogic accent; and syncopation resulting from tonal dissonance.

Rhythm and Dissonance

The stable character of consonance creates yet another layer of tonic accent. We commonly associate this tonic accent with metrically strong beats. Conversely, we find dissonance relegated to relatively weak beats. There, its unstable, embellishing character does not contradict the meter's regularity.

PASSING AND NEIGHBORING NOTES

As a rule, passing notes and neighbor notes arise in a weak position relative to the stable notes that surround them. We consider passing and neighboring notes that arise in this way *unaccented*.

P = unaccented passing note

LN = unaccented lower neighbor

UN = unaccented upper neighbor

Figure 4.3   Unaccented Passing and Neighboring Notes

When we place unstable notes on the pulse, they are *accented*. Such accented dissonances contradict the usual strong–weak pattern. They create an especially expressive form of syncopation called an *appoggiatura*.

An *appoggiatura* is an accented dissonance approached by a skip and left by a step. We will discuss it in chapter 10.

P = accented passing note

LN = accented lower neighbor note

UN = accented upper neighbor note

A = appoggiatura

Figure 4.4   Accented Passing and Neighboring Notes, and the Appoggiatura

RHYTHMIC DISPLACEMENT

Accented dissonances give us the impression that the strong beat has, in some way, been displaced, that its metrical position has been taken over by this dissonance. The expressive effect of the appoggiatura, for instance, arises in large part from this sense of delayed resolution. We call this *rhythmic displacement*.

Two additional forms of dissonant embellishment arise from the technique of *rhythmic displacement*. Given two successive stable notes, we may displace them rhythmically in two ways: with the *anticipation* or with the *suspension*.

The Anticipation. Beginning with the first (consonant) note (Figure 4.5a) on a relatively strong beat, we can move to the second (consonant) note (Figure 4.5c) *before* the next strong beat, creating a momentary dissonance called an *anticipation* (Figure 4.5b).

Figure 4.5   The Anticipation

The Suspension. Beginning with the first (consonant) note (Figure 4.6a) on a relatively strong beat, we can delay the arrival of the second (consonant) note (Figure 4.6c) until *after* the next strong beat. This creates a momentary dissonance called a *suspension* (Figure 4.6b).

Figure 4.6   Suspensions

We will discuss all of these dissonant embellishments further in chapter 10.

Phrase Structure

Patterns of stress and release, dissonance and resolution, act at all levels of tonal composition. Groups of measures form themselves into *phrases*, phrases group themselves into sections, and sections combine to form entire movements.

We often see two simple phrase types in tonal music, the *period* and the *sentence*.

THE PERIOD

The period is made up of two equal-length phrases.

Antecedent. The first phrase, or *antecedent*, is stressed, beginning in a stable position and then destabilizing (see Figure 4.7a).

Consequent. The second phrase, or *consequent*, is unstressed, beginning in an unstable position and then stabilizing (see Figure 4.7b).

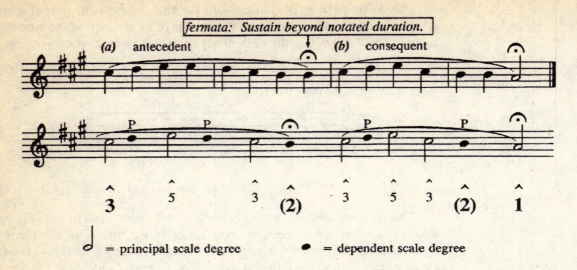

$\mathbf{d}$ = principal scale degree   ● = dependent scale degree

Figure 4.7   The Period: Bach, Chorale 233

In Figure 4.7, the antecedent begins on stable $\hat{3}$ but ends on the upper neighbor to $\hat{1}$, $\hat{2}$. The consequent begins again on $\hat{3}$ and then completes the passing motion from $\hat{3}$ through $\hat{2}$ down to $\hat{1}$.

THE SENTENCE

The sentence is more complex than the period. The sentence has three parts, the first two relating to each other as antecedent to consequent. The last phrase (as long as the first two combined) integrates the two.

Statement. The first phrase of the sentence is the *statement*. Like the *antecedent* of the period, it is stressed (see Figure 4.8a).

Continuation. The second phrase of the sentence is the *continuation*. Like the period's *consequent*, it is unstressed. The continuation is a varied repetition of the statement (see Figure 4.8b).

Dissolution. The last phrase of the sentence is the *dissolution*. It is the length of *statement* and *consequent* combined (see Figure 4.8c).

Figure 4.8   The Sentence: Bach, Chorale 7

In Figure 4.8, the continuation repeats the statement a fourth higher. The dissolution is the length of the statement and the continuation combined.

We will discuss the period and sentence further in chapter 15.

The regular flow of beats that we sense beneath a musical texture is called the pulse. The relative speed of those pulses is the tempo. The successive duration of musical events is rhythm. The organization of pulses into groups of equal duration is called meter.

Tonal music is isometric. Durations are an integral multiple of some smaller unit of duration (pulse). Those pulses group themselves into larger units of equal duration (measures). We find two kinds of meter in tonal music: simple and compound.

A meter signature or time signature suggests a meter. Those meters whose pulse divides naturally into two smaller note values are simple meters. In the time signature of a simple meter, the numerator gives the number of pulses in a measure and the denominator gives the note value of the pulse. Those meters whose pulses divide into three equal parts are compound meters. Their meter signatures are more difficult to interpret. In a compound meter, the numerator divided by three gives the number of pulses per measure. The denominator grouped in threes gives the note value of the pulse.

Accents form another layer of metrical organization. We find three kinds of accents in tonal music: tonic, agogic, and dynamic. Tonic accents result from harmonic or metrical emphasis. An agogic accent occurs when a duration is longer than those surrounding it. A dynamic accent results when a musical event is louder than those surrounding it.

Accents that arise in a relatively weak metrical position are syncopations. Syncopations that arise from the apparent displacement of a relative strong beat to a relatively weak one are called rhythmic displacements. We commonly find two kinds: anticipations and suspensions.

Harmonic consonance often coincides with strong metrical position. Harmonic dissonance usually arises in a relatively weak metrical position.

Selected Readings

Aldwell, Edward, and Carl Schachter. *Harmony and Voice Leading*. 2d ed. 2 vols. New York: Harcourt Brace Jovanovich, 1989. Chapter 3.

Bamberger, Jeanne Shapiro, and Howard Brofsky. *The Art of Listening: Developing Music Perception*. 5th ed. New York: Harper & Row, 1988. Chapters 2–3.

Benjamin, Thomas, Michael Horvit, and Robert Nelson. *Techniques and Materials of Tonal Music*. Belmont, CA: Wadsworth, 1992. Part I, Section 6.

Christ, William, et al. *Materials and Structure of Music*. 3d ed. Vol. I. Englewood Cliffs, NJ: Prentice-Hall, 1980. Chapters 1–2.

Cooper, Paul. *Perspectives in Music Theory*. 2d ed. New York: Harper & Row, 1981. Chapter 5.

Kostka, Stefan, and Dorothy Payne. *Tonal Harmony*. 2d ed. New York: Alfred A. Knopf, 1989. Chapter 2.

Lester, Joel. *The Rhythms of Tonal Music*. Carbondale, IL: Southern Illinois University Press, 1979. Chapters 1–3.

Mitchell, William J. *Elementary Harmony*. 2d ed. Englewood Cliffs, NJ: Prentice-Hall, 1948. Chapter 3.

Ottman, Robert W. *Elementary Harmony*. 4th ed. Englewood Cliffs, NJ: Prentice-Hall, 1989. Chapter 3.

Piston, Walter. *Harmony*. 5th ed. Revised and expanded by Mark DeVoto. New York: Norton, 1987. Chapter 13.

Sachs, Curt. *Rhythm and Tempo*. New York: Columbia University Press, 1953. Chapter 1.

5

The Basics of Four-Part Writing

*W*e begin the study of harmony with a four-voiced texture called chorale style. Two goals define this style: independence of voices and maintenance of tonality.

To create music in chorale style, we must control both the horizontal and vertical dimensions of the texture. Voice leading controls the relationship between voices. Rules of thumb concerning doubling and chord voicing shape the vertical disposition of the voices. A variant of chorale style called keyboard style alters both voice-leading and voicing rules to make practical performance by two hands at a keyboard.

THE FOUR VOICES

The study of harmony usually begins with a study of *chorale style*. Although strictly limited in scope, chorale style does provide basic training in the principles that govern a *polyphonic* (that is, many-voiced) texture. Those principles, along with the techniques associated with them, are called *voice leading*.

Disposition of the Four Voices   Each part of a four-part texture is called a *voice*. The name and ranges of these voices are derived from the four standardized singing ranges: *soprano*, *alto*, *tenor*, and *bass*. We notate the four voices on a grand staff.

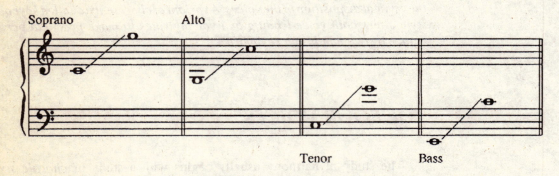

* Arrows point to doubled pitch classes.

Figure 5.1   Four Voices in Chorale Style (Bach, Chorale 293)

We place the soprano and alto on the treble staff with the soprano on top. All soprano stems ascend. All alto stems descend. This makes the two voices visually distinct. We place the tenor and bass on the bass staff. All tenor stems ascend, and all bass stems descend.

Range of the Four Voices

With the exception noted below (see "Keyboard Style," page 56), the four voices operate within restricted ranges, as shown in Figure 5.2.

Figure 5.2   Ranges of the Four Voices

Rhythm

In chorale style, all four voices move in *rhythmic unison*— that is, each voice moves at the same time as every other voice. A succession of four-voice chords results.

CHORD CONSTRUCTION

We use scale-degree triads to form the chords that result from the movement of the four voices.

Complete Triads

The bulk of a four-part texture consists of complete triads. Given a consonant, root-position triad, however, *you may omit the fifth* if this results in smoother voice leading. *You may not omit the third*.

Appendix L discusses the so-called horn fifths, which are a common exception to this last rule and are found in instrumental music of the eighteenth and nineteenth centuries.

Spacing

The distance between adjacent voices may not exceed an octave, *except between tenor and bass*.

OPEN POSITION

Disposing the voices evenly across the staff creates a chord in *open position*.

CLOSED POSITION

Disposing the voices so that the upper three are as close together as possible creates a chord in *closed position*.

Doubling

Given the three pitch classes of a triad distributed among four voices, we must give one pitch class to two different voices. When two voices have the same pitch class, we say that they are *doubling* each other (see Figure 5.1).

RULES FOR DOUBLING

The primary rule for doubling is simple: *Double the most stable note of the triad*. We apply this rule by considering the following alternatives in order:

Doubled Root. Double the root of the triad, when possible.

Doubled Fifth. Double the fifth of the triad *if this is warranted by some voice leading consideration*.

Doubled Third. Double the third *only for the most compelling voice leading reason*.

Remember: In a V or vii, *never* double $\hat{7}$. The leading tone is far too unstable to be doubled. It demands a resolution to $\hat{1}$, which, if supplied in both voices, would lead to (forbidden) parallel octaves (see "Forbidden Parallel Motions," page 61).

ALTERNATIVES TO DOUBLING

Tripled Root. If the fifth is omitted from the triad, and if that triad is in root position, you may *triple* the root, that is, place the root in three of the four voices, one of which is the bass. The remaining voice will, of course, have the third. As rule, composers reserve the tripled root for the end of a composition or, less often, for the end of a phrase.

Seventh Chords. In a later chapter we will discuss chords called seventh chords. Seventh chords contain four distinct pitch classes and therefore do not require doubling.

Figure 5.1 (page 54) illustrates these principles of doubling.

Keyboard Style

For performance on a keyboard instrument, we can use a variant of chorale style called *keyboard style*. In keyboard style, the upper three voices remain in closed position. At the same time, we *notate all three (soprano, alto,* and *tenor) on the treble staff.* As a result, a musician can perform all three upper voices with the right hand, leaving the bass to the left. The extreme closed position of the upper three voices—a position caused by the size of the hand— often places the tenor voice higher than we would normally find it in chorale style.

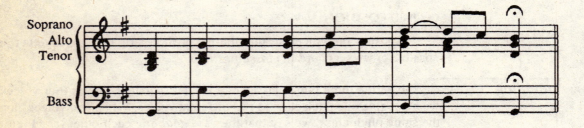

Figure 5.3   Figure 5.1 in Keyboard Style

VOICE LEADING

To create a four-voice texture in chorale or keyboard style, you must learn how to control each voice, as well as the relationship *between* the voices. The principles and techniques involved in this control are called *voice leading.* From the student's point of view, voice leading has two main goals: to establish and maintain the independence of the voices, and to establish and maintain a clear sense of tonality.

Soprano and Bass

The soprano and bass, or *outer voices*, define the chorale texture. The *inner voices* (alto and tenor) serve a supporting role. We must control the relation between the outer voices (see "Simultaneous Motion," page 58) precisely. Soprano and bass must not only be strong in themselves, but the relationship between them must be strong as well.

Function of the Individual Voice

Each voice forms a melody. The melodies in the outer voices are prominent, those of the inner voices supportive. The latter move primarily by step, or *conjunct motion*. They move only occasionally by skip, or *disjunct motion*.

CONJUNCT MOTION

When an individual voice moves by seconds, it moves *conjunctly*.

Consonant Seconds. A voice may move by any number of consecutive major or minor seconds.

Dissonant Seconds. But a voice may *not* move by an augmented second. As we saw in chapter 3, augmented seconds are ambiguous, unstable, and, therefore, dissonant.

Figure 5.4   Conjunct Motion

DISJUNCT MOTION

When an individual voice moves by an interval greater than a second, it moves *disjunctly* or by skip. (Some theorists call a skip a "leap." For our purposes, "skip" and "leap" are the same.)

Consonant Skips. A voice may skip any consonant interval *not larger than an octave*.

Dissonant Skips. Disjunct motion by a dissonant interval is possible, but strictly controlled. A voice may skip up a minor seventh if there is some compelling voice-leading reason to do so, *and* if it then moves down by consonant step. A voice may skip down a diminished fifth if there is some compelling voice-leading reason to do so, *and* if it then moves up by a consonant step.

Successive Skips. Since conjunct motion should be the norm, you should try to avoid successive skips. When used, successive skips work best if small and in opposite directions (Figure 5.5a). Still, you may use successive skips in the same direction if the combined skips do not exceed an octave, and if the combined skips do not outline a dissonant interval (Figure 5.5b). Commonly, successive skips outline (or arpeggiate) a triad (Figures 5.5c and 5.5d) and *a step in the opposite direction follows the second skip.*

Figure 5.5   Successive Skips

Approaching and Leaving Skips. As a rule, it is best to approach and leave any skip by step *in a direction opposite to that skip.* If this is impractical, you should at least follow the skip with a step in the same direction. The larger (or more dissonant) the skip, the more strictly this rule applies.

Figure 5.6   Disjunct Motion

SIMULTANEOUS MOTION

There are four ways in which two voices may relate to each other. Voice leading considerations grade these from weak to strong as follows: *parallel* motion, *similar* motion, *oblique* motion, and *contrary* motion.

PARALLEL MOTION

When two voices *move in the same direction by the same interval*, they move in *parallel motion*. Parallel motion is the weakest relative motion.

* Parallel perfect fourths permitted if lowest voice is NOT the bass.

Figure 5.7 Parallel Motion

You should *avoid parallel motion between outer voices*. Voices that move in parallel lose a degree of independence. Parallel motion between inner voices or between an inner voice and an outer voice is fine, providing that the parallel interval is not from the list of forbidden parallels.

Parallel motion in perfect unisons, octaves or fifths between any two voices is forbidden (see "Forbidden Parallel Motions," page 61).

SIMILAR MOTION

When two voices move in the same direction but *not* by the same interval, they move in *similar motion*. Similar motion is slightly stronger than parallel motion.

Figure 5.8 Similar Motion

Avoid similar motion between outer voices when moving into a perfect consonance (see "Hidden Parallel Octaves," page 63). Similar motion between inner voices or between an outer voice and an inner voice is fine.

OBLIQUE MOTION

When one voice moves while the other stays on the same note, *oblique motion* results.

Figure 5.9   Oblique Motion

Oblique motion has the advantage of emphasizing the independence of the voices involved. For this reason, oblique motion is relatively strong. The moving voice, however, takes precedence over the stationary one. Thus, to emphasize both the independence and the equality of each voice, we look to *contrary motion*.

CONTRARY MOTION

When two voices move in opposite directions, *contrary* motion results.

* Only bass and tenor may stand more than an octave apart.

Figure 5.10   Contrary Motion

Contrary motion is the strongest type of motion, since the two voices remain both equal and separate. Motion between outer voices should be primarily contrary.

FORBIDDEN PARALLEL MOTIONS

When voices move in parallel, one voice seems to track the other. The two sound less like equal voices than one voice imitated or doubled by another. When the interval that separates the two voices is a perfect consonance, the parallel voices fuse, losing any remaining sense of independence. Thus, tradition forbids the use of the three stronger perfect consonances—the unison, the fifth, and the octave—in parallel motion.

In the Bach Chorales, parallel perfect fourths appear in the upper three voices with regularity and in every conceivable configuration. Despite this, some theory texts (for example, Piston's *Harmony*), allow parallel fourths only when parallel *thirds* occur beneath them. Bach breaks this "rule" as often as he keeps it.

Forbidden Parallel Unisons. A pair of voices may move into or out of a unison, *but not by parallel motion.*

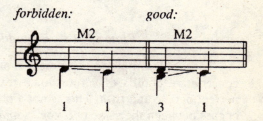

Figure 5.11   Forbidden Parallel Unisons

Parallel motion by the unison destroys all independence of voices. When moving in parallel by the unison, two voices merge into a single series of pitches.

Forbidden Parallel Octaves. Motion by parallel octaves creates the sense, not of *two* voices, but of one voice doubled at the octave. Since this destroys the independence of the "doubling" voice, we must avoid parallel octaves completely.

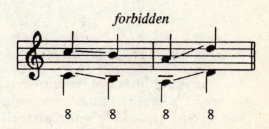

Figure 5.12   Forbidden Parallel Octaves

Forbidden Parallel Perfect Fifths. Like octaves, fifths in parallel convey the sense of a single voice doubled, and therefore parallel perfect fifths should be completely avoided (see Figure 5.13a). Two voices may move in parallel from a perfect fifth to a *diminished* fifth *if* the notes of the diminished fifth resolve (see Figure 5.13b). *Remember:* Diminished intervals resolve inward.

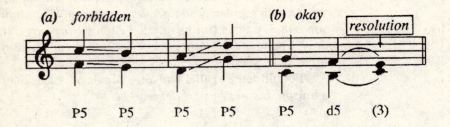

Figure 5.13 *Forbidden Parallel Fifths*

These rules apply to two voices moving in parallel motion. Given two consecutive chords of a four-voice texture, each will usually contain a perfect octave and fifth. This is not a problem unless the repeated interval occurs between the same two voices *and* the voices move in parallel.

Figure 5.14 *Permitted Successive Fifths*

Successive fifths that result from repeated notes pose no problem. In Figure 5.14a, the first fifth is between alto and bass, the second between alto and soprano. These fifths are *not* parallel fifths because they are not between the same two voices. Therefore, they are permitted. In Figure 5.14b, the first and second fifth *are* between the same two voices (alto and bass) but they do not move. This is not parallel *motion* but repetition. These repeated fifths are permitted.

Hidden Parallel Octaves. If, in the outer voices, we approach an octave by similar motion we create *hidden octaves*. These implicit octaves weaken the independence of our two most important voices. For this reason, avoid such voice leading, *except when the soprano moves by step*. A direct step in the upper voice destroys the implicit parallels that otherwise might result.

Figure 5.15   Hidden Parallel Octaves

VOICE CROSSING AND OVERLAP

Parallel motion is not the only challenge to the independence of voices. Registral confusion can lead to an equally serious loss of independence.

Voice Crossing. As a rule, adjacent voices should not cross. That is, the alto should not be higher than the soprano, nor the tenor higher than the alto, nor the bass higher than the tenor. When adjacent voices switch position, a voice crossing results. In chorale-style literature, composers occasionally cross voices (and this, most often, in the inner voices). As a student, however, you will do best to avoid voice crossings, *especially voice crossings that involve an outer voice*. Most theory texts forbid voice crossings.

Voice crossings do *not* correct forbidden parallels.

Figure 5.16   Voice Crossings

Voice Overlap. When the lower of two adjacent voices moves to a pitch higher than the previous pitch in the upper voice, we have a *voice overlap*. Voice overlaps occur regularly in the Bach Chorales. Many theory texts, however, forbid them. Since voice overlaps easily lead to a confusion of voices, and since they are usually unnecessary, you will do best to avoid them. *In keyboard style, however, voice overlaps are both unavoidable and appropriate.*

Figure 5.17   Voice Overlaps

General Guidelines for Composing Inner Voices

In *realizing*—that is, fleshing out—a four-voice texture, you should concern yourself primarily with the outer voices. If you create strong voice leading between soprano and bass, you will run into few problems realizing the inner voices.

GENERAL VOICING GUIDELINES

Whether to place a chord in open or closed position is a question of *voicing*. As a rule, you should keep the inner voices high. This leads both to a clearer sound and more easily realized part writing. Leave your voices room to maneuver, however. Continuous closed voicings force frequent voice overlaps and crossings. So, you are best off mixing closed with open voicings, favoring—all things being equal—the voicing that puts the inner voices higher. (In keyboard style, however, closed positions dominate, since overlaps are unproblematic.)

GUIDELINES FOR COMPOSING THE INDIVIDUAL VOICE

Broad rules regulate the composition of individual upper voices. (As we will see in the next chapter, the bass is a special case.) Govern your specific decisions by the following rules of thumb:

> *Rule:* When possible, repeat a note from one harmony to the next. If repetition is impossible, move by step. If you can neither repeat a note nor move by step, only then should you move by skip.

> *Rule:* If you must skip, skip by the smallest (consonant) interval possible.

Only when the above options fail should you consider a large or dissonant skip. If you follow these guidelines *in the order given*, you will find that skips are seldom necessary and that note repetition and conjunct motion are the norm within the upper voices.

The four voices of chorale style are soprano, alto, tenor, and bass. Except in keyboard style, adhere to their conventional ranges.

In creating music in chorale style, use complete triads. (If you omit any triad note, it should be the fifth.) Double (or— if omitting the fifth — triple) the root of the triad. Double the fifth only for some compelling voice-leading reason. Avoid doubling the third of a triad except in very special contexts (described in chapter 7). Do not double the leading tone ($\hat{7}$) in a V or vii.

Avoid parallel perfect unisons, fifths, and octaves completely. You may use parallel perfect fourths as long as they do not involve the bass. (If you are working from Piston's Harmony, *however, parallel fourths must always be accompanied by parallel thirds in a lower voice.) Avoid voice crossings and voice overlaps. When possible, move by step.*

Concern yourself primarily with the outer voices—the soprano and the bass. Maintain the independence of each and keep the relationship between them strong.

**Selected
Readings**

Aldwell, Edward, and Carl Schachter. *Harmony and Voice Leading*. 2d ed. 2 vols. New York: Harcourt Brace Jovanovich, 1989. Chapters 4–5.

Benjamin, Thomas, Michael Horvit, and Robert Nelson. *Techniques and Materials of Tonal Music*. Belmont, CA: Wadsworth, 1992. Part II, Sections 1–3.

Fux, Johann Joseph. *The Study of Counterpoint from Johann Fux's "Gradus ad Parnassum."* Translated and edited by Alfred Mann. New York: Norton, 1965. Part I, Sections I–II.

Jonas, Oswald. *Introduction to the Theory of Heinrich Schenker*. Translated and edited by John Rothgeb. New York: Longman, 1982. Chapters 1–2.

Komar, Arthur J. *Theory of Suspensions*. Princeton, NJ: Princeton University Press, 1971. Chapters 1–3.

Kostka, Stefan, and Dorothy Payne. *Tonal Harmony*. 2d ed. New York: Alfred A. Knopf, 1989. Chapter 5.

Mitchell, William J. *Elementary Harmony*. 2d ed. Englewood Cliffs, NJ: Prentice-Hall, 1948. Chapter 7.

Piston, Walter. *Harmony*. 5th ed. Revised and expanded by Mark DeVoto. New York: Norton, 1987. Chapter 3.

Salzer, Felix. *Structural Hearing*. New York: Dover, 1962. Chapters 2–3.

Schenker, Heinrich. *Counterpoint*. 2 vols. Edited by John Rothgeb. Translated by John Rothgeb and Jürgen Thym. New York: Schirmer Books, 1987. Part 1.

———. *Harmony*. Edited by Oswald Jonas. Translated by Elisabeth Mann Borgese. Chicago: University of Chicago Press, 1954. Section II.

Schoenberg, Arnold. *Theory of Harmony*. Translated by Roy E. Carter. Berkeley: University of California Press, 1983. Part II.

Westergaard, Peter. *An Introduction to Tonal Theory*. New York: Norton, 1975. Chapter 3.

6

Basic Harmonic Grammar

Harmonic progressions arise when the tonic triad is unfolded in time through arpeggiation. Dissonant passing notes prolong this process, which we call composing out. Root position harmonies provide consonant support for passing motions within the tonic triad. They create progressions of triads whose roots are related by fifth or third.

Functional tonality has two aims: maintaining voice independence and establishing a clear tonality. The voice leading guidelines outlined in the previous chapter concentrate on the former. Those in this chapter concentrate on the latter. However, you must remember that harmonic progressions arise from voice leading, and that voice leading expresses harmonic progressions.

$\frac{5}{3}$ TECHNIQUE

Tonal music does not merely begin and end in the same key. It extends the tonic triad of a key from the beginning of the musical work to its end. That process which extends and embellishes the tonic triad in time is called *composing out*.

Composing out has three stages: *unfolding, prolonging*, and providing *consonant support*. First, we unfold the triad in time by arpeggiating it. Next, we prolong the arpeggiated intervals by filling them in with passing notes. Linear progressions result. They begin and end on chord notes and the intervening scale degrees fill them in. Finally, we provide each of these (dissonant) passing notes with consonant support—that is, we provide each with its own triad, one that contains the former passing note as a chord member.

Composing Out: Unfolding and Prolongation

We can see this unfolding of the tonic triad in Figure 6.1. Mozart unfolds the tonic triad (Figure 6.1a) in time through arpeggiation (Figure 6.1b). To compose out further, he prolongs certain arpeggiated intervals with dissonant passing notes, creating linear progressions $\hat{5}-\hat{3}$, $\hat{3}-\hat{1}$, and $\hat{1}-\hat{3}$ (see Figure 6.1c).

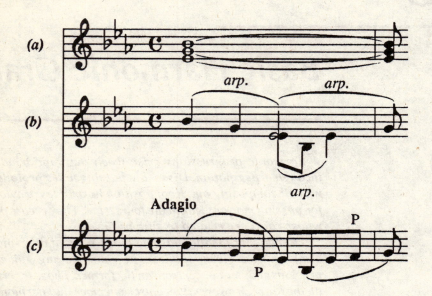

Figure 6.1   *Composing Out: Mozart, Piano Sonata, K. 570;*
second movement

Although this process results in melody alone, we begin to see how harmony (in this case, the tonic triad) finds expression through melody. In the next step, you will learn to unfold a triad in more than one voice. This process results in *counterpoint*.

Species Counterpoint

Traditionally, composers learn counterpoint in stages. Each stage is called a species of counterpoint and the counterpoint that results *species counterpoint*. Of the traditional five species, only the first two need concern us here. First- and second-species counterpoint will help you understand the proper relation between outer voices (soprano and bass). It will teach you as well how triads progress one to another in support of linear progressions.

FIRST SPECIES

In first-species counterpoint, the voices move in equal note-values, note-against-note. In addition, each voice remains consonant with the other.

If Figure 6.1 showed the upper voice of a first-species model, it would require a second, lower voice consonant with the first for its completion. As the lower voice, or bass, this new voice would have to support the unfolding of the upper voice. The bass provides this support with the root of the composed-out triad. In Figure 6.2, we see the tonic triad (6.2a) unfolded in first species counterpoint (6.2b).

> *Remember:* You may use only *consonant* intervals in first-species counterpoint.

Therefore, in Figure 6.2b we must omit the dissonant passing-note prolongations of Figure 6.1c.

Figure 6.2   Figure 6.1 as First-Species Counterpoint

SECOND SPECIES

Second-species counterpoint permits two notes in the upper voice for each note in the lower. The second note of each pair in the upper voice can be a dissonant passing note—that is, it can result from the prolongation of an arpeggiated interval.   Therefore, a *second*-species unfolding of Figure 6.1 would allow us to reintroduce the two passing-note prolongations of Figure 6.1.

(a)

(b)

5	3	(2)	8	(2)	3

Figure 6.3   Figure 6.1 as Second-Species Counterpoint

Notice that the dissonant passing notes make perfect sense. We hear them as prolongations of the linear progression $\hat{3}-\hat{1}$ and $\hat{1}-\hat{3}$.

Harmonic progression begins when, to prolong these linear progressions even further, we convert Figure 6.3 back to first species counterpoint (after we find some way to remove the dissonances).

The Fifth Divider

How can we accomplish this? First-species counterpoint must maintain consonance between the voices. Yet the passing notes of Figure 6.3 create dissonances against the bass.

By arpeggiation to $\hat{5}$ in the bass beneath each passing note, we provide *consonant support* for the previously dissonant passing notes (both $\hat{2}$). At the same time, we continue composing out the basic triad through bass arpeggiation.

5	3	5	8	5	8	5	3

*Figure 6.4   Mozart, Piano Sonata, K. 570;
second movement (showing consonant fifths)*

Notice how the new, consonant fifths support the formerly dissonant passing $\hat{2}$s of Figure 6.3. We call the harmony that results from the arpeggiation of the bass to $\hat{5}$ in support of a dissonant passing note the *upper-fifth divider*.

THE UPPER-FIFTH DIVIDER

Now each voice arpeggiates intervals from the tonic triad and helps prolong the linear progressions $\hat{3}$–$\hat{1}$ and $\hat{1}$–$\hat{3}$. However, the harmonic fifth between bass $\hat{5}$ and soprano $\hat{2}$ has no place in the tonic (E-flat) triad. In fact that fifth suggests the dominant triad (B-flat). In the complete version of this measure, we find that dominant triad fully realized.

Figure 6.5   Mozart, Piano Sonata, K. 570; second movement (as written)

The bass $\hat{5}$ supports not only a consonant fifth but also, with the second passing note, a complete dominant triad. In Figure 6.6 (page 72), a similar prolongation results in a similar upper-fifth divider.

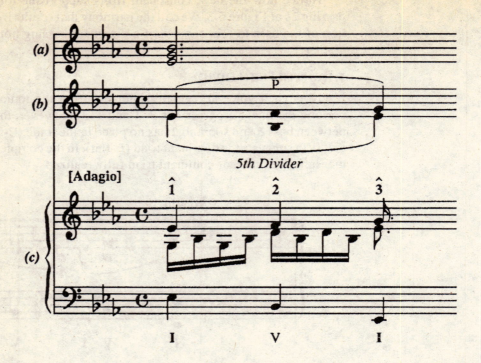

Figure 6.6   Mozart, Piano Sonata, K. 457; second movement, measure 2

Once again, the arpeggiated bass $\hat{5}$ creates a dominant triad in support of the passing $\hat{2}$ in the soprano.

THE LOWER-FIFTH DIVIDER

When $\hat{4}$ arises as a dissonant passing note, the upper-fifth divider cannot provide consonant support. In fact, no member of the tonic triad can create a consonance below $\hat{4}$. In this case, composers turn to the lower-fifth of the tonic—$\hat{4}$ itself—to provide consonant support.

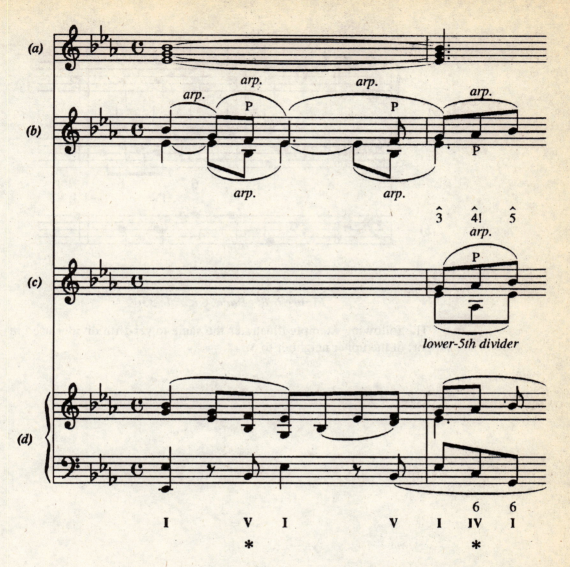

Figure 6.7   Mozart, Piano Sonata, K. 570; second movement

The lower-fifth divider provides consonant support for the ascending passing note $\hat{4}$ (see Figure 6.7c). The bass progression from $\hat{1}$ to $\hat{5}$ supports two passing notes ($\hat{2}$ and $\hat{4}$) with the upper- *and* lower-fifth dividers (see Figure 6.7d).

As a rule, however, the lower-fifth divider (IV) functions best as support for the upper neighbor to $\hat{5}$, $\hat{6}$. Figure 6.8b outlines the basic progression. Note how IV supports $\hat{6}$ in the $\hat{5}$–$\hat{6}$–$\hat{5}$ neighbor-note motion of the soprano.

Figure 6.8   Bach, Chorale 330

The following example illustrates the same lower-fifth divider used in support of the upper neighbor to $\hat{5}$.

Figure 6.9   Beethoven, Symphony No. 6; third movement, trio

FREE STYLE

The Beethoven example above and the previous Mozart examples illustrate a style based on both the voice-leading constraints of species counterpoint and the harmonic constraints of chorale style. Yet this composite style is freer and more flexible than either alone. Although we will concentrate on the more constrained chorale style for the moment, we will occasionally refer to realizations in what is called *free style*. For it is in free style that *all* the various techniques of functional tonality find full expression.

The Third Divider

Just as the fifth divider prolongs the repetition of a triad, the third divider prolongs the motion from a triad to its fifth divider. Two third dividers occur frequently: iii as the third divider of the upper-fifth divider I–V, and vi as the third divider of the lower-fifth divider I–IV.

THE UPPER-THIRD DIVIDER

The upper-third divider (I–iii–V) further prolongs the $\hat{3}$–$\hat{2}$–$\hat{1}$ linear progression already prolonged by the fifth divider (V) that supports $\hat{2}$ (Figure 6.10a). This prolongation is often accompanied by a voice-leading ii^6 (which we will discuss more thoroughly in the next chapter). The ii^6 helps balance the double prolongation of $\hat{3}$ with a double prolongation of $\hat{2}$ (see Figure 6.10b).

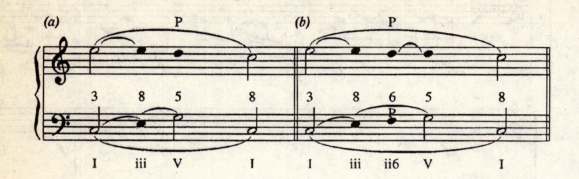

Figure 6.10   The Third Divider

The upper-third divider seldom occurs as a direct progression in chorale style, but we do see it in free style.

Figure 6.11   Brahms, Romance, *Op. 118, No. 5: measures 50-51*

THE LOWER-THIRD DIVIDER

Similarly, vi $\frac{5}{3}$ frequently functions as lower-third divider to the lower-fifth divider $\hat{4}$. This results in either a I–vi–IV (Figure 6.12a) or a I–vi–ii[6] (Figure 6.12b) progression.

Bach Chorales

(a) No. 209   (b) No. 334

I   vi   IV   V   I   I   vi   ii⁶₅   V   I

Figure 6.12   vi: Lower-Third Divider

THE CADENCE

The harmonic and voice-leading formulas that serve as punctuation marks at the end of phrases or compositions are called *cadences*. We will distinguish among three cadences: the *authentic cadence*, the *half cadence*, and the *plagal cadence*.

The Authentic Cadence

The progression V^5_3– I^5_3 at the end of a phrase is referred to as an authentic cadence. If the soprano ends on $\hat{1}$, the cadence is a *perfect* authentic cadence. If the soprano ends on $\hat{3}$ or $\hat{5}$, the cadence is an *imperfect* authentic cadence.

THE PERFECT AUTHENTIC CADENCE

In a perfect authentic cadence, a root-position V–I progression supports soprano $\hat{7}$–$\hat{1}$ or $\hat{2}$–$\hat{1}$. With the former, we find conventional voice leading.

Bach Chorales
No. 11

Figure 6.13   Perfect Authentic Cadences: $\hat{7}$–$\hat{1}$

In the Bach chorales, the $\hat{2}$–$\hat{1}$ motion of the soprano often provokes unusual voice leading in the tenor or alto. The leading tone ($\hat{7}$) sometimes leaps to the third (Figure 6.14a) or the fifth (Figure 6.14b). Although unusual, this voice leading does avoid a tripled root and creates a complete triad.

Bach Chorales

(a) No. 9   (b) No. 40   (c) No. 38

Figure 6.14   Perfect Authentic Cadences: $\hat{2}$–$\hat{1}$

THE IMPERFECT AUTHENTIC CADENCE

The perfect authentic cadence signals a full stop, whereas the *imperfect* authentic cadence signals a temporary pause or partial stop. *Only when both outer voices reach $\hat{1}$ together will a musical motion be complete.* Most imperfect authentic cadences end on $\hat{3}$ in the soprano. We cannot provide the neighbors of $\hat{5}$ with consonant support from V. Therefore, most cadences to $\hat{5}$ will be plagal or half cadences (see below) rather than imperfect authentic cadences.

Figure 6.15   Bach, Chorale 6

The Half Cadence	When the prolongation of a linear progression occupies more than a single musical phrase, an interior phrase may end on V. In Figure 6.16a and b, the soprano's $\hat{3}$–$\hat{2}$–$\hat{1}$ motion pauses on $\hat{2}$. We call the resulting I–V cadence a half (or semi) cadence. (We will discuss the half cadence and associated techniques in a later chapter.)

Figure 6.16   Half Cadences

A half cadence requires completion (to I) in a later phrase. The terminal $\hat{2}$ of the soprano must eventually complete its passing motion (usually) to $\hat{1}$. Frequently, it returns first to $\hat{3}$ (see Figure 6.16a).

The Plagal Cadence

The cadence from the lower-fifth divider to I is called a plagal cadence. The I–IV–I plagal cadence is ambiguous. Is this a plagal cadence in C (I–IV–I) or is it an imperfect authentic cadence in F (I–V–I)? For this reason, we see the plagal cadence rarely and under two conditions: when the soprano cadences to $\hat{5}$ from its upper neighbor ($\hat{6}$), or at the end of a composition (after the final perfect authentic cadence) and as a final prolongation of the tonic triad.

THE IMPERFECT PLAGAL CADENCE

V contains neither $\hat{4}$ nor $\hat{6}$, the neighbors of $\hat{5}$. The step-wise approach to a terminal $\hat{5}$ supported by I, then, needs the *lower*-fifth divider, IV. IV contains *both* neighbors to $\hat{5}$–$\hat{4}$ and $\hat{6}$. As a rule, plagal cadences result from a $\hat{5}$–$\hat{6}$–$\hat{5}$ neighbor motion in the soprano (see Figure 6.17a).

THE PERFECT PLAGAL CADENCE

When a plagal cadence comes at the end of a composition, it usually follows a perfect authentic cadence. It provides lower-fifth-divider support for a repeated soprano $\hat{1}$. (The "Amen" added to the end of hymns is a cadence of this sort.) As a terminal cadence with $\hat{1}$ in the soprano, this sort of plagal cadence is called perfect (see Figure 6.17b).

Bach Chorales

(a) No. 32   *(b)* No. 239

Figure 6.17 Plagal Cadences

The Deceptive Cadence

In the imperfect authentic cadence, the bass completes its motion to $\hat{1}$ but the soprano does not. The deceptive cadence reverses this by allowing the soprano to cadence to $\hat{1}$ but by stopping the bass on $\hat{6}$. In fact, the deceptive progression V$\frac{5}{3}$–vi$\frac{5}{3}$ allows all the voices (save the bass) to resolve as if to I. The bass, however, moves to $\hat{6}$—the root of vi and the one member of the vi triad that is not a member of I.

Bach Chorales

(a) No. 196   *(b)* No. 321

Figure 6.18   Deceptive Cadences: V–vi

Note that in both Figures 6.18a and 6.18b, the upper voices move as if realizing a perfect authentic cadence. The bass move to $\hat{6}$ creates the "deception." The phrase does not end on the expected terminal I but on vi. Notice that this cadential vi must then complete its inevitable motion back to V and, eventually, to I in a subsequent progression.

METRICAL CONSIDERATIONS

As we have seen, harmonic changes create tonic accents. The accent pattern created by a harmonic progression is the *harmonic rhythm* of the progression. The play of harmonic rhythm with and against the strong–weak metrical accents of any time signature is the stuff of music. We must, therefore, avoid *unintentional* conflicts between the two.

Bass Repetition

In particular, any repeated bass note should repeat from a strong to a weak beat. When we repeat the bass note from weak to strong *even if the harmony changes*, we create a syncopation (see Figure 6.19a).

Figure 6.19   Unintentional Syncopations

Chord Repetition

We risk similar accidental syncopations by repeating the same chord in different inversions from a weak to a strong beat (see Figure 6.19b). Even though the bass changes, the repeated chord diminishes the importance of the metrically strong beat. It does so by accenting the weak beat that begins the chord. We would do better to replace both the bass repetition of 6.19a and the harmonic repetition of 6.19b with discrete harmonies (see Figure 6.19c). This solution not only removes the unintentional syncopations, but also provides stronger support for the soprano.

Common Exceptions

Free composition abounds with exceptions to the harmonic principles just discussed. As a rule, these exceptions are unique to their context. However, two are so common as to warrant mention here.

OPENING CHORD REPETITION

Often a composition opens with a weak-to-strong rhythm that we call a *pickup*. These opening weak–strong motions often involve repeated harmonies or bass notes (see Figure 6.20a).

Bach Chorales

Figure 6.20   Two Common Exceptions to Rules Restricting Chord Repetition

BASS REPETITION INTO A DISSONANCE

We may repeat a bass note from a strong to a weak beat *if* the second bass note is dissonant. This is most often the case with a bass suspension (see Figure 6.20b). We will discuss suspensions further in a later chapter. The bass dissonance generates a tonic accent that reinforces the naturally occurring metrical accent.

Notice that the 4 below the final harmony has a slash through it. A slash through a figure indicates that the pitch class represented by that figure has been raised by a half step.

Appendix J outlines the conventions and abbreviations of figured-bass notation.

We can compose out the tonic triad by unfolding it in time through arpeggiation. We may prolong it by inserting passing or neighboring notes between members of the arpeggiated triad.

We support passing and neighboring notes between root, third, and fifth by bass arpeggiations to the upper-fifth divider. We may compose out the upper-fifth divider by arpeggiating up to it through the upper-third divider. Authentic and half cadences result from a terminal bass arpeggiation to the upper-fifth divider and back to the tonic.

The lower-fifth divider supports neighboring notes to the tonic triad. We may prolong the motion to the lower-fifth divider by arpeggiating down to it through the lower-third divider.

Half cadences arise when we end the passing motion $\hat{3}–\hat{2}–\hat{1}$ prematurely on $\hat{2}$, completing the motion to $\hat{1}$ in a later progression.

When we cadence to I from IV, we create a plagal cadence. A plagal cadence beneath repeated $\hat{1}$s is perfect. A plagal cadence beneath $\hat{6}–\hat{5}$ is imperfect.

The deceptive cadence completes all voice-leading motions from V (or V^7) to I except in the bass. It substitutes the lower-third divider (vi) for I, and $\hat{6}$ for $\hat{1}$ in the bass. The composing out of the lower fifth or a direct return to V follows in a later progression.

Avoid repeating a chord or a bass note from a weak to a strong beat. Such repetitions could result in unintentional syncopations.

Selected Readings

Aldwell, Edward, and Carl Schachter. *Harmony and Voice Leading.* 2d ed. 2 vols. New York: Harcourt Brace Jovanovich, 1989. Chapters 6, 8, 9, 11, and 13.

Benjamin, Thomas, Michael Horvit, and Robert Nelson. *Techniques and Materials of Tonal Music.* Belmont, CA: Wadsworth, 1992. Part I, Sections 3–7.

Christ, William, et al. *Materials and Structure of Music.* 3d ed. Vol. I. Englewood Cliffs, NJ: Prentice-Hall, 1980. Chapter 12.

Cooper, Paul. *Perspectives in Music Theory.* 2d ed. New York: Harper & Row, 1980. Chapters 15–16.

Jonas, Oswald. *Introduction to the Theory of Heinrich Schenker.* Translated and edited by John Rothgeb. New York: Longman, 1982. Chapters 2–3.

Kostka, Stefan, and Dorothy Payne. *Tonal Harmony.* 2d ed. New York: Alfred A. Knopf, 1989. Chapter 6.

Ottman, Robert W. *Elementary Harmony.* 4th ed. Englewood Cliffs, NJ: Prentice-Hall, 1989. Chapters 4–10.

Piston, Walter. *Harmony.* 5th ed. Revised and expanded by Mark DeVoto. New York: Norton, 1987. Chapter 3.

Salzer, Felix. *Structural Hearing.* New York: Dover, 1962. Chapters 2–5.

Schenker, Heinrich. *Harmony.* Edited by Oswald Jonas. Translated by Elisabeth Mann Borgese. Chicago: University of Chicago Press, 1980. Division II, Sections I–III.

Schoenberg, Arnold. *Structural Functions of Harmony.* Rev. ed. Edited by Leonard Stein. New York: Norton, 1969. Chapters 1–2.

———. *Theory of Harmony.* Translated by Roy E. Carter. Berkeley: University of California Press, 1983. Chapter 4.

7

Contrapuntal Progressions and Voice-Leading Harmonies

The $\frac{5}{3}$ techniques discussed so far allow us to support dissonant passing- and neighboring-note prolongations in the upper voice with root-position triads. This results in a bass line that moves mainly by skip. The inversions of a triad, especially second inversions, are less stable than its root position. For this reason, inversions provide ideal support for stepwise passing and neighbor motions in the bass. Inversions also provide us with a variety of cadential effects, allowing us to avoid premature or unwanted cadences.

Progressions that involve inversions are known as contrapuntal progressions—that is, progressions that result from linear embellishment. The inversions that create these passing linear embellishments are called passing and neighboring harmonies, by analogy with passing and neighboring notes. The harmonies that result from such passing motions are called voice-leading harmonies because stepwise motion places voice-leading emphasis on the bass.

VOICE-LEADING CONSIDERATIONS

Contrapuntal progressions make no sense apart from good part writing since they arise from voice leading necessity. Therefore, all voices should move as strongly as possible. To effect this, we suspend the doubling rules (discussed in chapter 5) when dealing with contrapuntal progressions.

When reviewing the examples, you should remember that figured bass is a kind of short hand. When a roman numeral has *no* figures it is in $\frac{5}{3}$ or root position. When the figure is simply 6, it is in $\frac{6}{3}$ or first inversion. (See Appendix J for a review of figured-bass notation.)

$\frac{6}{3}$ TECHNIQUE

When we place the third of a triad in the bass, that triad is in first inversion. In that position, the pitch class of the root stands a sixth above the bass, and the fifth stands a third above the bass. Therefore, the figure $\frac{6}{3}$ represents the first-inversion triad.

The $\frac{6}{3}$ inversion of a consonant triad is itself consonant. However, with the third rather than the root in the bass, it is unstable. Being both consonant and unstable, first inversion triads embellish stable $\frac{5}{3}$ progressions.

Bass Arpeggiation

We can prolong a bass motion by unfolding a root position triad to first inversion.

BASS ARPEGGIATION

A root-position triad can prolong itself by unfolding to $\frac{6}{3}$ and then back again.

In Figure 7.1a, Bach prolongs a root position I–V by allowing bass $\hat{1}$ to arpeggiate up to $\hat{3}$ and then back again. There results a I $\frac{5}{3}$ –I $\frac{6}{3}$ –I $\frac{5}{3}$ (or, in figured bass short hand, I–I^6–I) progression. Similarly, in Figure 7.1b, Bach prolongs a I–IV progression by unfolding I to its first inversion and then back again.

Figure 7.1   Bass Arpeggiation: $\frac{5}{3} - \frac{6}{3}$

$\frac{6}{3}$ AS THIRD DIVIDER

A $\frac{6}{3}$ can substitute for a $\frac{5}{3}$ as a third divider. In Figure 7.2a, the bass moves from root-position I to root-position V. Bach breaks the bass $\hat{1}-\hat{5}$ (F–C) leap with an arpeggiation through $\hat{3}$ (A). Since this note prolongs the motion to $\hat{5}$, Bach supports it with a passing $\frac{6}{3}$ (in this case, I⁶).

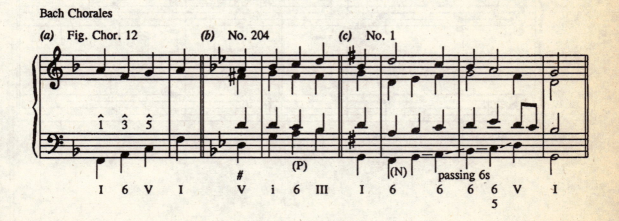

Figure 7.2 $\frac{6}{3}$ Usage

Passing $\frac{6}{3}$s

A first inversion chord provides ideal support for a bass passing note. In Figure 7.2b, root-position i (G minor) moves to root-position III (B-flat). Bach fills in the resulting $\hat{1}$–$\hat{3}$ bass with a passing $\hat{2}$. A $\frac{6}{3}$ (VII^6) provides support for this bass passing note. Since it is in first inversion and is less stable than the two root-position triads that surround it, this $\frac{6}{3}$ has a passing character.

We often see strings of passing $\frac{6}{3}$s in parallel. In Figure 7.2c, Bach supports a linear progression from bass $\hat{1}$ (G) to $\hat{5}$ (D) with parallel passing $\frac{6}{3}$s. This creates a series of passing chords that span the fifth from root-position I to root-position V.

Neighbor $\frac{6}{3}$s

Before the bass of Figure 7.2c begins its ascent to $\hat{5}$, it prolongs its root position with a lower-neighbor note (G–F-sharp–G or $\hat{1}$–$\hat{7}$–$\hat{1}$). Bach supports this neighbor with another $\frac{6}{3}$, creating a neighboring chord above the neighbor-note F-sharp.

BASS NEIGHBOR NOTE

In this way, $\frac{6}{3}$s frequently support neighbor note prolongations in the bass. Figure 7.3a provides another example of a bass neighbor supported by a neighboring $\frac{6}{3}$. The bass prolongation of $\hat{1}$ ($\hat{1}$–#$\hat{7}$–$\hat{1}$) receives the same $\frac{6}{3}$ support as in Figure 7.2c.

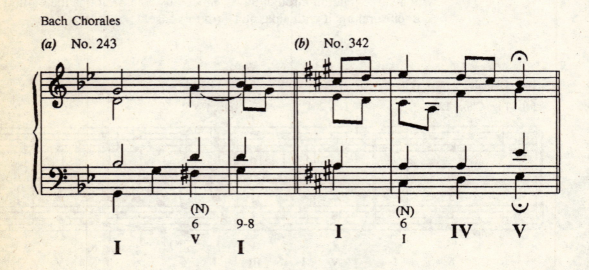

Figure 7.3   Neighbor $\frac{6}{3}$s

INCOMPLETE NEIGHBOR NOTES

When a voice leaps from one note to the neighbor of another, we consider this neighbor note *incomplete*. "Incomplete" in this case does not refer to the chord above the incomplete neighbor; it can contain all its pitches. We frequently see incomplete neighbors in the bass when it is progressing between two $\frac{5}{3}$s. If the bass of the first $\frac{5}{3}$ leaps *down* to the second $\frac{5}{3}$, we can embellish that leap with an incomplete lower neighbor. We support this neighbor with a $\frac{6}{3}$.

In Figure 7.3b, the bass progresses from $\hat{1}$ (A) to $\hat{4}$ (D, its lower-fifth divider), moving first to the incomplete lower neighbor of $\hat{4}$, $\hat{3}$ (C-sharp). To maintain the clarity of the $\frac{5}{3}$ progression (I–IV) progression, Bach supports the neighboring $\hat{3}$ with a $\frac{6}{3}$.

$\frac{6}{4}$ *TECHNIQUE*

The $\frac{6}{4}$ functions like the $\frac{6}{3}$ but, as a dissonant inversion, has a stronger passing character. In general, $\frac{6}{4}$s either function as dissonant passing chords or result from double neighbor note prolongations in the upper voices.

Passing $\frac{6}{4}$

We often see $\frac{6}{4}$s support passing note prolongations of a bass arpeggiation. In Figure 7.4a, Bach fills in the bass of a ii–V^6 progression with a passing note. By supporting that passing note with a $\frac{6}{4}$—an inversion more dissonant and unstable than the $\frac{6}{3}$ to which it passes—he creates a passing harmony between ii and V^6.

Bach Chorales

(a)   No. 85   *(b)*   No. 80

Figure 7.4 $\frac{6}{4}$ *Usage*

COMMON-NOTE $\frac{6}{4}$

Often $\frac{6}{4}$s arise not from passing motions in the bass but from neighbor note motions in the upper voices. These $\frac{6}{4}$s arise above a repeated bass note. For this reason, they are called common-note $\frac{6}{4}$s.

In Figure 7.4b, a motion to $\hat{1}$ (D) in the bass receives a supporting I$\frac{5}{3}$ only on the final quarter note. Bach delays the arrival of I by moving $\hat{5}$ (A) and $\hat{3}$ (F-sharp) to their upper neighbors. This creates a $\frac{6}{4}$ above $\hat{1}$. As the neighboring $\hat{6}$ moves to $\hat{5}$ and the neighboring $\hat{4}$ to $\hat{3}$, the root-position tonic emerges and the phrase ends.

CADENTIAL $\frac{6}{4}$

The most familiar common-note $\frac{6}{4}$ embellishes the V of an authentic cadence. As the bass reaches $\hat{5}$, the upper voices remain on the upper neighbors of the third and fifth of V. This creates a fleeting $\frac{6}{4}$. However, as the bass repeats $\hat{5}$, these upper neighbors resolve down by step to the third and fifth of V proper.

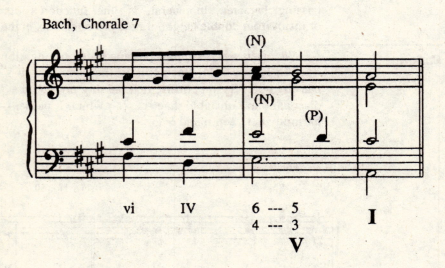

Figure 7.5   The Cadential $\frac{6}{4}$

In Figure 7.5 we see a perfect authentic cadence in A major. The bass moves directly to $\hat{5}$, but the soprano and alto move to a $\frac{6}{4}$ position above that $\hat{5}$. These are upper neighbors that delay the arrival of V itself. As each neighbor resolves down to a $\frac{5}{3}$ position, the V is formed and can now complete its motion to I.

> *Remember:* A cadential $^6_4$ results from a neighbor note embellishment of V in the upper voices. Therefore, the 6 and 4 above the bass must *act* like neighbors and resolve down by step to the 5 and 3 above bass $\hat{5}$.

THE DOMINANT SEVENTH (V^7)

All dissonance has a passing character. It takes us from one consonant position to another, enhancing the voice leading. The most common dissonant prolongation of the upper-fifth divider is the passing V^{8-7}. In a perfect authentic cadence, the upper voice that doubles the root of V ($\hat{5}$) naturally descends through a passing note ($\hat{4}$) to the third of I ($\hat{3}$) (see Figure 7.6a).

Figure 7.6   Origins of the V^7

Origin of the Seventh Chord   The V^7 arises when the composer drops the initial $\hat{5}$ (the doubled root of the V) from this passing 8–7 (Figure 7.6b). We may then move directly to the passing $\hat{4}$. There results a dissonant chord, one that adds a seventh above the root of the V. In general, such chords are known as seventh chords. In particular, we call the V^7 a *dominant seventh*. ("Dominant seventh" is another name for a major-minor seventh chord.)

> *Remember:* We cannot separate seventh chords from their voice-leading origins. A seventh chord takes on the passing character of the dissonance that it incorporates.

Appendix G lists triad and seventh chord types and qualities.

Voice Leading and the Seventh Chord

Three special voice leading considerations govern the V^7.

THE SEVENTH

The seventh (that pitch class a seventh above the root) must resolve down by step. Usually, this resolution is to the third of the succeeding chord.

DOUBLING

Since a seventh chord has four notes, none need be doubled. However, we may omit the fifth of a root-position seventh chord and double the root. This often makes for better voice leading. If we invert the seventh chord, however, we do best to leave the chord complete. *Never double the seventh.*

THE TRITONE

The dissonant tritone formed by the seventh of the V^7 ($\hat{4}$) and the third ($\hat{7}$) resolves predictably. The dissonant $\hat{4}$ resolves down to $\hat{3}$ and the leading tone ($\hat{7}$) resolves up to $\hat{1}$.

Inversions of the V^7

A seventh chord has three inversions. The third ($^6_4$, abbreviated $^4_2$) holds the seventh in the bass. As a dissonant chord in an unstable position, the passing character of the third inversion is very strong.

VOICE LEADING

The voice leading functions of the inversions of the V^7 result from the scale degree in the bass. In the V $^6_5$ the $\hat{7}$ in the bass functions as the lower neighbor to $\hat{1}$ (see Figures 7.7a and 7.8a). In the V $^4_3$, the bass $\hat{2}$ serves as a passing note between $\hat{1}$ and $\hat{3}$. Less frequently it provides an upper neighbor to $\hat{1}$ (see Figures 7.7b and 7.8b). The bass $\hat{4}$ acts as upper neighbor to $\hat{3}$ (see Figures 7.7c and 7.8c).

Figure 7.7   *Inversions of V^7*

Remember: The dissonant seventh must complete its passing motion to $\hat{3}$ no matter in what voice it occurs.

Bach Chorales

(a) No. 32   **(b)** No. 1   **(c)** No. 27

Figure 7.8   Resolution of the Seventh

DOUBLING

As rule, neither omit nor double any notes when using the inversions of a V^7. Notice not only that each inversion of V^7 in Figure 7.8 is complete, but also that the seventh always resolves down by step.

V^7 in the Cadence

The V^7 frequently substitutes for V in the authentic cadence. But because it is dissonant, V^7 seldom replaces V in the half cadence. Still, the half cadence to V^7 does provide a potent, dramatically inconclusive cadence, especially when used to illustrate a text.

Bach Chorales

No. 83   No. 142

Figure 7.9   Rare Half Cadences to Inversions of V^7

These examples illustrate not merely half cadences to V^7, but to inversions of this already dissonant sonority! The text of Chorale 83 considers Christ's sadness, pain, and death. The half cadence arises on the word *acht* ("take care" or "heed"). The cadence from Chorale 132 occurs on *entrückt* ("carried away" or "delivered"). Christ "delivers" the sinner from that pain represented here by the unstable $\frac{4}{2}$. We see the half cadence to V^7 frequently in free style.

The $V\frac{4}{3}$ and vii ^{6}

The active interval of the V^7 (the tritone between $\hat{4}$ and $\hat{7}$) forms the defining fifth of vii. In fact, the leading tone triad (vii) contains all the notes of the V^7 save its root ($\hat{5}$). We use vii^6 as a substitute for the $V\frac{4}{3}$ when voice leading considerations require that we double some member of the harmony.

Notice that in each of these examples not only is one note of the vii^6 doubled, but also that doubling allows step-wise motion in the doubling voice. Remember, however: *Do not double the leading tone in a V, V^7 or vii.*

Figure 7.10   *vii^6 as a Substitute for $V\frac{4}{3}$*

Noncadential V^{7}s

Because of the rhythmic regularity of chorale style, incidental V^7–I progressions may, accidentally, sound cadential. To avoid unwanted cadential effects, we should make the voice-leading role of these non-cadential V^7s clear by placing them in inversion. The $V\frac{6}{5}$ functions well as a voice leading chord to I without suggesting a premature cadence (see Figures 7.8a and 7.8c, page 93).

THE CONTRAPUNTAL CADENCE

A cadence to I in which the bass moves by step rather than by fifth is called a *contrapuntal cadence*. The contrapuntal cadence is useful as a way of ending a phrase on I while also postponing the final perfect authentic close. Most often, contrapuntal cadences use V^6_5 (see Figure 7.11a and b).

We seldom see V^4_3 at a contrapuntal cadence, however, but vii^6 instead (see Figure 7.11c). The doubled bass of the vii^6 provides stronger voice leading for the doubling voice.

Bach Chorales

(a) No. 42   *(b)* No. 46   *(c)* No. 40

Figure 7.11   Contrapuntal Cadences

We support stepwise passing and neighboring motions in the bass with inversions. The consonant inversion ($^6_3$) is the most flexible, functioning either as support for passing and neighboring notes or bass arpeggiations. The dissonant inversions ($^6_4$, $^6_5$, $^4_3$, and $^4_2$) function in more restricted (usually stepwise) voice-leading contexts.

We can avoid unwanted cadential effects by using inversions of V^7 when moving to I before the cadence. Similarly, contrapuntal cadences allow us to postpone the perfect authentic cadence to a later point.

Selected Readings

Aldwell, Edward, and Carl Schachter. *Harmony and Voice Leading.* 2 vols. 2d ed. New York: Harcourt Brace Jovanovich, 1989. Chapters 6, 8, 13, 15, and 16.

Bamberger, Jeanne Shapiro, and Howard Brofsky. *The Art of Listening: Developing Music Perception.* 5th ed. New York: Harper & Row, 1988. Chapter 5.

Benjamin, Thomas, Michael Horvit, and Robert Nelson. *Techniques and Materials of Tonal Music.* Belmont, CA: Wadsworth, 1992. Part I, Sections 8–14.

Jonas, Oswald. *Introduction to the Theory of Heinrich Schenker.* Translated and edited by John Rothgeb. New York: Longman, 1982. Chapters 3–4.

Kostka, Stefan, and Dorothy Payne. *Tonal Harmony.* 2d ed. New York: Alfred A. Knopf, 1989. Chapters 6–9.

Ottman, Robert W. *Elementary Harmony.* 4th ed. Englewood Cliffs, NJ: Prentice-Hall, 1989. Chapter 9.

Piston, Walter. *Harmony.* 5th ed. Revised and expanded by Mark DeVoto. New York: Norton, 1987. Chapter 6.

Salzer, Felix. *Structural Hearing.* New York: Dover, 1962. Chapters 5–6.

Schoenberg, Arnold. *Structural Functions of Harmony.* Rev. ed. Edited by Leonard Stein. New York: Norton, 1969. Chapter 3.

———. *Theory of Harmony.* Translated by Roy E. Carter. Berkeley: University of California Press, 1983. Chapters 6–7.

Westergaard, Peter. *An Introduction to Tonal Theory.* New York: Norton, 1975. Chapters 4–6.

8

Scale-Degree Triads in Context

As we have seen, harmonic progressions arise from voice leading. We can describe, for example, "the function of a IV⁶" only in relation to a particular musical context. In this chapter and the next, we will examine each of the diatonic scale-degree triads and various musical contexts in which they may arise.

THE TONIC TRIAD (I)

Linear progressions unfolded from the tonic triad define sections and entire compositions. The *voice-leading* functions of I are, therefore, limited.

$I \frac{5}{3}$ The root-position tonic functions principally *as* tonic—that is, as the source and destination of all tonal movement. Occasionally the $I\frac{5}{3}$ functions as fifth divider to IV and V. When it does, it provides support for the passing notes that prolong unfoldings of IV or V.

UPPER-FIFTH DIVIDER OF IV

As upper-fifth divider of IV, $I\frac{5}{3}$ supports passing motions that prolong the arpeggiation of IV. In this context, I often sounds like the V *of* IV (see Figure 8.1a).

Bach Chorales

Figure 8.1 $I\frac{5}{3}$ as Fifth Divider

LOWER-FIFTH DIVIDER OF V

I may serve to prolong V, acting as its lower-fifth divider. In this role, I_3^5 supports passing- and neighboring-note motions within the dominant triad (see Figure 8.1b).

$I\frac{6}{3}$ I_3^6 frequently appears as support for bass arpeggiations to $\hat{3}$ and bass passing and neighboring motions to $\hat{2}$ and $\hat{4}$.

UPPER-THIRD DIVIDER

We often find the motion from I to its upper-fifth divider V prolonged by a bass arpeggiation through $\hat{3}$. A bass passing note often intervenes between I_3^6 and V (see Figure 8.2a).

LOWER NEIGHBOR TO BASS $\hat{4}$

We can prolong a motion to the lower-fifth divider by moving from $\hat{1}$ to $\hat{3}$, the lower neighbor of $\hat{4}$. We support this incomplete neighbor with I_3^6. (See Figure 8.2b, where a bass passing note fills in the skip between $\hat{1}$ and $\hat{3}$). The skip *down* a sixth to the unstable I_3^6 makes for a dramatic opening gesture (see Figure 8.2c). We see this leap down to the lower neighbor of $\hat{4}$ frequently in both chorale and free styles.

Bach Chorales

Figure 8.2　*Voice-Leading Role of I$\frac{6}{3}$*

The Cadential "I$\frac{6}{4}$"

Frequently, we find the V of an authentic cadence prolonged by some voice-leading motion that delays its arrival. The most common method of prolongation is the *cadential* $\frac{6}{4}$. In a cadential $\frac{6}{4}$, the bass arrives on the root of the dominant ($\hat{5}$), while the upper voice delays the arrival of the expected $\frac{5}{3}$ with a neighboring $\frac{6}{4}$. As a prolongation of V$\frac{5}{3}$, the initial cadential $\frac{6}{4}$ must resolve. Usually, the 6 resolves down to 5 and the 4 down to 3.

Figure 8.3　*Cadential* $\frac{6}{4}$

Objectively, this $\frac{6}{4}$ built on $\hat{5}$ is a I$_4^6$. However, many theorists argue that it makes more sense to think of this "I$_4^6$" as part of the dominant harmony. The student may sometimes see the cadential $\frac{6}{4}$ progression labeled not I$_4^6$–V$_3^5$–I, but V$_{4-3}^{6-5}$–I. In the latter, the analyst understands the $\frac{6}{4}$ as a dissonant prolongation of the $\frac{5}{3}$ rather than as a separate chord.

THE SUBDOMINANT TRIAD (IV)

The subdominant triad (IV) supports various prolongations of the tonic triad as its lower-fifth divider.

IV $\frac{5}{3}$

We discussed the lower-fifth-divider role of IV$_3^5$ in chapter 6. It supports $\hat{4}$ and $\hat{6}$ as neighbors to $\hat{3}$ and $\hat{5}$ in a prolongation of I. We discussed the plagal cadence in chapter 6 as well. However, in free composition we occasionally see an exceptional and dramatic variant of the plagal cadence. It exemplifies a technique called *harmonic contraction*.

We often find the plagal I–IV–I at the end of a work, after the final perfect authentic cadence. It functions there like the *Amen* at the end of a hymn. It roots the tonic securely between its lower *and* upper fifths. In free composition, we occasionally find this final plagal cadence contracted. The composer omits the initial I (which succeeds the V and precedes the plagal IV). This results in a dramatic deceptive cadence to IV$_3^5$. Only after IV's immediate resolution to I do we hear the contracted plagal cadence.

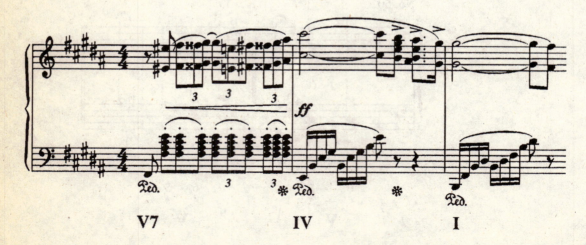

Figure 8.4 *Wagner,* Tristan und Isolde: *final scene (piano reduction)*

By omitting the middle I of this V–I–IV–I plagal progression, Wagner achieves both the drama of the deceptive cadence and a tonic firmly fixed between its upper and lower fifths.

IV$\frac{6}{3}$

IV$\frac{6}{3}$, like all $\frac{6}{3}$s, provides passing and neighboring support for the bass.

IV$\frac{6}{3}$ AS LOWER-THIRD DIVIDER

We often see the IV$\frac{6}{3}$ serving as third divider in a descent from I to its lower fifth. In such a case, IV$\frac{6}{3}$ can simply move to the lower-fifth divider (IV$\frac{5}{3}$). Or it can move to a voice-leading substitute—usually, ii^6 (see Figure 8.5a).

Bach Chorales

Figure 8.5   Voice-Leading Role of IV^6

IV$\frac{6}{3}$ AND V

We frequently find the passing note that prolongs the motion from V to V^6 prolonged by a passing IV^6 (see Figure 8.5b).

IV$\frac{6}{3}$ IN A DECEPTIVE PROGRESSION

Less frequently, IV^6 substitutes for vi in a deceptive progression from V (see Figure 8.6a).

Figure 8.6   *Deceptive Progression: IV⁶*

Like the vi of a deceptive cadence, the IV^6 completes its voice-leading motion to V in the next progression.

iv$^6_3$ IN THE MINOR

In the minor, iv^6 has an additional function. As a minor triad, its third ($\hat{6}$) is now only a half step from $\hat{5}$. As a result, we often find iv^6 functioning as upper neighbor to $\hat{5}$ (see Figure 8.6b).

IV $^6_4$

We see IV$^6_4$ most often as a support for a neighbor-note prolongation of I. (See the discussion of neighboring $^6_4$s in chapter 7.)

THE DOMINANT AND DOMINANT-SEVENTH (V AND V⁷)

In chapters 6 and 7 we discussed the dominant's primary function as upper-fifth divider of I, as well as its crucial cadential role. The inversions of V and V^7 serve not only these functions but also more varied contrapuntal functions.

V $^6_3$ and V $^6_5$

With $\hat{7}$ (the leading tone) in the bass, V^6 and V$^6_5$ function primarily as lower neighbors to I. As such they serve either in a contrapuntal progression to I$^5_3$ or as part of a bass arpeggiation of V (see Figures 7.7a and 7.8a, pp. 92–93).

$V\frac{6}{4}$ *and* $V\frac{4}{3}$

In general, the second inversions of V and V^7 most often function as passing chords prolonging the bass arpeggiation $I_3^5 - I^6$ (see Figures 7.7b and 7.8b, pp. 92–93). However, Bach seems to prefer vii^6 for this role.

$V\frac{4}{2}$

With the seventh—the dissonance—in the bass, the V_2^4 functions exclusively as a neighboring chord to I^6 (see Figures 7.7c and 7.8c, pp. 92–93).

THE SUPERTONIC TRIAD (ii)

$ii\frac{5}{3}$

$II\frac{5}{3}$ AS UPPER-FIFTH DIVIDER TO V

In the major, ii_3^5 serves as upper-fifth divider to V (see Figure 8.7a).

Bach, Chorale 125

Figure 8.7   Bach, Chorale 125

$ii\frac{5}{3}$ AND $I\frac{5}{3}$

Students often find ii_3^5 irresistible as a passing chord between I and I^6. It functions poorly in this role. (V_3^4 or vii^6, on the other hand, is ideal.) At first glance, Figure 8.7a seems to contradict this. In the more detailed analysis of 8–7b, however, we notice how the 5-6 motion above the bass $\hat{2}$ converts the ii_3^5 into the more appropriate passing vii^6 before the bass completes its motion to I^6 (see "5–6 Technique," page 104).

$ii\frac{6}{3}$

The ii_3^6 functions as lower neighbor to V (Figure 8.8a) or, just as often, as a passing chord between I^6 and V.

Bach Chorales

(a)   No. 22   (b)   No. 264

      I   ii6   V   V   I   vi   iii   vi

Figure 8.8   Voice-Leading Role of ii$\frac{6}{3}$ and iii

5–6 TECHNIQUE

IV$^5_3$ and ii^6 function similarly as lower neighbors to V. And although IV is the stronger chord, it creates greater voice-leading problems. Any time we create successive root position triads, we risk forbidden parallel perfect fifths or octaves.

One common technique retains the best of both these motions to V while reducing the threat of unwanted parallels. If we begin on IV$^5_3$, we can convert the harmony to a ii^6 by moving the 5 to a 6 in the procedure known as *5–6 technique*. In Figure 8.7b (page 103) for example, a root-position ii prolongs a V. A pair of 5–6 motions above the V–ii progression creates passing motions in the inner voices that propel the progression toward the I^6. (If we look at the rest of the phrase in Figure 8.7a we see that Bach reproduces in the *bass* as it approaches V those upward passing notes created by this 5–6 technique first in the tenor and then in the alto.)

THE MEDIANT TRIAD (iii)

In the major, we seldom find iii in any but root position, where it serves as upper-fifth and upper-third divider. (See chapter 10 for a discussion of III in the minor.)

**iii as Fifth
Divider of vi**

iii$^5_3$ often serves as upper-fifth divider of vi, as it does in Figure 8.8b.

**iii as Third
Divider**

Root-position iii can function as third divider in the progression I–V. A ii^6 or IV^7 often passes between the third divider and V: I–iii–ii^6–V–I. In Figure 8.9, Bach divides the progression from root-position i to root-position V♯ with III.

* The figures between staves are Bach's.

Figure 8.9   Bach, Figured Chorale 59

VII^6 supports the bass passing note between $\hat{1}$ and $\hat{3}$. A ii^6 supports the bass passing note between $\hat{3}$ and $\hat{5}$.

In Bach's figures, we see that the ii^6 becomes a IV^7 as the soprano moves to $\hat{1}$. We will discuss IV^{7}s in chapter 12. As a dissonant chord, a IV^7 does not always behave like a lower-fifth divider, but can as often have a passing character.

**Neighboring
and Passing iiis**

In a bass arpeggiation from $\hat{4}$ to $\hat{6}$, iii^6 may support a bass passing note between $\hat{4}$ and $\hat{6}$ (see Figure 8.10a).

Bach Chorales

Figure 8.10   iii: Uncommon Functions

When the root of vi (6̂) functions as third divider between a bass 1̂ and 4̂, Bach often prolongs that vi with its upper-fifth divider, iii⁵₃. The root of iii (3̂) then moves directly to bass 4̂ as the lower neighbor (see Figure 8.10b).

THE SUBMEDIANT TRIAD (vi)

vi in the Major

In the major, vi functions most often as upper-fifth divider to ii or as lower-third divider to I.

Bach Chorales

Figure 8.11   vi in the Major

UPPER-FIFTH DIVIDER

As upper-fifth divider, vi supports a prolongation of ii (see Figure 8.11a).

LOWER-THIRD DIVIDER

A vi can divide the bass progression from $\hat{1}$ *down* to $\hat{4}$ with a bass $\hat{6}$ (see Figure 8.11b).

Notice that the bass $\hat{4}$ supports either the lower-fifth divider (IV) or neighboring ii^6.

NEIGHBORING CHORD

Frequently, Bach contracts the bass $\hat{1}$–$\hat{6}$–$\hat{4}$–$\hat{5}$ progression, omitting the lower-fifth divider $\hat{4}$ (supported by IV or ii^6) altogether. The lower-third divider (vi), then, moves directly to V as V's upper neighbor.

The vi can function directly as a neighboring chord to V as in Figure 8.11c. Here, V^7 approaches vi as if approaching I. The upper voices resolve as if to I—only the bass moves to the upper neighbor of $\hat{5}$ instead. The resulting vi functions as a neighboring chord as it moves immediately back to V and then on to the cadential I.

DECEPTIVE SUBSTITUTE FOR I

The deceptive progression throws us back to the lower-third divider while mimicking a cadence to I (see Figure 8.12a).

Bach Chorales

Figure 8.12   vi and vii

This progression leaves a potential authentic cadence unresolved: We have not cadenced V–I but V–vi. This propels us forward into the next progression in search of the avoided tonic.

VI in the Minor

In the minor, VI retains its role as third divider and deceptive substitute for I. VI, in the minor, is a major triad, however. The deceptive progression from a major triad on V♯ up a half step to a major triad on VI is startling. For this reason, the deceptive cadence is even more distinctive in the minor than in the major. Compare the sound of the deceptive progression (V–vi) of Figure 8.12a in the major with the minor example in 8.12b.

THE LEADING TONE TRIAD (vii)

As a diminished triad, dissonant in all positions, vii functions purely as a voice-leading (that is, passing or neighboring) chord. (For a discussion of VII in the *minor*, see chapter 9.) As a result, we seldom see vii in any but the first inversion.

vii$^6_3$

As a dissonant chord with $\hat{2}$ in the bass, vii^6 passes between $\hat{1}$ and $\hat{3}$ or $\hat{3}$ and $\hat{1}$, occasionally acting as an incomplete neighbor to either (see Figure 8.12c).

vii^6 and the Contrapuntal Cadence

The vii^6 often replaces V$^4_3$ in a contrapuntal cadence (see Figure 7.11c).

*R*oot-position I, IV, and V form the background of most progressions. In inversions, each of these primary triads serves broader voice-leading roles. I occasionally functions as a fifth divider of IV and V. IV^6 functions as a passing chord within a prolongation of V. The inversions of V and V^7 function as passing and neighbor chords within an expansion of I. The vii^6 serves as a substitute for the passing V$^4_3$.

The ii, iii, and vi function either as fifth dividers or, in inversion, as passing or neighboring chords. The iii and vi function as third dividers as well. In that role they prolong motions to the upper-fifth divider or the lower-fifth divider of I. The vi functions additionally as a deceptive substitute for I.

Selected Readings

Aldwell, Edward, and Carl Schachter. *Harmony and Voice Leading*. 2d ed. 2 vols. New York: Harcourt Brace Jovanovich, 1989. Chapter 16.

Benjamin, Thomas, Michael Horvit, and Robert Nelson. *Techniques and Materials of Tonal Music*. Belmont, CA: Wadsworth, 1992. Part II, Sections 9–14.

Christ, William, et al. *Materials and Structure of Music*. 3d ed. Vol. I. Englewood Cliffs, NJ: Prentice-Hall, 1980. Chapters 15–19.

Jonas, Oswald. *Introduction to the Theory of Heinrich Schenker*. Translated and edited by John Rothgeb. New York: Longman, 1982. Chapter 4.

Kostka, Stefan, and Dorothy Payne. *Tonal Harmony*. 2d ed. New York: Alfred A. Knopf, 1989. Chapters 6–9.

Ottman, Robert W. *Elementary Harmony*. 4th ed. Englewood Cliffs, NJ: Prentice-Hall, 1989. Chapters 4–11.

Piston, Walter. *Harmony*. 5th ed. Revised and expanded by Mark DeVoto. New York: Norton, 1987. Chapters 5–13.

Salzer, Felix. *Structural Hearing*. New York: Dover, 1962. Chapters 4–7.

9

The Minor Mode

The minor mode requires special attention. First, the altered notes create complex and dissonant relations not present in the major. Second, without these altered notes, the minor will pull to its relative major. We must learn to use these altered notes without creating unwanted linear dissonances or unintended shifts in key.

ALTERED NOTES

In the proper context, we may raise both the sixth and seventh scale degrees of a minor key.

Cross-Relations In successive harmonies, if the same scale degree appears in two different forms, we have a *cross-relation*. When, say, $\hat{7}$ follows raised $\hat{7}$, we are uncertain of the exact nature of the seventh scale degree and, for that matter, of the key. However, if we maintain the cross-relation in the same voice, the ambiguity resolves itself in the voice leading.

As a rule, you should avoid cross-relations except when they arise in a single voice, as they do in each of the three excerpts of Figure 9.1.

Figure 9.1   Cross-Relations in Chorale Style

In free style, composers often use the cross-relation between outer voices for dramatic effect.

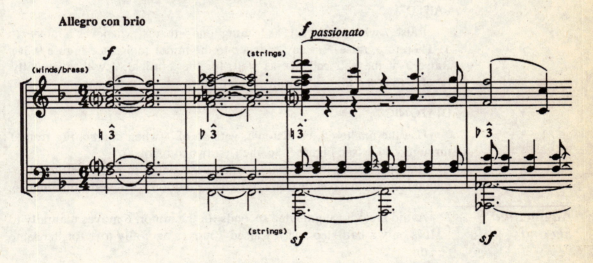

Figure 9.2   Brahms, Symphony No. 3; first movement

Each measure of Figure 9.2 gives us a new version of the third scale degree (A). We can follow the changes from one measure to the next until, in the fourth measure, the A-natural from the highest voice on beat 5 of measure 3 shifts to the A-flat in the lowest.

Seventh Scale Degree in the Minor

A special ambiguity surrounds the seventh scale degree. When do we raise $\hat{7}$ and when do we leave it unaltered? The answer is quite simple and direct.

Bach Chorales

Figure 9.3   *Leading Tone in the Minor*

RAISED $\hat{7}$

Raise $\hat{7}$ whenever it acts as leading tone—that is, whenever it moves to $\hat{1}$. Therefore, raise $\hat{7}$ in any cadence to the minor tonic (see Figure 9.3a). Raise $\hat{7}$ at the half cadence as well, for the terminal V will, eventually, resolve to i (see Figure 9.3b).

DIATONIC $\hat{7}$

Use the unaltered, or diatonic, version of $\hat{7}$ when *descending* from $\hat{1}$ through $\hat{7}$ to $\hat{6}$ (see Figure 9.3c, the first two alto notes).

Raised $\hat{7}$ offers no advantage when descending to $\hat{6}$. In fact, the augmented second that results from a raised $\hat{7}$–$\hat{6}$ motion is a melodic dissonance.

Augmented Second

Avoid melodic augmented seconds. In the minor, $\hat{6}$ moves naturally to $\hat{5}$. It is only a half step away. Raised $\hat{7}$ moves naturally to $\hat{1}$ for the same reason.

Remember: Unaltered $\hat{6}$ descends to $\hat{5}$ and raised $\hat{7}$ ascends to $\hat{1}$.

Clearly, the motions $\hat{6}$–raised $\hat{7}$ and raised $\hat{7}$–$\hat{6}$ which create the augmented second contradict the natural voice leading tendencies of the scale degrees involved.

The simplest way to avoid the augmented second is to approach and leave the raised seventh scale degree from above. As a rule, raised $\hat{7}$ should either move directly to $\hat{1}$ or should move to another scale degree that does. For example, we frequently see the melodic progression raised $\hat{7}$–$\hat{2}$–$\hat{1}$ in the minor.

Raised $\hat{6}$

Similarly, you should remember that the raised $\hat{6}$ arises from our effort to *avoid* the augmented second (see chapter 3, the "Melodic Minor"). When passing from $\hat{5}$ to $\hat{1}$ in the minor, we require raised $\hat{7}$—and raised $\hat{6}$ to approach raised $\hat{7}$. *If you must approach raised $\hat{7}$ from below, do so from raised $\hat{6}$.*

Figure 9.4   Bach, Chorale 57

As a voice moves *up* by step toward $\hat{1}$, Bach raises $\hat{7}$ to create the leading tone and raises $\hat{6}$ to avoid the augmented second. When a voice moves *down* by step from $\hat{1}$ to $\hat{5}$, Bach leaves both $\hat{6}$ and $\hat{7}$ unaltered. When a voice skips from raised $\hat{7}$, the augmented second is not a concern (see the final tenor G-sharp of Figure 9.4).

The Linear Dissonance

The dissonance created by altered notes in the minor can, in special instances, provide dramatic contrast to our free flowing voice leading. Though more common in free style, such exceptional voice leading has its place even in chorale style.

Recall that *all melodic dissonances, like harmonic dissonances, require resolution.* Diminished intervals resolve inwards—that is, in the opposite direction of the skip. Augmented intervals resolve outwards—that is, in the same direction as the skip (see chapter 3, "Active Intervals").

We see in Figure 9.5 three dissonant skips to the raised seventh scale degree, each in the bass. Notice the similarities.

Bach Chorales (bass and soprano, only)

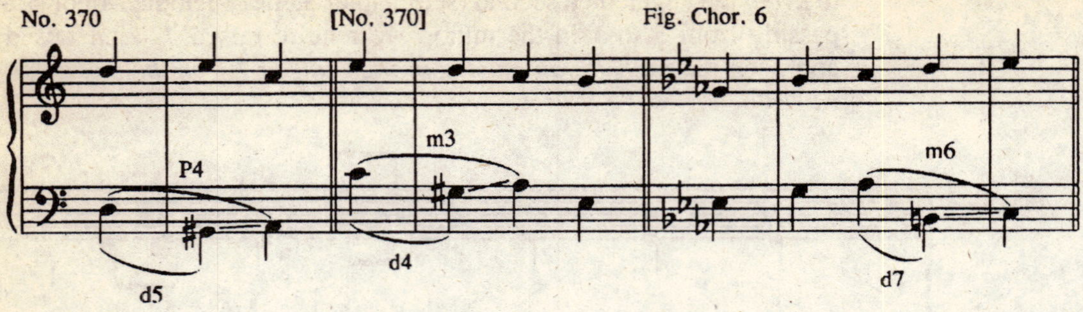

Figure 9.5   Linear Dissonances in the Bass

DESCENDING TO THE LEADING TONE

First, each example *descends to raised* $\hat{7}$, creating a diminished interval.

RESOLVING THE LEADING TONE

Second, the leading tone of each example *resolves to* $\hat{1}$. This motion "resolves" each of the dissonant intervals to a consonant interval.

BALANCING CONJUNCT MOTION IN SOPRANO

Third, the dissonant skip in the bass is *balanced by a step in the soprano*, usually in the opposite direction.

As you learned in chapter 5, a skip—especially a dissonant one—should be followed by a step in the opposite direction. Recall that diminished intervals resolve inwards. They resolve naturally by step in the opposite direction, creating just that preferred voice leading. For this reason, we see diminished melodic intervals more frequently than augmented melodic intervals.

III: THE RELATIVE MAJOR

In the minor, we alter scale degrees to avoid the natural pull of the minor mode toward its relative major. As the relative major of each minor key, III is a potential tonic.

Bach Chorales

Figure 9.6   Diminished ii and Tonicized III

Diminished ii

The major has a single naturally occurring diminished triad, vii. It functions as a voice-leading triad (almost always in $\frac{6}{3}$ position) to I or I^6. The diminished triad on ii in the minor poses a special problem. It will pull toward III, for the moment making it sound like a tonic. We call this process *tonicization*.

DIMINISHED ii $\frac{6}{3}$

We may use diminished ii in first inversion as a passing chord to V♯ (see Figure 9.6a).

ROOT POSITION DIMINISHED ii

Avoid any diminished triad in root position. Root position emphasizes the (dissonant) diminished fifth above the bass. For this reason, *diminished-ii cannot function adequately as the upper-fifth divider of V.* (Root-position diminished triads arise frequently in the *diatonic sequences* discussed in chapter 16, however.)

DIMINISHED ii–III

Just as vii resolves naturally to I in the major, diminished ii resolves naturally to III in the minor. This tonicization of III poses a challenge to the minor tonic (see "Tonicized III," page 116).

The Subtonic Triad

Similarly, the major triad on (unaltered) $\hat{7}$ easily takes on the appearance of an upper-fifth divider of III. The resulting VII–III progression, however, mimics the V–I progression of the relative major. This, too, creates tonal ambiguity and a momentary tonicization of III, the relative major.

In Figure 9.6b, Bach supports the bass passing note between $\hat{1}$ and $\hat{3}$ with a VII^6. This major triad sounds, for the moment, like V^6 in the key of F major (that is, the key of III). Thus the VII^6–III in i (D minor) sounds like V^6–I in III, (F major). The C–C-sharp cross-relation of the alto ($\hat{7}$– $\sharp\hat{7}$) immediately draws us back into D minor (i), however, creating a V$^4_3$ passing dominant to the true tonic.

When using VII as upper-fifth divider of III, be aware of this implicit tonicization of III.

Tonicized III

For the minor tonic to remain tonic, you should *tonicize III only when the voice-leading function of III in relation to its minor tonic is clear.* For this reason, we find III tonicized most frequently when it functions as the third divider of the progression i–V$\sharp$ or when III substitutes for i^6 in a prolongation of i.

In a i–III–V$\sharp$ progression, you can prolong the motion from i to III with a passing VII$^6_3$ that tonicizes III. If, then, you move directly from III to V$\sharp$, you create a cross-relation between the unaltered $\hat{7}$ of III and the raised $\hat{7}$ of V$\sharp$. Thus, a ii$^6_3$ often passes between III and V$\sharp$. If, however, you move directly from III to V$\sharp$, you should keep the cross-relation ($\hat{7}$–$\sharp\hat{7}$) in the same voice (see Figure 9.6b). In free composition (and, on occasion, in chorale style), the tonicization of the third divider can be extensive.

Figure 9.7   Bach, Chorale 13

Here, Bach tonicizes III with the same i–VII^6–III progression. This sounds like V^6–I in III (C major). Bach prolongs this III with a III^6. (At the moment, this sounds more like I^6 in C major than III^6 in A minor.) The voice-leading bass F-sharp that begins the last measure destroys the tonicization. Bach reestablishes tonic A minor with a contrapuntal cadence to i, approached in the bass by a raised $\hat{6}$–raised $\hat{7}$–$\hat{1}$ linear progression.

We will discuss tonicization techniques more thoroughly in chapter 13.

*I*n the minor, you must be certain that the raised seventh scale degree functions as neighbor to $\hat{1}$. When approaching the raised seventh scale degree, avoid the augmented second between raised $\hat{7}$ and $\hat{6}$.

Remember that both the diminished triad on ii and the major triad on VII can tonicize III. A tonicization of III need not compromise the minor tonality as long as III functions clearly as a voice-leading prolongation of the minor tonic.

Selected Readings

Christ, William, et al. *Materials and Structure of Music*. 3d ed. Vol. I. Englewood Cliffs, NJ: Prentice-Hall, 1980. Chapter 3.

Ottman, Robert W. *Elementary Harmony*. 4th ed. Englewood Cliffs, NJ: Prentice-Hall, 1989. Chapter 5.

Piston, Walter. *Harmony*. 5th ed. Revised and expanded by Mark DeVoto. New York: Norton, 1987. Chapters 4–5.

Schenker, Heinrich. *Harmony*. Edited by Oswald Jonas. Translated by Elisabeth Mann Borgese. Chicago: University of Chicago Press, 1980. Section I, Chapters 1–3.

Schoenberg, Arnold. *Structural Functions of Harmony*. Rev. ed. Edited by Leonard Stein. New York: Norton, 1969. Chapters 1–4.

———. *Theory of Harmony*. Translated by Roy E. Carter. Berkeley: University of California Press, 1983. Chapter 5.

10

Melodic Figuration

*T*onal music contains many passing and neighboring motions that remain unsupported. These melodic figures smooth and sometimes even correct voice leading from one chord to the next. We distinguish between two types of melodic figuration: chordal skips and nonharmonic notes. Passing notes and neighboring notes are the two types of nonharmonic notes.

Chromatic figurations often serve to tonicize scale degrees other than the tonic. These tonicizations highlight the primary triads V or IV within a larger unfolding of I.

CHORDAL SKIPS

Often a voice moves from one chord note to another chord note within the same chord. Such a motion is a *chordal skip*.

General Function

When a voice must skip between two harmonies, we may "fill in" that skip with a chordal skip (see Figure 10.1a). When a voice moves by step between harmonies, a chordal skip intensifies that motion by providing the other neighbor to the final note (see Figure 10.1b).

Figure 10.1   Chordal Skips

Remember: A chordal skip moves to a note in the same chord. Thus, all chordal skips are consonant.

Chordal Skips and Faulty Voice Leading

What smooths out the voice leading in one voice may create problems with another voice. Be careful not to create faulty parallel motions when adding chordal skips. Each of the chordal skips below creates forbidden parallels.

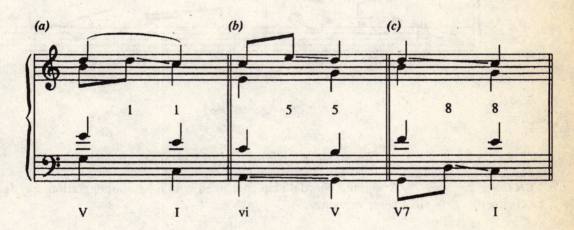

Figure 10.2   Chordal Skips and Forbidden Parallels

The alto's chordal skip creates parallel perfect unisons with the soprano in Figure 10.2a. Similarly, a chordal skip in the soprano creates parallel fifths with the bass in Figure 10.2b. In Figure 10.2c, parallel octaves arise with the chordal skip in the bass.

All such parallels are forbidden. The note that results from a chordal skip is itself a chord note. The voice leading between it and the next chord must be sound. It may not contain faulty parallels.

Correction for Faulty Parallels

However, chordal skips can also *correct* faulty parallels that arise in basic part writing. In Figure 10.3a, Bach eliminates parallel octaves between soprano and tenor with a chordal skip. As a result, the tenor moves into the octave Cs in contrary motion with the soprano rather than in parallel. Bach corrects the parallel fifths of Figure 10.3b in much the same way. Here the tenor skips to the fifth of the iv (D) before moving to the root of V (A). In this way it approaches the fifth with the soprano in similar rather than parallel motion.

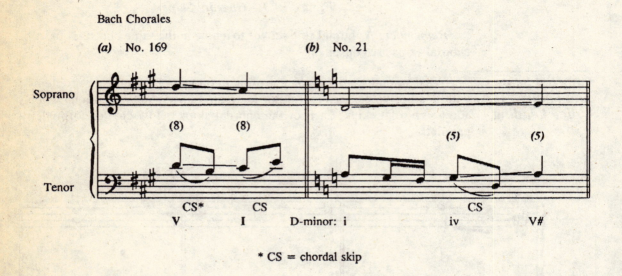

Figure 10.3   *Chordal Skips Correct Forbidden Parallels*

Voice Exchange

A soprano chordal skip combined with a bass arpeggiation may result in a *voice exchange*.

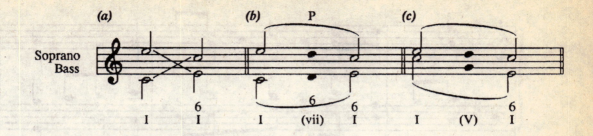

Figure 10.4   Origin of the Voice Exchange

In Figure 10.4a, the outer voices exchange chord notes. Passing motions fill in the resulting arpeggiations (10.4b). Often a fifth divider serves as a sort of "leaping passing note" in the bass of a voice exchange (10.4c).

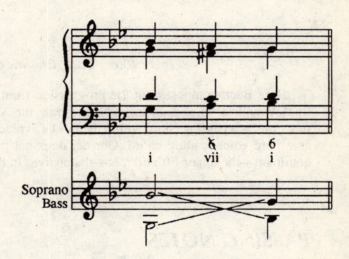

Figure 10.5   Bach, Chorale 261

Using the voice exchange, we can compose out a soprano chordal skip or a bass arpeggiation. In Figure 10.5, the bass moves from G to B as the soprano moves from B to G. Bach prolongs the voice exchange with a passing A in each voice. Often a voice exchange provides the framework for an extended progression.

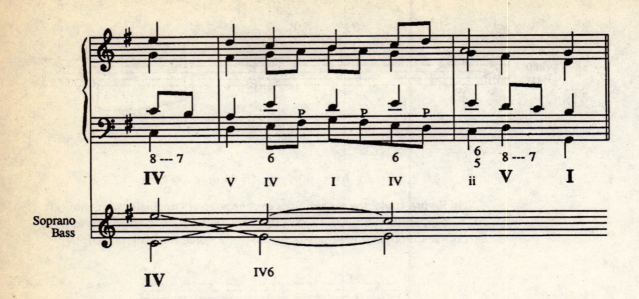

Figure 10.6   Bach, Chorale 65

Here Bach composes out the progression from the opening IV to the final V with a voice exchange. Notice how the V_3^5 (measure 1, beat 1) functions as a passing chord within the IV–IV[6] voice exchange, functioning as a pure voice-leading chord. Our ear does not confuse it with the true dominant—the upper fifth divider—that arrives in the last measure.

PASSING NOTES

When a voice skips by third (or fourth) from a note of one chord to a note of the next, we may fill in the space between them with passing notes. Passing notes that act as melodic figurations, however, do not receive consonant support from the bass. In this way they differ from the passing notes that we have discussed thus far.

We distinguish between two types of passing notes: unaccented and accented. Unaccented passing notes move between two accented chord notes. (The passing notes of Figure 10.6 are all unaccented.) Accented passing notes arise on a metrical accent. In Figure 10.7, passing notes fill in the third skip in soprano and alto simultaneously. Bach places the passing G and E on the beat, creating a pair of accented passing notes.

Bach, Chorale 338

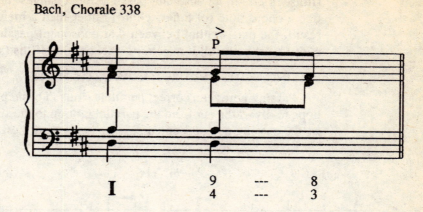

$$\begin{array}{ccc} 9 & --- & 8 \\ 4 & --- & 3 \end{array}$$

I

Figure 10.7   Accented Passing Notes

Passing Notes and Parallel Fifths

Both accented and unaccented passing notes can be either dissonant or consonant. The dissonance of a dissonant passing note clearly confirms its passing character. The consonant passing note, however, can create problems.

PASSING NOTES AS CAUSE OF PARALLEL FIFTHS

Passing notes often create parallel fifths. If the basic part writing is solid and the passing note is dissonant, then these fifths cause no problem. Parallel fifths created by dissonant passing notes result from melodic figuration and not basic part writing (see Figure 10.8a).

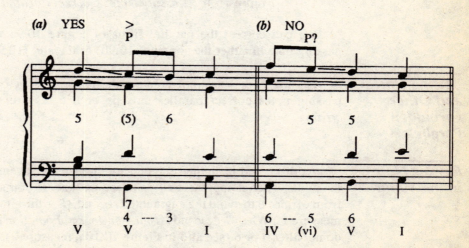

Figure 10.8   Passing Notes and Faulty Parallel Fifths

However, do not allow the *consonant* passing note to create parallel fifths. In effect, a consonant passing note changes the harmony, sounding like a chord note (of a new chord) rather than a melodic figuration. As a result, the part writing between that consonant passing note and the next chord must be solid. It may *not* create parallel fifths (see Figure 10.8b).

PASSING NOTES AS CURE FOR PARALLEL FIFTHS

Passing notes can correct parallels fifths in basic part writing. Since we hope to divert the ear from the parallel motion to the similar motion created by the passing note, accented passing notes work best in this role.

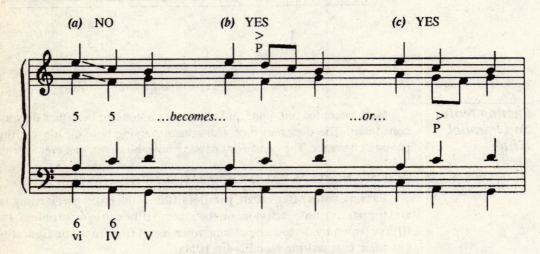

Figure 10.9   Passing Notes Correct Parallel Fifths

We can correct the parallel fifths of Figure 10.9a with an accented passing note in either the soprano (10.9b) or the alto (10.9c).

Passing Notes and Other Forbidden Parallels

Passing notes may not create parallel unisons or octaves. Nor may passing notes correct parallel unisons or octaves present in basic part writing.

Passing Notes in the Minor

As discussed in chapter 9, you should raise the seventh scale degree in the minor when it approaches $\hat{1}$ as a leading tone. If you approach raised $\hat{7}$ from $\hat{6}$, raise $\hat{6}$ to avoid the augmented second. (See the alto in Figure 10.10a, measure 1.) When $\hat{7}$ descends from $\hat{1}$ *or does not function as a leading tone*, do not alter it or $\hat{6}$ (see alto in Figure 10.10a, measure 2).

Figure 10.10   Passing Notes in the Minor

However, when unaltered $\hat{6}$ is the principal chord note, passing from $\hat{6}$ through $\hat{7}$ to $\hat{1}$ causes problems. In Figure 10.10b, Bach expands VI of B minor with its lower-fifth divider, ii. Diatonic $\hat{6}$ is the root of this prolonged triad. By raising $\hat{7}$ to create a leading tone as diatonic $\hat{6}$ moves to $\hat{1}$, Bach creates an augmented second. Presumably, Bach allows this here because the sequence of parallel passing notes between bass and alto helps mask this last linear dissonance.

NEIGHBORING NOTES

Neighboring notes embellish the repetition of a single pitch between successive chords. Neighboring notes may be unaccented (bass, Figure 10.11a) or accented (tenor, 10.11b). Their motion may be complete (Figures 10.11a and 10.11b) or incomplete. In Figure 10.11c, Bach begins a neighbor note motion above the soprano C. Rather than return the upper neighbor (D) to C and complete the neighbor-note motion, he skips from D to A, leaving the neighbor incomplete.

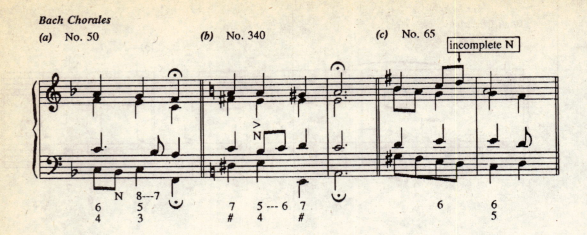

Figure 10.11   Neighboring Notes

Neighboring Notes and Parallel Fifths

Like passing notes, neighboring notes can be consonant or dissonant. Consonant neighbors create greater problems than dissonant neighbors.

NEIGHBORING NOTES AS CAUSE OF PARALLEL FIFTHS

Avoid parallel fifths that result from consonant neighbors for the same reasons that you avoid parallel fifths that result from consonant passing notes. A consonant neighbor note, in effect, changes the harmony. Any parallels that result, therefore, are between chord notes. In Figure 10.12a, a consonant alto neighbor note creates parallel fifths with the soprano. Since we may hear a consonant neighbor as a chord note, these parallel fifths are incorrect. Parallel fifths that result from *dissonant* neighbor notes, however, create no problems. In Figure 10.12b, the alto neighbor note is dissonant (with the tenor G). As a result, we will not hear these notes as parallel fifths.

NEIGHBORING NOTES AS CURE FOR PARALLEL FIFTHS

A neighbor note can break up parallel fifths in the basic part writing. Like accented passing notes, the accented neighbor functions better in this role. Bach breaks up the parallel fifths of Figure 10.12c with an accented neighbor note. The parallel fifths have become parallel sixths.

Figure 10.12 Neighboring Notes and Parallel Fifths

Parallel Octaves and Unisons

Like passing notes, neighboring notes can not create parallel unisons or octaves. Nor can neighboring notes correct parallel unisons or octaves present in basic part writing.

OTHER TYPES OF MELODIC FIGURATION

Traditionally, theorists have further distinguished two special types of incomplete neighbors.

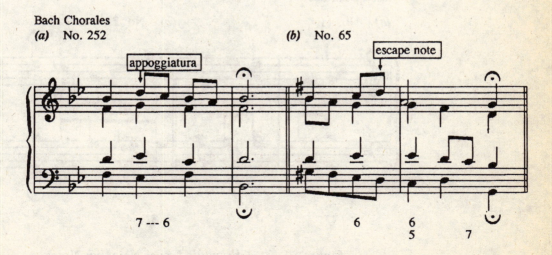

Figure 10.13 Special Types of Melodic Figuration

The Appoggiatura

When we have a voice skip to an accented incomplete neighbor, we create an *appoggiatura*. More often than not, this accented incomplete neighbor is dissonant as well. In Figure 10.13a, the soprano embellishes its B♭–C motion by skipping to the dissonant upper neighbor of C before arriving on C. This incomplete neighbor is an appoggiatura because (1) it is accented, (2) the voice skips into it, and (3) it resolves by step.

The Escape Note

When we have a voice skip *from* an unaccented incomplete neighbor, we create an *escape note*. In Figure 10.13b, Bach embellishes a soprano C–A motion with an incomplete neighbor above C. Instead of returning to C, the neighbor (D) skips to A. This incomplete neighbor is an escape note because (1) it is unaccented, (2) we approach it by step, and (3) we skip from it.

CHROMATIC FIGURATION

Often altered scale degrees serve as passing or neighboring notes. We call this procedure *chromatic figuration*.

Chromatic Lower Neighbor

The chromatic lower neighbor is the most common chromatic figuration. A half step provides the strongest neighboring motion. The chromatic lower neighbor provides this half-step neighbor where one does not exist naturally.

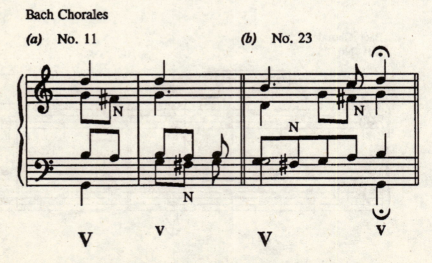

Figure 10.14   Chromatic Lower Neighbor Notes

In Figure 10.14a, both alto and bass in turn embellish a repeated G with a chromatic lower neighbor, F-sharp. We see the same in Figure 10.14b, this time in alto and tenor.

Melodic Tonicization

So effective is the chromatic lower neighbor in strengthening the scale degree it embellishes that this scale degree may become *tonicized*.

TONICIZATION

A tonal composition has one tonic. However, we may occasionally emphasize a certain scale degree by treating it, momentarily, like a tonic. The technique that creates this fleeting "tonic" is known as *tonicization*. Two types of tonicization occur: harmonic tonicization and melodic (or linear) tonicization. (See "Tonicized III" in chapter 9. In chapter 13 we will discuss harmonic tonicization in more detail.)

When we tonicize a scale degree, we do not "change the key." Rather, we temporarily emphasize one scale degree at the expense of the tonic. Any scale degree can be tonicized. However, tonicizations of V (and IV) are by far the most common. Why? Because tonicization serves a greater end. It provides a technique for reinforcing the primary scale degrees in the prolongation of the tonic triad.

MELODIC TONICIZATION OF V

We frequently see $\hat{5}$ embellished by a chromatic lower neighbor (see Figures 10.14a and 10.14b). This chromatic neighbor provides a linear tonicization of V by providing it (momentarily) with a leading tone. In free style such linear tonicizations may be extensive.

Figure 10.15   Mozart, Piano Sonata, K. 283:
third movement, measures 13–16

In Figure 10.15, Mozart repeatedly embellishes $\hat{5}$ (D) with its chromatic lower neighbor (C-sharp). This raised-$\hat{4}$ not only provides $\hat{5}$ with a leading tone, but forms a tritone with the real tonic (G). This new tritone denies (for the moment) G's tonic function by tonicizing $\hat{5}$ (D).

LINEAR TONICIZATION OF IV

When I serves as the upper-fifth divider of IV, we frequently see a passing note that lowers the seventh scale degree.

Figure 10.16   Linear Tonicization of IV

In Figures 10.16a and 10.16b, Bach flats the $\hat{7}$ (marked with an arrow)

that passes between $\hat{1}$ and $\hat{6}$. By destroying the leading tone and creating a new tritone (between $\hat{3}$ and lowered $\hat{7}$), these altered $\hat{7}$s create momentary tonicizations of IV. Like all tonicizations, this tonicized IV serves to prolong the composing out of IV. It does so by—for the moment—providing IV with the quality of a tonic. (For an example of the linear tonicization of IV in free style, see the top staff of Figure 6.9: the brief, melodic E-flat serves to impart a fleeting "tonic" character to the lower-fifth divider of measure 3.)

*W*e distinguish between two kinds of melodic figuration: chordal skips and nonharmonic notes. Chordal skips move from one chord note to another of the same chord. Nonharmonic notes embellish the motion from a chord note of one chord to a chord note of the next. We distinguish between two basic types of nonharmonic notes: the passing note and the neighbor note.

Chordal skips break up large skips. When introduced, they must not create forbidden parallel motions. However, they can break up faulty parallels present in basic part writing.

Passing and neighboring notes can be complete or incomplete. They can be accented or unaccented, consonant or dissonant. Parallel fifths that result from dissonant passing and neighboring notes (and not from basic part writing) are permitted, but those that result from consonant passing notes are not permitted. Passing and neighboring notes can break up parallel fifths present in basic part writing. However, they are not strong enough to break up parallel unisons or octaves present in basic part writing.

When we have a voice skip to an accented incomplete neighbor, we create an appoggiatura. When we have a voice skip from an unaccented incomplete neighbor, we create an escape note.

Chromatic figurations can tonicize certain scale degrees, creating a melodic tonicization. A chromatic lower neighbor frequently tonicizes $\hat{5}$. Lowered $\hat{7}$ frequently tonicizes IV.

Selected Readings

Aldwell, Edward, and Carl Schachter. *Harmony and Voice Leading.* 2d ed. 2 vols. New York: Harcourt Brace Jovanovich, 1989. Chapter 20.

Christ, William, et al. *Materials and Structure of Music.* 3d ed. Vol. I. 3d ed. Englewood Cliffs, NJ: Prentice-Hall, 1980. Chapter 8.

Kostka, Stefan, and Dorothy Payne. *Tonal Harmony.* 2d ed. New York: Alfred A. Knopf, 1989. Chapters 10–11.

Ottman, Robert W. *Elementary Harmony.* 4th ed. Englewood Cliffs, NJ: Prentice-Hall, 1989. Chapter 11.

Piston, Walter. *Harmony.* 5th ed. Revised and expanded by Mark DeVoto. New York: Norton, 1987. Chapter 8.

11

Rhythmic Figuration

*E*very chord has a duration called its time span. Delaying or anticipating the arrival of a new time span creates tension or drama. We can overlap one time span with another in one voice, while allowing the other voices to proceed normally. This procedure creates a rhythmic figuration. The three basic types of rhythmic figurations are: the suspension, the anticipation, and the pedal point.

A voice embellished by a suspension delays the new note until after the new time span has begun. A voice that is embellished by an anticipation reaches the new time span too early.

The pedal point overlays a succession of time spans with a single time span. There results a sustained note around which the other voices unfold a succession of harmonies.

TIME SPANS

Within a composition, each chord has a definite duration called its *time span*. The successive time spans of a progression together create that progression's *harmonic rhythm*.

The chords of Figure 11.1a have time spans of the same duration. That is, the harmonic rhythm moves uniformly by quarter note. These regular time spans are characteristic of chorale style.

(a) Bach, Chorale 1

(b) Beethoven, Piano Sonata, Op. 111, Arietta

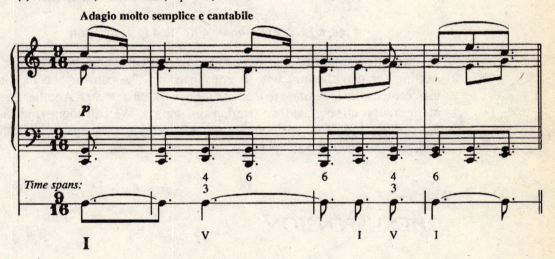

Figure 11.1   Time Span Examples

In free style, time spans are more varied. The harmony of Figure 11.1b, for instance, shows a variety of time spans. As a result, the harmonic rhythm of Figure 11.1b is complex. Although the bass moves uniformly in dotted eighth notes, the harmony does not. The first tonic triad lasts a total of two dotted eighths. The following dominant lasts for a dotted quarter plus a dotted eighth. The next two chords span single dotted eighths. The final tonic spans a duration of a dotted quarter plus a dotted eighth, and so on.

We say that a chord controls or governs its time span. Within the confines of its time span, a chord controls both consonance and dissonance. The same scale degrees may be consonant in one time span (Figure 11.2a) and dissonant in another (11.2b).

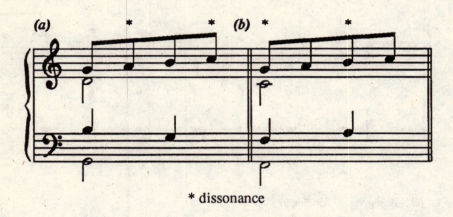

* dissonance

Figure 11.2   Dissonance Related to Time Span

Melodic figurations arise in relation to a particular time span. That is, a passing (or neighboring) note is consonant or dissonant or accented or unaccented *only in relation to the time span in which it occurs*. Another class of figuration arises when we overlap time spans. We call them *rhythmic figurations*, and distinguish among three basic types: the suspension, the anticipation, and the pedal point.

THE SUSPENSION

As a rule, the suspension begins with a voice that moves by step from a chord note in one time span to a chord note in another, as in the soprano of Figure 11.3a. If we delay this stepwise motion, notice what happens. We *suspend* the first note into the time span of the second (see Figure 11.3b), arriving late on the expected second note (11.3c). The delay creates a dissonance at the beginning of the second time span (11.3b) as well as a sense of expectation and, finally, dramatic resolution (11.3c).

Figure 11.3   Origin of the Suspension

We create a suspension, then, by overlapping time spans. Notice that the suspension of Figure 11.3 does *not* arise from adding a note to the voice. It arises from suspending a note into the next time span. For a suspension to work clearly, then, its metrical position must be clear.

Elements of the Suspension

A suspension has three parts: the preparation, the suspension, and the resolution, each distinguished by its relative metrical position.

THE PREPARATION

To suspend a note, we must first prepare it as a consonance. Thus the first (consonant) note of the suspension is called its *preparation*. Figure 11.3a shows the basic, consonant, voice leading. The soprano C becomes the preparation for the subsequent suspension (11.3b) and resolution (11.3c).

THE SUSPENSION

We then tie the preparation into the new harmonic span, where it becomes the *suspension* proper. In Figure 11.3b, we have suspended the soprano C into the time span occupied by soprano B in Figure 11.3a to create a suspension.

THE RESOLUTION

The suspended dissonance then resolves *down* by step to a consonance, called its *resolution*. The suspended C resolves to the consonant B at (c) in Figure 11.3.

Metrical Position of the Suspension

As a rule, both the preparation and the suspension arise in metrically accented positions. That is, the preparation arises at the beginning of the first time span, and the suspension appears at the beginning of the second. In contrast, the resolution arises in a metrically weak position. Note that each of the resolutions *(z)* in Figure 11.4 arises in a weak metrical position relative to the suspension *(y)* that precedes it.

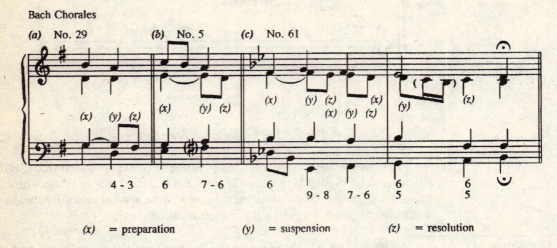

(x) = preparation   (y) = suspension   (z) = resolution

Figure 11.4   Suspensions

Doubling and the Suspension

Since the suspension *delays* the note of resolution, we do best not to double the note of resolution in another voice. If we double the note of resolution, we *anticipate the note of resolution*, thereby weakening its dramatic effect. Notice that, in each suspension of Figure 11.4, Bach avoids doubling the note of resolution.

The Suspension and Parallel Fifths

Dissonant suspensions can break up parallel fifths in basic part writing. In Figure 11.5, Bach destroys the sense of parallel fifths (outlined in 11.5a) by suspending the first fifth into the time span of the second (alto, 11.5b). By adding the suspension, Bach creates a dissonance below D on the first beat of the measure. The accented dissonance between the two fifths makes it difficult for us to hear the fifths as parallel.

(a)   *(b)*   Bach, Chorale 284

Figure 11.5   Suspensions and Parallel Fifths

A suspension may not create parallel unisons or octaves with another voice. Nor can a suspension correct parallel unisons or octaves in the basic part writing.

The Bass Suspension

Most suspensions arise in the upper voices. Although we see bass suspensions less often, they can be very effective. Bass suspensions require, however, special attention.

SUSPENDING THE BASS OF A $\frac{5}{3}$

The bass defines a $\frac{5}{3}$ chord. If we suspend that bass, we create harmonic ambiguity. What is the root of this triad? We do not know until the bass suspension resolves. For this reason, it is best to *anticipate the resolution of a bass suspension if the triad is in $\frac{5}{3}$ position*. Although this weakens the effect of the suspension, it clarifies the harmony.

SUSPENDING THE BASS OF A $\frac{6}{3}$

The $\frac{6}{3}$ provides the most successful bass suspension. The root and fifth define a triad. The root and the fifth of a $\frac{6}{3}$ triad lie in the upper voices, so they are unaffected by a bass suspension. Therefore, we need not anticipate the resolution of the bass third, but can treat the bass suspension of a $\frac{6}{3}$ like a suspension in an upper voice.

Figure 11.6   Bass Suspensions

In Figure 11.6a, I moves to V^6. Bach suspends the bass of the V^6. The suspension works just as it would in an upper voice. Figure 11.6b is more complex, however. The suspended F is the root of the final harmony. Bach anticipates the note of resolution (F) in the alto to keep the root of the triad present even while it is suspended in the bass. In Figure 11.6c, Bach suspends the bass of the final $\frac{5}{3}$ as well. But since this $\frac{5}{3}$ is a voice-leading chord (an augmented triad), the root of the triad is less important. (Voice-leading chords, remember, have only passing significance. The identity of their roots is less important than their linear function.) Here, Bach does *not* anticipate the resolution, doubling the third of the G-augmented triad rather than its root.

SUSPENSIONS AND FIGURED BASS

We identify suspensions by the figures they create.

The 4–3 Suspension. Suspending that note a third above the bass creates a 4–3 suspension. The suspension in Figure 11.4a is a 4–3 suspension.

The 6–5 Suspension. Suspending that note a fifth above the bass creates a 6–5 suspension. (We will discuss the 6–5 suspension in "The Consonant Suspension" below. See also Figure 11.9c.)

The 7–6 Suspension. Suspending the sixth above the bass creates a 7–6 suspension. The suspension in Figure 11.4b is a 7–6 suspension.

The 9–8 Suspension. Suspending the note that doubles the bass creates a 9–8 suspension. (The bass always anticipates the resolution of the 9–8 suspension.) The suspension on the second quarter note of Figure 11.4c is a

9–8 suspension. Note that the resolution of the suspended alto E-flat is anticipated by the bass E-flat.

Figures and the Bass Suspension. The figures of figured bass show intervals above the bass. When we suspend the bass note, then, unusual figures result. A $\frac{6}{3}$ with a bass suspension and with the resolution *not* anticipated begins as a $\frac{5}{2}$ before resolving to a $\frac{6}{3}$ (see Figure 11.6a, above). A $\frac{5}{3}$ with a bass suspension and with an anticipated resolution begins as a $\frac{7}{4}$ before resolving to a $\frac{5}{3}$ (see Figure 11.6b, above). If the resolution is *not* anticipated, the figures move $\frac{4}{2} \underline{} \frac{5}{3}$ (see Figure 11.6c).

Figure 11.6d is an excerpt from one of Bach's figured chorales. (In the figured chorales, Bach gives only soprano, bass, and figures, but this is all we need to determine the harmonic motion.) The $\frac{5}{2}$ figures are puzzling until we realize that when the bass moves down to B, those figures become $\frac{6}{3}$. Thus we have a $\frac{6}{5}$ chord with a suspended bass.

The Double Suspension

It is possible to suspend more than one note at a time. We risk obscuring the basic harmonic motion, however, when we suspend two notes of a triad. For this reason, it is best to *use double suspensions only when the bass progression is strong and unambiguous*. As a rule, do not suspend the bass in a double suspension.

In Figure 11.7, Bach suspends both the tenor and alto at the cadence, creating a simultaneous 4–3 and 6–5 suspension.

Bach, Chorale 197

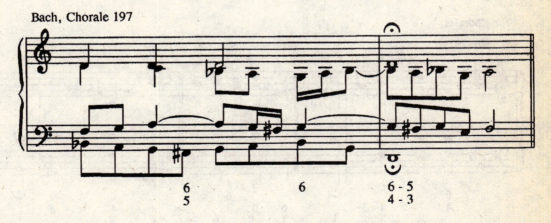

Figure 11.7   The Double Suspension

The Upward-Resolving Suspension

Save for the direction of resolution, the upward resolving suspension works like any other. The upward-resolving suspension can suspend the motion $\hat{7}$–$\hat{1}$ (in a V–I or vii^6–I progression). Usually, the upward-resolving suspension is a 7–8 suspension, the bass anticipating the note of resolution (see Figure 11.8).

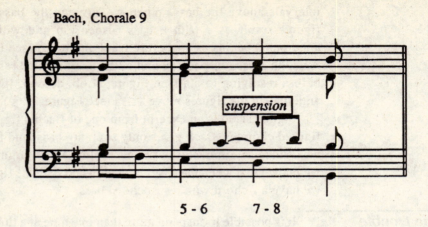

Figure 11.8   The Upward-Resolving Suspension

Variants of the Suspension

The preparation, suspension, and resolution of a suspension can vary according to the context. Several common variants follow.

(x) = preparation   (y) = resolution

Figure 11.9   Variants of the Suspension

THE INDIRECT SUSPENSION

When the preparation lies in one voice and the suspension and resolution in another, we have an *indirect suspension*.

In Figure 11.9a, the "preparation" for the soprano suspension is in the tenor. We might correctly call this an appoggiatura (see chapter 10). But we can see that the soprano D is not so much an incomplete neighbor of the C that follows as a suspension of the D of the previous harmony. Figure 11.9b represents a more extreme case. Here Bach suspends all three upper voices above the passing vii^6. Not only that, but all three suspensions are prepared in the "wrong" voice. Bach prepares the suspended soprano D in the bass of the preceding I. Similarly, the tenor prepares the suspended B♮ of the alto, while the alto prepares the suspended F in the tenor.

DECORATED RESOLUTION

We often see the resolution of a suspension embellished by a chordal skip or incomplete neighbor note. We call these variants *decorated resolutions*. In Figure 11.9c, Bach suspends the opening alto B into the cadence. Before the B resolves to A-sharp, however, it leaps to the *lower* neighbor of A-sharp, G-sharp. (A-sharp is raised $\hat{7}$ of B-minor. Therefore, to avoid the augmented second, its lower neighbor must be raised $\hat{6}$—in this case, G-sharp.)

SUSPENDED P'S AND N'S

The suspension principle can also be applied to nonharmonic notes. We might, for example, suspend a passing note by delaying its motion to the next chord note.

Bach Chorales

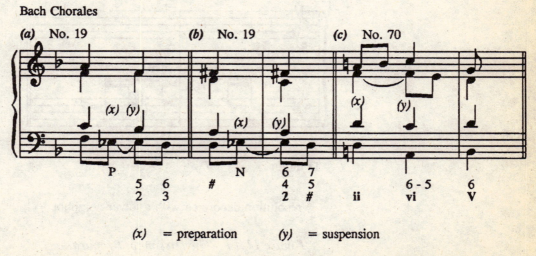

(x) = preparation   *(y)* = suspension

Figure 11.10   Variants of the Suspension

In Figure 11.10a, Bach suspends the passing E-flat of the bass, delaying the arrival of the chord note, D.

In Figure 11.10b, Bach turns a bass neighbor note (E-flat) into a suspension.

THE CONSONANT SUSPENSION

Not all suspensions are dissonant. If the bass motion between the two time spans is strong enough to define the harmonies, a suspended note is effective even if the suspension itself is consonant. We might analyze the second beat of Figure 11.10c as a IV^6 that becomes a vi as the eighth note F moves to E in the alto. That alto F, though, is approached and left as if it were a suspension. As a result, we are more likely to hear that harmony as a vi with a 6–5 suspension *even though the suspended 6 is consonant with the other voices.*

THE DISSONANT PREPARATION

As a rule, the preparation of a suspension is consonant. On occasion, though, we see dissonant preparations. Commonly, this results from suspending the seventh of a V^7 into the I that follows.   Thus the 4–3 suspension that results has a *dissonant* preparation. Bach prepares the tenor suspension in the last measure of Figure 11.11 with the seventh of a V^7. That seventh is, of course, dissonant. Still, Bach suspends it into the final tonic where it resolves to the third, creating a 4–3 suspension.

Bach, Chorale 133

D minor: #   7   4 - #

* resolution decorated with a lower neighbor

Figure 11.11   The Dissonant Preparation

ANTICIPATIONS

The anticipation reverses the suspension. A (consonant) note from one time span moves by step to a (consonant) note of the next time span *but before that time span arrives*. We call this early arrival an *anticipation* (see Figure 11.12). Usually, anticipations are dissonant.

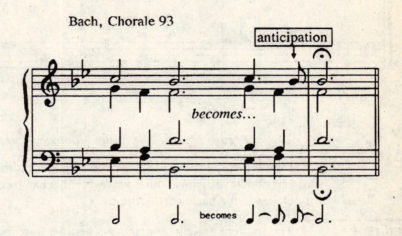

Figure 11.12   The Anticipation

Metrical Considerations

The anticipation arises in a metrically weak position within the first time span. Unlike the suspension, however, the anticipation is not tied into the second time span. Rather, we repeat the anticipated note as the second time span begins. In the metrical arrangement of Figure 11.12, above, the anticipation arises on the last eighth of the first time span.

The Anticipation and Parallel Fifths

Parallel fifths that arise between the anticipation and passing or neighboring notes in another voice create no problem *if* the anticipation is dissonant (see Figure 11.13a).

On occasion, Bach allows an anticipation to break up parallel fifths in the basic part writing (see Figure 11.13b).

Bach Chorales

Figure 11.13   The Anticipation and Parallel Fifths

Like the suspension, however, the anticipation may not create parallel unisons or octaves with another voice. Neither can it correct parallel unisons or octaves in the basic part writing.

The Indirect Anticipation

The indirect anticipation arises when we transfer the repetition of the anticipated note to another voice. Some theorists call the indirect suspension an *anticipatory arpeggiation*. If we begin a chordal skip from the second time span, *before* the first span is over, we create such an anticipatory arpeggiation.

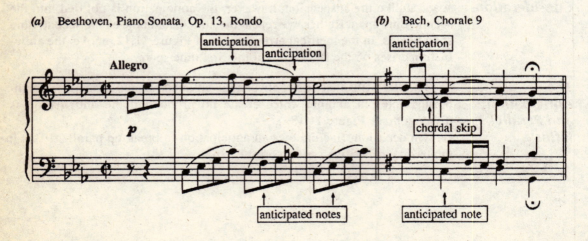

Figure 11.14   The Indirect Anticipation

In Figure 11.14a, the anticipations in the soprano actually anticipate pitches two octaves lower (in the bass staff) as the soprano skips to a different chord note. There results a chordal skip in the soprano—but one that begins an eighth note too early.

Many of the so-called escape notes (described in chapter 10) are in fact indirect anticipations. The soprano C of Figure 11.14b is less an incomplete neighbor of the soprano B than it is an anticipation of the subsequent C in the bass. Thus, soprano C–A is a chordal skip within the $\frac{6}{5}$ chord, but one that begins an eighth note too soon.

THE PEDAL POINT

When a sustained note in one voice accompanies a continuing chord progression in the other voices, that sustained note is a *pedal point*. As a rule, pedal points arise when a composition has reached an important harmonic goal. We find pedal points most often in either the soprano or the bass. Pedal points usually arise on the dominant or tonic and usually at the beginning or end of a phrase, section, or composition. The pedal point both firmly establishes the root of this harmonic goal and dramatically delays the resolution of the upper voices.

In Bach's Chorale 55 we find a soprano pedal point on the dominant. It precedes a half cadence in B minor.

Figure 11.15   Bach, Chorale 55

The lower voices simply prolong the i that precedes the final V♯ of the half cadence.

The voices above or below the pedal point frequently form harmonies that do not contain the pedal point note. The following dominant pedal point prolongs V in preparation for an authentic cadence.

Figure 11.16   Bach, Chorale 91

Notice that the long dominant pedal in the bass does not belong to all the voice-leading harmonies in the upper voices.

Every chord has a duration called its time span. We can overlap one time span with another in one voice, while allowing the other voices to proceed normally. This procedure creates a rhythmic figuration of which there are three basic types: the suspension, the anticipation, and the pedal point.

The three parts of a suspension are: the preparation, the suspension proper, and the resolution. The consonant preparation arises on a relatively strong beat. The suspension results from a change of harmony that creates a dissonance out of the consonant preparation. The resolution arises on a relatively weak beat as the (dissonant) suspension moves by step to a consonant note.

Avoid doubling the note of resolution (called "anticipating the resolution") so as not to weaken the effect of that resolution. Usually, the parallel fifths that arise from suspensions are no problem. However, avoid creating parallel unisons or octaves with any suspension.

Bass suspensions work best in $\frac{6}{3}$ position. You may suspend two or even three notes at a time. A suspension may resolve upward. Most upward resolving suspensions are 7–8 suspensions. Indirect suspensions arise when the preparation and suspension are in two different voices. The seventh of the V^7 occasionally serves as a dissonant preparation for a I^{4-3} suspension.

In the anticipation, the note of the second time span arrives early, on a weak beat of the first time span. The anticipated note repeats itself as the second time span arrives. Parallel fifths that arise between a dissonant anticipation and melodic figuration in another voice cause no problem. An anticipation may not create parallel unisons or octaves. An anticipation may break up parallel fifths present in the basic part writing.

A note sustained in one voice throughout a continuing progression in the other voices is called a pedal point. Pedal points serve to accent the arrival of important scale degree triads (usually V or I).

Selected Readings

Aldwell, Edward, and Carl Schachter. *Harmony and Voice Leading*. 2d ed. 2 vols. New York: Harcourt Brace Jovanovich, 1989. Chapter 21.

Christ, William, et al. *Materials and Structure of Music*. 3d ed. Vol. I. Englewood Cliffs, NJ: Prentice-Hall, 1980. Chapter 14.

Kostka, Stefan, and Dorothy Payne. *Tonal Harmony*. 2d ed. New York: Alfred A. Knopf, 1989. Chapters 10–11.

Piston, Walter. *Harmony*. 5th ed. Revised and expanded by Mark DeVoto. New York: Norton, 1987. Chapter 8.

12

Diatonic Seventh Chords

Diatonic seventh chords arise on all scale degrees. Remember that seventh chords arise from voice leading. The dissonant seventh must resolve down by step. Similarly, the remaining chord notes of the seventh should make clear voice-leading sense.

SUPERTONIC AND SUBDOMINANT SEVENTH CHORDS

Seventh chords on the supertonic and subdominant lead naturally to V or vii.

Supertonic Seventh   The supertonic seventh functions as upper-fifth divider to V. The seventh ($\hat{1}$) of the ii^7 resolves naturally down to the leading tone ($\hat{7}$).

Bach Chorales

Figure 12.1   Supertonic Seventh Chords

In both excerpts of Figure 12.1, the seventh of the supertonic seventh is in the alto. In each case it resolves down by step to the third of V.

Subdominant Seventh

The subdominant seventh functions the same in major and minor. It supports a soprano $\hat{3}$–$\hat{2}$–$\hat{1}$ cadential motion as part of a IV^7–V^7–I progression. The seventh of the subdominant ($\hat{3}$, in the soprano) resolves to $\hat{2}$. The other chord notes move by step to those of V (see Figure 12.2).

Bach Chorales

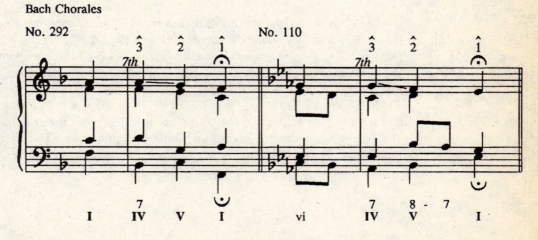

Figure 12.2   Subdominant Seventh Chords

MEDIANT SEVENTH CHORDS

The mediant seventh chord serves as the upper fifth divider of vi (or vi^7). More often than not, iii^7 supports $\hat{5}$ in a soprano $\hat{5}$–$\hat{4}$–$\hat{3}$ motion. Usually, the passing $\hat{4}$ provides an accented passing note above the vi, creating a 6–5 motion above $\hat{6}$ in the bass.

* decorated resolution of the seventh

Figure 12.3   Mediant Seventh Chords

In Figure 12.3a, the alto holds the seventh (G) of the supertonic seventh. It resolves down by step to $\hat{1}$, the third of vi. We might read the vi$^{6-5}$ that follows iii^7 as IV^6–vi since the passing soprano $\hat{4}$ (B-flat) is consonant. The bass moves clearly by descending fifths, however, so we will tend to hear this harmony as vi rather than IV^6.

In Figure 12.3b, the seventh (C) of iii^7 is in the tenor. It, too, resolves down by step to $\hat{1}$ (B-flat), but not before leaping to the lower neighbor of $\hat{1}$. This is a decorated resolution of the seventh (see "The Decorated Resolution," page 154).

SUBMEDIANT SEVENTH CHORDS

The submediant seventh chord functions as a voice-leading harmony to V, V^7 or vii. It often substitutes for or becomes a IV^6. We find the seventh ($\hat{5}$) most often in the soprano as part of a soprano $\hat{5}$–$\hat{4}$–$\hat{3}$ or $\hat{5}$–$\hat{4}$–$\hat{5}$ motion (see Figure 12.4a).

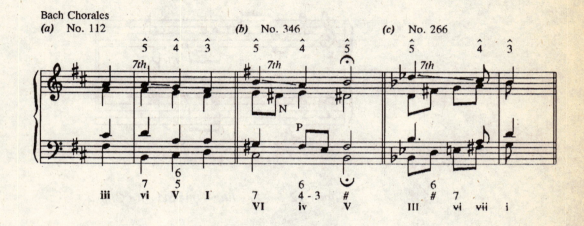

Figure 12.4   Submediant Seventh Chords

In the minor, diatonic VI^7 supports the same $\hat{5}$–$\hat{4}$ soprano motion that it does in the major. However, in the minor, VI^7 is more closely associated with iv^6 than ii. In Figure 12.4b, VI^7 serves to prolong iv^6 above a common-note bass.

In the minor, we find yet another version of vi^7. If we build a triad above raised $\hat{6}$ we create a diminished triad. A seventh added to this triad increases its dissonant, voice-leading character. When we hear this seventh chord built on raised $\hat{6}$, its voice-leading character is unmistakable. Note that it still supports a $\hat{5}$–$\hat{4}$–$\hat{3}$ motion in the soprano, as in Figure 12.4c. (The hash marks through vi and vii in Figure 12.4c indicate that these triads are built upon altered scale degrees.)

LEADING-TONE SEVENTH CHORDS

The leading-tone seventh chord functions like the leading-tone triad. Whereas vii functions most often as a $^6_3$ (serving as a voice-leading substitute for V^4_3), vii[7] often functions in root position as a voice-leading substitute for V^6_5. As a rule, the seventh ($\hat{6}$) of the vii[7] resolves to $\hat{5}$ (see Figure 12.5).

Bach, Chorale 69

Figure 12.5   Leading-Tone Seventh Chord

TONIC SEVENTH CHORDS

Usually, the tonic seventh arises within a lower-fifth divider prolongation of I. If the soprano moves from $\hat{1}$ to $\hat{6}$ as I moves to IV, we may support the passing $\hat{7}$ that connects $\hat{1}$ and $\hat{6}$ with a I[7] (see Figure 12.6).

Bach, Chorale 12

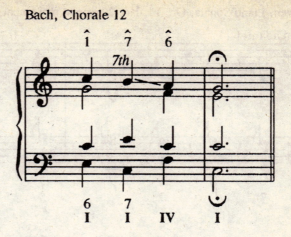

Figure 12.6   Tonic Seventh Chord

RESOLUTION OF THE SEVENTH: VARIANTS

As a rule, *the seventh must resolve down by step in the next chord.* However, in free style we see three common variants of this resolution.

Transferred Resolution

The seventh can resolve in another voice *if the resolution is by step and to the expected pitch.* Such a resolution is called a *transferred resolution.*

In Figure 12.7, the sevenths arise in the top voice of the bass staff but resolve in the middle voice. Notice that the transferred resolutions are by step to the expected pitch—they are simply not in the same voice. Though they are rare in chorale style, we see transferred resolutions often in free style.

Beethoven, Piano Sonata, Op. 14, No. 2, second movement, measures 17-19

Figure 12.7 Transferred Resolutions of the Seventh

The Decorated Resolution

We often see the resolution of the seventh embellished with one or more incomplete neighbors. Such a *decorated resolution* resembles the decorated resolution of the suspension (see Figure 12.3).

The Delayed Resolution

We may delay the resolution of the seventh by maintaining the unresolved seventh as a common note between chords. Eventually, however, the dissonant seventh will resolve. Figure 12.8 is a classic (and extreme) example of the delayed resolution.

Note that the seventh, though unresolved until measure 7, remains dissonant. Although the nature of the dissonance changes, the demand for resolution remains.

Beethoven, Piano Sonata, Op. 31, No. 3, first movement

Figure 12.8   The Delayed Resolution

Apparent Seventh Chords

In free style, notes of figuration in an upper voice often create what appear to be seventh chords. However, these *apparent sevenths* neither act nor sound like true seventh chords. Apparent sevenths arise often as the result of pedal points, dissonant passing and neighboring notes, or bass suspensions. The apparent $^6_5$ is the most common (see Figure 12.9).

By placing simple melodic figurations in accented positions, Chopin creates an apparent $^6_5$ above $\hat{4}$ in the bass. The open fifth above $\hat{4}$ (D), however, creates the effect of a IV in root position—not a seventh chord in first inversion. (If the $^6_5$ above IV were, in fact, a seventh chord, the tenor A would have to be the seventh. But the A sounds, in fact, stable and consonant.)

Chopin, Mazurka, Op. 6, No. 1

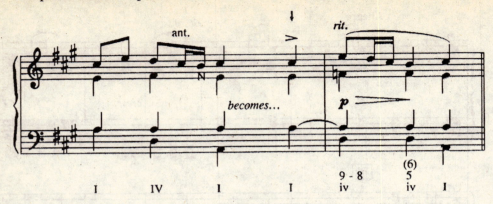

Figure 12.9   Apparent Seventh Chords

In the chorales, Bach shows a particular fondness for an embellished $\frac{6}{3}$ that the student may easily confuse with a $\frac{4}{3}$.

Bach Chorales

(a)   No. 57   *(b)*   No. 59

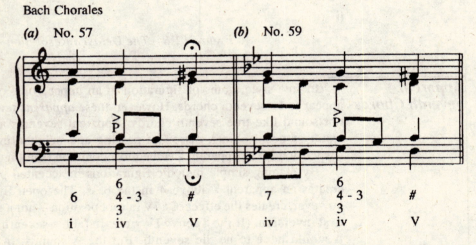

Figure 12.10   The Apparent $\frac{4}{3}$

In Figure 12.10a, an accented passing note (tenor, B) creates a momentary $\frac{4}{3}$. If this indeed were a ii$\frac{4}{3}$, A would be the seventh. Notice, however, that the B sounds dissonant, not the A. In fact, the B seems to resolve to the A. As a result, the chord does not sound like a $\frac{4}{3}$ on ii, but a $\frac{6}{3}$ on iv. In Figure 12.10b, the same $\hat{1}$–raised $\hat{7}$ soprano receives similar treatment. Once again, the apparent $\frac{4}{3}$ resolves itself into a iv$\frac{6}{3}$.

Supertonic and subdominant seventh chords resolve to the dominant. The seventh of the ii^7 resolves to the leading tone. The seventh of the IV^7 resolves to the supertonic.

Mediant and submediant seventh chords support $\hat{5}$ in a soprano $\hat{5}$–$\hat{4}$–$\hat{3}$ motion. The mediant seventh serves as upper-fifth divider to vi. The submediant seventh serves as upper-fifth divider to ii.

The leading tone seventh chord intensifies the voice leading of vii as it moves to I.

The tonic seventh chord arises as a passing motion to IV within a lower-fifth divider prolongation of I. It supports $\hat{7}$ in a soprano $\hat{1}$–$\hat{7}$–$\hat{6}$ motion from I to IV.

When we resolve the seventh in another voice, we have transferred the resolution. When we keep the seventh as a dissonant common note between chords before resolving it, we have delayed the resolution. We can treat the resolution of the seventh as a suspension (with a dissonant preparation).

Pedal points, dissonant passing or neighboring notes, and bass suspensions sometimes create figures that look like sevenths. These so-called apparent sevenths do not behave or sound like true sevenths. The most common apparent sevenths are the "$\frac{6}{5}$" (which, in sound, is a decorated $\frac{5}{3}$) and the "$\frac{4}{3}$" (which, in sound, is a decorated $\frac{6}{3}$).

Selected Readings

Aldwell, Edward, and Carl Schachter. *Harmony and Voice Leading*. 2d ed. 2 vols. New York: Harcourt Brace Jovanovich, 1989. Chapters 23–24.

Benjamin, Thomas, Michael Horvit, and Robert Nelson. *Techniques and Materials of Tonal Music*. Belmont, CA: Wadsworth, 1992. Part II, Sections 17–19.

Kostka, Stefan, and Dorothy Payne. *Tonal Harmony*. 2d ed. New York: Alfred A. Knopf, 1989. Chapters 12–14.

Ottman, Robert W. *Elementary Harmony*. 4th ed. Englewood Cliffs, NJ: Prentice-Hall, Inc. 1989. Chapter 17.

Schenker, Heinrich. *Harmony*. Edited by Oswald Jonas. Translated by Elisabeth Mann Borgese. Chicago: University of Chicago Press, 1980. Section IV, Chapter 1.

13

Harmonic Tonicization and Modulation

*W*e can highlight a scale degree triad by treating it, for the moment, like a tonic. We do so with techniques called linear tonicization (discussed in chapter 10) and harmonic tonicization (discussed in this chapter). Toniciz-ing a scale degree creates a brief, temporary "tonic." We call a longer-last-ing tonicization modulation.

Tonicization and modulation are the extremes of a continuum. If a new key area seems temporary or fleeting, we consider it a tonicization. If the new key area seems of greater significance, we consider it a modulation. It is important to remember, however, that neither tonicization nor modulation "changes the key" of a composition. Rather, each represents just another technique of composing out the true tonic triad.

HARMONIC TONICIZATION

We can tonicize any consonant triad. To make a consonant triad other than the tonic *sound* like the tonic, we must approach it as if it *were* the tonic.

Applied Dominants

The authentic cadence defines a tonic. We can create an artificial authentic cadence to any consonant triad by approaching it from *its* dominant.

APPLIED V

An artificial dominant created to tonicize a triad is called an *applied dominant*. (Some theorists call applied dominants "secondary dominants.")

Structure of the Applied V. The dominant of a key must be both a perfect fifth above its tonic and a major triad. (See Figure 13.1, below. In the examples, a curved arrow connects the applied chord to the triad that it tonicizes. The chord that precedes the arrow is the applied chord. The chord that follows it is the tonicized triad.)

Bach Chorales

(a) No. 4   (b) No. 366   (c) No. 139

I6   vi   V ⤸ V6   V   V ⤸ vi   V6   I   IV   I   V6   ii ⤸

* applied leading tones

Figure 13.1   Applied V

In Figure 13.1a, Bach raises $\hat{4}$ (A) to create a leading tone to $\hat{5}$ (B). The ii triad beneath is now a major triad. It serves as an applied V of V. Similarly in Figure 13.1b, a raised $\hat{5}$ (E-sharp) provides a leading tone to $\hat{6}$ (F-sharp). This major III serves as an applied V of vi.

Inversion and the Applied V. Applied chords serve as voice-leading chords, intensifying the motion to a diatonic scale degree. For this reason, they arise naturally in first inversion, placing the applied leading tone in the bass. In Figure 13.1c, the applied V of ii arises in first inversion as a chromatic passing note between $\hat{1}$ (bass G) and $\hat{2}$ (bass A).

Voice Leading and the Applied V. The applied dominant must *behave* as if it were a dominant. That is, the chord notes of the applied dominant should move strongly to its "tonic." In particular, the new "leading tone" should act like one and resolve to the root of the tonicized triad. (When the applied dominant is in first inversion, this is always the case. However, when the applied dominant is in root position and the applied leading tone is in an inner voice, the resolution is less constrained.)

The Cross Relation. When a cross relation arises during tonicization, we do best to keep the cross relation in the same voice. If we cannot, we should pass the changing scale degree from a weak (inner) voice to a strong (outer) voice (see the discussion of Figure 13.5, page 166).

APPLIED V^7

Far more common than the applied V is the applied V^7. The applied V^7 tonicizes a triad more effectively than a simple V. The V^7 adds to the V the minor seventh above its root. The V^7 thus contains the tritone that occurs naturally between $\hat{4}$ (the seventh of the V^7) and $\hat{7}$ (the third of the V^7) of the new key area or tonicized degree. There is but one tritone in any key. As a result, a key's tritone *defines* that key. When we add a minor seventh to the applied V, we provide not only the "dominant" of the new "tonic," but the defining tritone as well.

Structure of the Applied V^7. The V^7 must be a perfect fifth above its "tonic" and a major triad. The seventh must stand a minor seventh above the root.

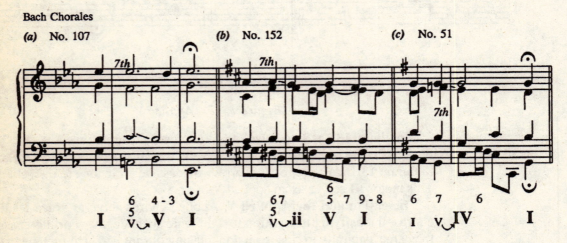

Figure 13.2   Applied V^7

Notice that in Figures 13.2a and 13.2b the applied leading tone arises and resolves in the bass. In Figure 13.2a, bass A-natural arises as the applied leading tone of a V$^6_5$ of V. Notice that it resolves to the root of V (B-flat). Similarly, the bass D-sharp of Figure 13.2b arises as the leading tone within a V$^6_5$ of ii. Here, before resolving, the D-sharp makes a chordal skip to B, the root of the V of ii. The resolution to $\hat{2}$ follows immediately. Notice that the seventh of each applied V$^6_5$ resolves down by step.

The applied V^7 of Figure 13.2c tonicizes IV. I is the upper fifth of IV and will serve as the applied chord. I is already a major triad, so Bach does not need to alter it to create the necessary leading tone to $\hat{4}$. Bach must lower $\hat{7}$ (F-sharp to F-natural), however, to create the necessary *minor* seventh above the applied V^7 on C.

Notice how this F-natural creates a tritone with B. This is the key-defining tritone of C. In gaining this C-defining tritone, we lose that tritone formed between F-sharp and C—the tritone that defines G.

Voice Leading and the Applied V^7. Like all sevenths, the seventh of the V^7 resolves down by step to the third of the tonicized triad. Note that in Figure 13.2, each applied seventh does just this. (In Figure 13.2a, however, Bach suspends the applied seventh into the tonicized V *before* its resolution.)

As a voice-leading harmony, V^7 arises most often in first inversion. When in an outer voice, the applied leading tone must resolve to the tonicized scale degree. In any inversion, the seventh must resolve down by step.

Other Applied Chords

So powerful a tonic-defining interval is the tritone that it can tonicize a triad by itself.

APPLIED vii AND vii^7

The leading-tone triad contains as its defining fifth the key-defining tritone. We frequently see a seventh added to vii to enhance its voice-leading potential. Both vii and vii^7 move naturally to I. We can tonicize any consonant triad with an applied vii or vii^7.

Structure of the Applied vii and vii^7. The root of the applied vii or vii^7 must be a minor second below its applied tonic—that is, it must be built on an applied leading tone. The applied vii must be a diminished triad.

Voice Leading and the Applied vii and vii^7. The applied leading tone (the root of vii) should resolve to the new "tonic" (see Figure 13.3a). Similarly, the seventh of the applied vii^7 should resolve down by step to the fifth of the new "tonic" (see Figure 13.3b).

* applied leading tones

Figure 13.3   Applied vii and vii⁷

Inversions of the Applied vii and vii^7. We see the applied vii most often in $^6_3$ position, where it substitutes for an applied V$^4_3$. The applied vii^7, however, arises just as often in root position, substituting for applied V$^6_5$.

THE FULLY-DIMINISHED vii^7

The structure of the leading tone triad is the same in both major and minor since, in the minor, the triad is built on raised $\hat{7}$. However, the structure of the vii^7 differs between the two modes.

vii^7 in the Major. In the major, the seventh of the vii^7 stands a minor seventh above its root. Adding a minor seventh to a diminished triad creates a *half-diminished seventh chord*.

vii^7 in the Minor. The seventh of the leading tone triad is the sixth scale degree. That seventh must resolve down by step. In the minor, therefore, we do not use raised $\hat{6}$ for the seventh of the vii^7 but unaltered $\hat{6}$. That unaltered sixth stands a *diminished seventh* above its root, raised $\hat{7}$. Whenever we add a diminished seventh to a diminished triad, we create a *fully diminished seventh chord*.

Thus, vii^7 has two forms depending on whether we derive it from the major or the minor mode. When creating an applied vii^7, which form do we use?

Triad Quality and Tonicization. The diatonic quality of the new "tonic" determines whether the new key area is to be major or minor.

If the tonicized triad is a major triad, the tonicization is major. In Figure 13.3b, an applied vii^7 tonicizes V. V is a major triad, so Bach uses a half-diminished vii^7 to tonicize it.

If the tonicized triad is a minor triad, the tonicization is minor. Therefore, a vii^7 applied to a minor triad should be the fully-diminished seventh found in the minor mode. In Figure 13.3c, an applied vii^7 tonicizes ii. Since ii is a minor triad, Bach uses a fully-diminished vii^7 to tonicize it.

Structure of the Applied vii^7 in a Minor Tonicization. When it is tonicizing a minor triad, the applied vii^7 should be a fully-diminished seventh. The root should stand a minor second below the new "tonic." It should support both a diminished triad and a diminished seventh.

Voice Leading and the Applied vii^7 in a Minor Tonicization. The diminished seventh of the applied vii^7 in a minor tonicization must resolve down by step to the fifth of the new "tonic." In Figure 13.3c, soprano D stands a diminished fifth above the root of the applied vii$^6_5$. It resolves down by step to C. Notice that although this applied vii^7 is in first inversion, the applied leading tone (tenor G-sharp) resolves to the new "tonic" and the diminished seventh (alto E-natural) resolves down by step.

MODULATION

On occasion, a tonicization occupies an entire phrase or even an entire section of a composition. Such an extensive tonicization is called a *modulation*. A modulation creates a new *key area*.

General Considerations

Modulation, like tonicization, arises from the composing-out process. Tonicization provides only a momentary emphasis of the tonicized scale degree. Modulation, on the other hand, establishes a new key area. Within this new key area, the tonicized scale degree reigns as "tonic."

A new key area relates to a work's main key area in the same way that the triad on which we base that new key area relates to the tonic triad of the main *key area.* Any consonant scale degree can be tonicized for local emphasis, but usually modulation is limited to the primary scale degrees. These scale degrees play the most prominent role in composing out the true tonic.

CLOSELY RELATED KEYS

Notice that the key signatures of the primary scale degrees (I, V, and IV) of a given key differ from each other by no more than one sharp or flat. Keys related in this way are called *closely related keys*.

For example, the following keys are considered closely related to C major: V (G major, one sharp), IV (F major, one flat), vi (A minor, no flats or sharps), iii (E minor, one sharp), and ii (D minor, one flat). Notice that the tonic triad of each of these keys is a scale degree triad within C major.

Note as well that *the quality of the tonicized scale degree triad determines the mode of the new key area.*

Both iii and V are closely related key areas to I. As a scale degree triad, however, V serves a much more important role than does iii. Therefore, we will see a modulation to V much more frequently than a modulation to iii. Any modulation to iii prolongs a prominent iii within a larger progression. (For example, within a prolonged I–iii–V progression, the third divider, iii, may become tonicized. If the prolongation is extensive enough, the progression might even modulate to iii before completing its motion to V.)

MODULATION AND THE LEADING-TONE TRIAD

We *cannot* tonicize or modulate to the leading tone triad, because the leading-tone triad is a diminished triad. A dissonant triad cannot serve as a tonic triad.

In the minor, however, we can tonicize or modulate to the subtonic triad (that is, the unaltered seventh-scale-degree triad). As a major triad, it can serve as a temporary tonic. But, once again, it does so only by prolonging a prominent subtonic triad within a larger progression.

Modulatory Techniques

To modulate, we must create a definitive progression in the new key area. This is called *establishing* the new key.

ESTABLISHING THE NEW KEY AREA

Usually an applied chord is necessary in a modulation. However, it is not enough in itself to establish a new key area. We need a more extensive, confirming progression. This often takes the form I–IV–V–I (or I–ii^6–V–I) *in the new key*. For example, to modulate to V we must first *tonicize V* with an applied chord. Then we must establish V as a new key area with a confirming progression within the key of V.

TYPES OF MODULATION

Traditionally, two modulatory techniques are used. The first uses what we call a *pivot chord* between the new key and the old. This technique, in effect, overlaps a progression in the old key with the establishing progression in the new key. The second technique is more abrupt, tonicizing the new key with a cross-relation before the establishing progression.

The Pivot-Chord Modulation. A chord held in common between two keys is a *common chord*. Any common chord can serve as a pivot chord.

Figure 13.4   Bach, Chorale 20

Bach follows the perfect authentic cadence of measure 1 with a modulation to V. In measure 3, he confirms and establishes V as a key area with a perfect authentic cadence to V. The final I of the initial cadence serves as the pivot chord. On reaching the applied dominant to V on the second beat of measure 2, we interpret the weak I–iii motion in the old key area as IV–vi–V in the new key area. The *pivot chord modulation* (sometimes called a "common-chord modulation") is by far the most common modulatory technique.

Modulation By Cross-Relation. We can, on the other hand, avoid a pivot chord by moving directly from a chord found in the old key but not in the new key to a chord found in the new key but not the old. When we use this technique to modulate between closely related keys, a cross-relation results. Such a modulation is abrupt and dramatic by comparison with the pivot-chord modulation.

G minor: V i   V   I   IV I   ii V I
C major:

Figure 13.5   Bach, Chorale 74

The first part of Figure 13.5 provides a half cadence in G minor. Bach leaves the cadential V with a chord that clearly contradicts the G tonic, however. On the last quarter of the second full measure, the soprano leaps from A up to F-natural. This F-natural creates both a cross-relation with the F-sharp leading tone (alto) that preceded it, and a dissonance (diminished fifth) above the bass B-natural. This major-minor $\frac{6}{5}$ on G cannot be tonic. The F-natural destroys the leading tone of G at the same time it creates an applied $V\frac{6}{5}$ that points to C. The F–B tritone (between soprano and bass) is the key-defining tritone of C. It immediately (measure 3) resolves to C (IV), tonicizing it. Bach makes of this tonicization a modulation, by continuing to progress as if *in* C. He confirms C as tonic with an imperfect authentic cadence at the end of measure 4.

This modulation hinges on the cross-relation of measure 2. Therefore, Bach makes the cross-relation clear by passing the changing scale degree from a weak inner voice (alto) to a strong outer voice (soprano). The effect is startling but, at the same time, perfectly clear. (If the cross-relation does not pass from an inner voice to an outer voice, it should be kept within the same voice.)

We can intensify a scale degree triad by tonicizing it. We do so by approaching it from an applied chord. An applied chord reproduces the V, V^7, vii, or vii^7 that is found in the key of the tonicized triad. The applied chord behaves as if the tonicized triad were, in fact, "tonic."

The quality of the tonicized triad determines the mode of tonicization. In a major key, vii^7 is a half-diminished seventh. In a minor key it is a fully-diminished seventh. So when creating an applied vii^7 to a major triad, we construct a minor seventh above the applied leading tone. When creating an applied vii^7 to a minor triad, we construct a diminished seventh above the applied leading tone.

A modulation is an extended tonicization. Usually, a modulation begins with a tonicization. However, after tonicizing a triad, we must then establish the new key area. We do so with a confirming progression in the new key area. This confirming progression may be an authentic or half cadence. It may simply involve the principal triads of the new key area. In either event, it must do more than merely provide an applied chord to the tonicized triad.

Modulation can be either gradual or abrupt. We effect a gradual modulation by using a chord or succession of chords, called pivot chords, shared by the old and the new key areas. An abrupt modulation with a cross-relation takes us immediately from a chord not found in the new key area to a chord not found in the old key area. We must be careful either to keep the cross-relation in the same voice or to pass it from an inner voice to an outer voice.

Selected Readings

Aldwell, Edward, and Carl Schachter. *Harmony and Voice Leading*. 2d ed. 2 vols. New York: Harcourt Brace Jovanovich, 1989. Chapter 25.

Christ, William, et al. *Materials and Structure of Music*. 3d ed. Vol. I. Englewood Cliffs, NJ: Prentice-Hall, 1980. Chapters 20–21.

Kostka, Stefan, and Dorothy Payne. *Tonal Harmony*. 2d ed. New York: Alfred A. Knopf, 1989. Chapters 16–19.

Ottman, Robert W. *Elementary Harmony*. 4th ed. Englewood Cliffs, NJ: Prentice-Hall, 1989. Chapter 12.

Piston, Walter. *Harmony*. 5th ed. Revised and expanded by Mark DeVoto. New York: Norton, 1987. Chapters 14–16.

Schoenberg, Arnold. *Structural Functions of Harmony*. Rev. ed. Edited by Leonard Stein. New York: Norton, 1969. Chapters 3–4.

——— . *Theory of Harmony*. Translated by Roy E. Carter. Berkeley: University of California Press, 1983. Chapters 9–10.

14

Harmonizing a Melody

Harmonizing a chorale melody gives you the opportunity to call on all the techniques and skills covered in the prior chapters. Harmonization is a three stage process. First, analyze the given melody. (That is, determine how the tune composes out its tonic triad.) From this you can determine the nature and location of any cadences. Next, compose a bass against the given soprano. (This bass arises from analysis of the melody.) Finally, realize the inner voices.

MELODIC ANALYSIS

Consider the following chorale tune:

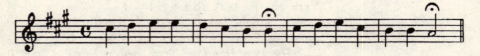

Figure 14.1   Chorale Tune, Werde munter, meine Gemüthe;
first two phrases

To harmonize this tune, we must first understand it as an expression of its tonality. That is, we must understand the way in which it composes out its tonic triad. First, we analyze this tune through its tonic triad (Figure 14.2a). When we do, we uncover a series of arpeggiations filled in by passing notes.

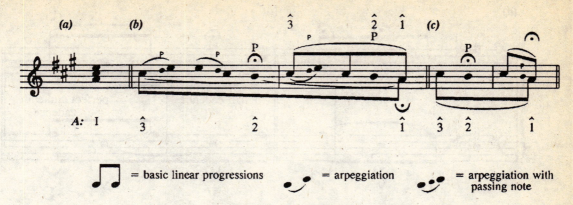

Figure 14.2   Basic Analysis of Figure 14.1

The first phrase (Figure 14.2b, measure 1) arpeggiates from $\hat{3}$ to $\hat{5}$ and back again, filling in the arpeggiations with passing notes. The half cadence arises as this prolonged $\hat{3}$ begins its descent to $\hat{1}$. The tune pauses on the $\hat{2}$ that passes between them to create this half cadence. The second phrase (Figure 14.2b, measure 2) begins like the first phrase with an arpeggiation from $\hat{3}$ to $\hat{5}$. However, the repetition of the first phrase is abbreviated, returning to $\hat{3}$ without a repetition of $\hat{5}$ and without the second passing $\hat{4}$ (D). This allows the second phrase the time needed to complete the passing motion from $\hat{2}$ to $\hat{1}$. The second phrase ends on a perfect authentic cadence, having completed the motion from prolonged $\hat{3}$ (first phrase) through a passing $\hat{2}$ (half cadence) to $\hat{1}$.

Notice that all these embellishments seem to form themselves around a single $\hat{3}$–$\hat{1}$ arpeggiation, prolonged with a passing note and becoming $\hat{3}$–$\hat{2}$–$\hat{1}$ (see Figure 14.2c). The first phrase stops prematurely on $\hat{2}$ with a half cadence. The arpeggiation reaches $\hat{1}$ only at the end of the tune and after a repetition of the same basic $\hat{3}$–$\hat{2}$–$\hat{1}$ motion.

ESTABLISHING THE BASS

Begin establishing the harmonic structure by sketching the bass.

Structure of the Bass

We support the basic $\hat{3}$–$\hat{2}$–$\hat{1}$ soprano progression (illustrated in Figure 14.2c) with the tonic and its upper-fifth divider in the bass (see Figure 14.3a).

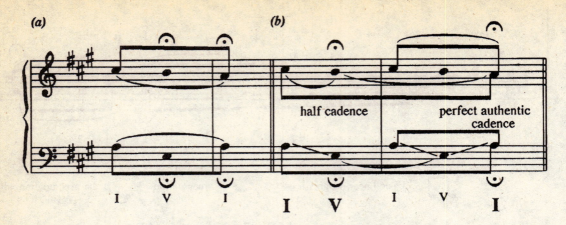

Figure 14.3   Analysis with Cadences

We support the repetition of that structure in the second phrase the same way (see Figure 14.3b). The tonic prolonged by its fifth divider will form the backbone of any complete tonal structure.

The Cadences

The simple analysis in Figure 14.2c now allows us to choose appropriate cadences (Figure 14.3b). The final move to $\hat{1}$ should involve a perfect authentic cadence. This appropriately reinforces the completion of the large-scale arpeggiation from $\hat{3}$ to $\hat{1}$. Notice that the bass line of Figure 14.3b already provides the necessary V–I progression below the soprano $\hat{2}$–$\hat{1}$.

But what of the first phrase cadence to $\hat{2}$? *A cadence to the passing note between $\hat{3}$ and $\hat{1}$ signals the half cadence* (see chapter 6). The cadence to V (measure 2) provides consonant support for that passing $\hat{2}$. Notice that our working bass already provides the necessary progression for this half cadence as well.

Voice-Leading Connections

This is how the working bass line stands against the melody:

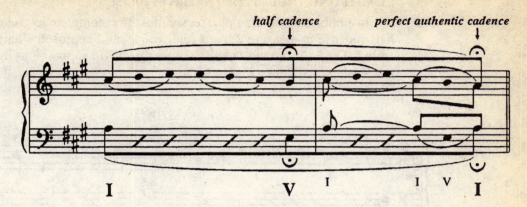

Figure 14.4   Melody with Working Bass

COMPLETING THE BASS OF THE SECOND PHRASE

The bass of the second phrase is now almost complete. We need only provide some sort of voice-leading connective between the root-position tonics that begin the second measure of Figure 14.4. We might accomplish this by dropping to the lower-third divider (vi or IV^6) and then moving through a passing $\hat{7}$ back to $\hat{1}$ (see Figure 14.5).

Figure 14.5   Second Phrase with Bass

Here, a first-inversion IV is preferable to a root-position vi. The inversion is less stable and more clearly a voice-leading harmony. Similarly, the V^6 that follows makes clear the linear origin of these harmonies.

COMPLETING THE BASS OF THE FIRST PHRASE

In completing the first phrase, we must first complete its cadence—the half cadence in measure 2. As a rule, you should approach a half cadence from I. The $\hat{3}$–$\hat{2}$ soprano cadence allows this. I will support $\hat{3}$ as it moves to the V-supported $\hat{2}$ (see Figure 14.6a).

Figure 14.6   Approaching the Half Cadence

However, root-position I does not function well as a voice-leading chord. Therefore, we will place it in first inversion (see Figure 14.6b, above). Now this new I arises in inversion on a weak beat as a voice-leading harmony to the cadential V. In this way it cannot be confused with the root-position tonics that support the basic $\hat{3}$–$\hat{1}$ structure.

We now must complete measure 1. We need a voice-leading progression that takes us from the opening root-position tonic to the final cadential dominant.

Consider what this means. First, each chord must be a voice-leading chord. (That is, it will not be part of the basic harmonic structure outlined above.) Second, each voice-leading chord must *lead* somewhere. Each must take us closer to the cadential V. (These voice-leading chords will *not* lead to the I⁶ on beat 2 of measure 2. Remember, this I⁶ is part of the same *voice-leading* motion to the cadential V. I⁶ is not the goal here; V is.)

From chapters 6 and 7, we know that IV (or ii) provides the best approach to V. Placing either IV or ii on the strong first beat of measure 2, creates a IV(or ii)–V progression between the strong beats of the measure. We have two choices: a bass $\hat{4}$ (IV or ii⁶, Figure 14.7a) or a bass $\hat{2}$ (ii, Figure 14.7b).

Figure 14.7   First Phrase One: Measure 2 Bass

Neither IV nor ii^6 (14.7a) will work. If we are to move from bass $\hat{4}$ (measure 2, beat 1) to bass $\hat{5}$ (measure 2, beat 3), the bass $\hat{3}$ makes no sense. It moves in the wrong direction—not toward bass $\hat{5}$ but *away* from it. (Even if it made sense, the parallel octaves that result between bass and soprano rule out this alternative.) A root-position ii, however, makes sound voice-leading sense (14.7b). Root-position ii serves as a fifth divider to V. In this context, the following I^6 takes us closer to bass $\hat{5}$. In fact, by adding an unaccented passing note between the bass of this I^6 and V, we create a nice fourth progression from root-position ii to V (14.7c).

We now have a strong approach to the half cadence of measure 2. Let us return to measure 1.

Figure 14.8   Completing the Bass

The $\hat{3}$–$\hat{5}$ arpeggiation of the first measure calls for a lower-fifth divider prolongation (see Figure 14.8a). However, the root-position I below the soprano $\hat{5}$ gives undue emphasis to the $\hat{5}$ (which is *not* an element of the basic $\hat{3}$–$\hat{2}$–$\hat{1}$ structure). We therefore convert this I to a voice-leading I^6 (see Figure 14.8b). Remember: A voice-leading chord must lead somewhere. Hence we use the lower octave for this bass $\hat{3}$ where it serves as a upper neighbor to the bass $\hat{2}$ that follows in measure 2 (see Figure 14.8c).

The approach to measure 2 is now strong. However, the opening bass $\hat{1}$ remains separate from the voice-leading progression that follows. (That is, we have skipped from it down to a lower register). Converting the lower-fifth divider (IV) to first inversion creates a voice-leading connection between the initial $\hat{1}$ and the final $\hat{5}$ (at the end of the phrase) in Figure 14.8c, where slurs outline this connection.

Now we have only one chord to go. The bass (measure 1, beat 3) stands only a step away from the first beat of measure 2. We cannot make the bass line move any more easily from $\hat{3}$ to $\hat{2}$. We must, therefore, prolong either the chord we are leaving (that is, the I^6 on beat 3) or the chord to which we are moving (ii on beat 1 of measure 2). Root-position ii, as fifth divider to the cadential V, is the more important chord, because it is in root position and it helps prolong an even more important chord—the cadential V. So, it is best to prolong that ii back into the last beat of measure 1. We accomplish this with the upper-fifth divider of ii or vi, marked with an asterisk in Figure 14.9.

Figure 14.9   The Completed Bass Line

Soprano $\hat{5}$ becomes the dissonant seventh of that vi. The dissonance enhances the voice-leading quality of the vi. The resolution of the dissonant $\hat{5}$ to $\hat{4}$ above ii helps provide a tonic accent on ii, the principal voice-leading connection to the cadential V.

The Completed Bass

Our bass is now complete. Compare it with a bass provided for this same tune by J. S. Bach.

BACH'S OWN VERSION

Bach wrote five different harmonizations of this tune. Let us look at the bass from the one that most resembles our own.

Figure 14.10 Bach, Chorale 233, soprano and bass only

Bach's bass differs from ours in two details. First, he adds a passing note to connect the I–IV^6 progression of measure 3. Compare (a) in Figure 14.10 with Figure 14.9. He makes a more significant change in measure 1, however, at (b) in Figure 14.10. Bach *uses not a I^6 but a root-position iii.* (He keeps the same bass, but provides different harmonic support.) If you consider the bass line, ignoring the figures, you will see why. A succession of descending fifths moves from the third beat of measure 1 (bass $\hat{3}$) all the way to the cadential V (bass $\hat{5}$) (see Figure 14.11). The fifths continue on from that bass $\hat{5}$ to the following root-position I (measure 3, beat 1)—and even further, to the root of the following IV^6.

Figure 14.11 Bach, Chorale 233, bass and soprano

Except for our I⁶, then, each chord approaches the next as its upper-fifth divider. This sequence of upper-fifth dividers ends only at the beginning of the second phrase. By using iii instead of I⁶ as harmonic support for the bass $\hat{3}$ (measure 1, beat 3), Bach provides the missing upper-fifth divider for vi.

> *Remember:* As support for a voice-leading harmony, the scale
> degree in the bass is much more important than the chord
> that it supports.

Thus, the iii that replaces I⁶ does not change the voice-leading function of the line. Rather, it continues and makes clear that succession of descending fifths that leads us to cadential V—and then on to I.

The Inner Voices

Before we begin adding the inner voices, let us look at Bach's complete harmonization of these two phrases.

Figure 14.12   Bach, Chorale 233

Notice that (except for the second phrase tenor) both alto and tenor have very simple lines, moving mainly by step and common notes. As a rule, *the inner voices arise naturally from the completed bass and soprano if the voice leading of the bass in relation to the soprano is strong.*

INNER VOICES OF THE FIRST PHRASE

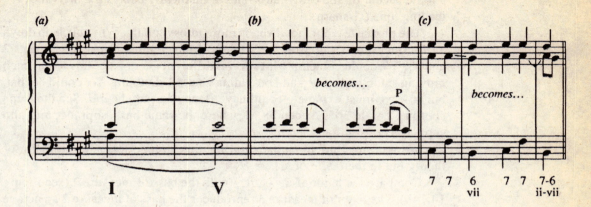

Figure 14.13   First Phrase: Alto and Tenor

Bach's bass is strong, so let us begin examining the inner voices by looking at the relationship between the beginning and end of the phrase (see Figure 14.13a).

By establishing a clear voice leading relationship between the initial tonic and the final dominant, Bach makes it possible for the inner voices to move simply by step or common note. Notice that the tenor does leap a third between the third and fourth beats of measure 1. Bach fills in this leap with a passing note (see Figure 14.13b). On beat 1 of measure 2, Bach suspends the previous A of the alto (see Figure 14.13c).

INNER VOICES OF THE SECOND PHRASE

* suspension

Figure 14.14   Second Phrase: Alto and Tenor

Bach's phrase-2 alto is straightforward. The only embellishment is a suspension at the cadence (see Figure 14.14a). The dissonance both provides a tonic accent on the cadential V and dramatically delays the arrival of the leading tone (G-sharp).

The phrase-2 tenor, however, is more idiosyncratic. Why this leap down a fifth (measure 3, into beat 3)? Why the doubled thirds (measure 3, beats 2 and 4)? We could come up with several different versions of this tenor, each moving smoothly by step and providing "better" doubling. We could do that, but so—we must assume—could have Bach. (In fact, he *did*. See the same spot in Chorale 365, Appendix M, where the same bass, soprano, *and* alto support a conventional tenor.)

We will not find an explanation for this strange tenor in the realm of theory but in the realm of art.

Compare the tenor of measure 3 with the bass of measure 2 (see Figure 14.14b). The tenor of measure 3 reproduces the bass of measure 2 an octave higher. As a result, the bass motion that brought us to the half cadence (measure 2, beat 3) now moves to the tenor. There it sets up the cadential dominant of the final authentic cadence (measure 4, beat 3).

We might say that the tenor here answers a much higher call than just "good voice leading." It turns an exercise into a composition—one whose parts relate to the whole in rich and unexpected ways.

Other Harmonizations

Take time now to inspect the four additional Bach harmonizations of this tune found in Appendix M. Notice that, although each differs in detail, three reflect a similar understanding of the harmonic structure of the tune. Chorale 121, however, stands apart. It delays the arrival of the first tonic until the second beat of measure 2. That delayed tonic seems to function as fifth divider of that root position V that precedes and follows it. As a result, the first phrase of Chorale 121 seems to prolong the descent from $\hat{5}$ to $\hat{2}$.

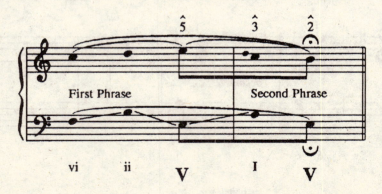

Figure 14.15   Bach, Chorale 121, analysis of the first phrase

Note *how* Bach delays the arrival of the tonic. The vi–ii–V–I–V motion that begins, in the other harmonizations, only on the last beat of measure 1 begins here on the first beat. Tonally, Chorale 121 begins as if in left field, eventually homing in on the tonic, but only as lower-fifth divider to a cadential V. It is not until the second phrase that Bach locates the tonic securely beneath $\hat{3}$, and completes the $\hat{3}$–$\hat{2}$–$\hat{1}$ motion that spans both phrases.

Harmonizing a tune requires three steps.

First, analyze the tune to determine how the tune composes out its tonic triad and to determine the basic structure, the framework on which the composer built the tune.

Second, construct the bass. The bass should reflect the basic structure by outlining the basic scale-degree motion of the chords. Complete the bass with voice-leading chords that connect the harmonies of the basic progression.

Third, realize the inner voices. Our goal is "good voice leading." But as we saw in our Bach example, broader compositional goals can excuse deviations from basic voice-leading guidelines. Such deviations do not arise from the need for "variety," however, but from the effort to create a richer and more complex relationship among the parts.

Selected Readings

Cooper, Paul. *Perspectives in Music Theory*. 2d ed. New York: Harper & Row, 1981. Chapter 19.

Ottman, Robert W. *Elementary Harmony*. 4th ed. Englewood Cliffs, NJ: Prentice-Hall, 1989. Chapter 11.

Piston, Walter. *Harmony*. 5th ed. Revised and expanded by Mark DeVoto. New York: Norton, 1987. Chapters 9–10.

Schoenberg, Arnold. *Theory of Harmony*. Translated by Roy E. Carter. Berkeley: University of California Press, 1983. Chapter 16.

15

Motive, Phrase, and Melody

In free composition, we concern ourselves with techniques that control larger musical structures. We do this by combining melodic and harmonic organization.

Melody and harmony work together to create a phrase. There are two basic phrase types: the period and the sentence. Composers often create more complex structures by combining the two.

We now move from chorale style to free composition. Up to this point, we have concerned ourselves almost exclusively with voice leading. In free composition, we will consider broader tonal constructs and more complex means of organization. Our source for examples will no longer be the chorales of Bach but the piano sonatas of Mozart. We identify the works of Mozart with a "K" or "Köchel" number. Ludwig Köchel's catalogue of Mozart's works (*Chronologisch-thematisches Verzeichnis*, 6th ed., Wiesbaden: Breitkopf & Härtel, 1964) is the standard.

We begin with the basic unit of free composition, the motive.

THE MOTIVE

A motive is the smallest melodic unit that remains identifiable. Although identifiable, it is not complete in itself. The motive is a part of a larger melodic structure, the *phrase*. (We discuss the phrase in the next section.) The motive has both a melodic and a rhythmic aspect. Although we usually find both together, either may serve to represent the motive within a composition.

Figure 15.1   Mozart, Piano Sonata, K. 545: third movement

In Figure 15.1, a descending third (the melodic aspect) and three staccato eighth notes (the rhythmic aspect) make up the motive. The motive of Figure 15.2a is more complex.

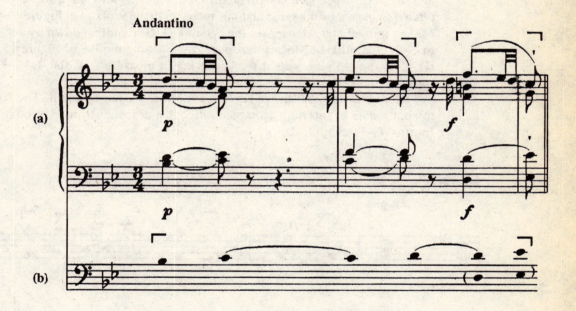

Figure 15.2   Mozart, Fantasy, *K. 475: measures 93–95*

The melodic aspect of this motive consists of a descending fourth filled in with passing notes. The rhythmic aspect consists of a dotted eighth note followed by two thirty-seconds and an eighth.

In Figure 15.1, the motive saturates the music: we find nothing *but* the motive in either voice. Although the motive of Figure 15.2a is more complex, its setting appears simpler. The lower voices seem to provide nothing but harmonic support. A more detailed look at the bass line, however, reveals a rhythmic and intervallic transformation of the motive (see Figure 15.2b). The motive lasts six and a half beats instead of one and a half. The descending fourth of the soprano becomes an ascending fourth in the bass. This bass transformation is considerably more abstract than the repetitions of the motive found in the soprano. However, it is exactly in these more abstract applications of the motive that we encounter the shaping forces of tonal music. *Composers do not simply repeat motives, they transform them.*

The Basic Transformations

We can transform the rhythmic or the intervallic aspect of a motive or both. However, we will consider each aspect separately.

PITCH TRANSFORMATIONS

Transposition. Mozart does not merely repeat the motives of Figure 15.1 and 15.2a, he transposes them. That is, they keep both their intervallic and rhythmic aspects, but begin on different scale degrees, each successive pitch *transposed* by the same diatonic interval. In the soprano of Figure 15.1, Mozart immediately transposes the opening G–G–E motive down by a step to F–F–D. Similarly, Mozart transposes the opening motive of Figure 15.2 (D–C–B-flat–A) *up* a step at the beginning of measure 2 (E-flat–D–C–B-flat).

Retrogression. When we reverse a motive, we retrograde it. The following sonata begins with a simple motive that descends by step through a fourth—G–F-sharp–E–D.

X = motive, Y = retrograde of X

Figure 15.3   Mozart, Piano Sonata, K. 284; first movement

The second theme of the movement begins with the same motive (intervallic aspect only)—but in reverse—that is, *retrograded*. G–F-sharp–E–D becomes D–E–F-sharp–G (see Figure 15.3b).

Look again at Figure 15.2. The bass (15.2b) *retrogrades* the motive found in measure 2, beat 1 of Figure 15.2a. In fact, the intervallic aspect of the motive from Figure 15.3 matches that of the motive in Figure 15.2. Each fills in a descending fourth. However, the rhythmic aspect of each differs. Play the motives from Figures 15.2 and 15.3 and compare them. Notice that this slight rhythmic difference creates a great musical difference when combined with differences in tempo and articulation.

Inversion. To invert a motive, we use the same succession of intervals but reverse their direction. This creates a mirror image of the motive, where *up* becomes *down*.

X = motive, X' = X (second interval inverted), Y = X inverted

Figure 15.4   Mozart, Piano Sonata, K. 282; second movement

This movement begins with a simple motive (X) and its transposition (see Figure 15.4a). The first theme ends with a varied repetition of the opening motive (X′) and then its inversion (Y) (see Figure 15.4b). X, the opening motive, begins on D, ascends by a step, descends by a third, and then descends by another step (see the second stave of Figure 15.4 for the pitch aspect of the motives discussed). The inverted motive (Y, Figure 15.4b) begins on D as well, but then *descends* by a step, *ascends* by a third, and then *ascends* by another step. The intervals of Y are the same as those of X except that they move in the opposite direction.

RHYTHMIC TRANSFORMATIONS

Augmentation. If we double (or triple, and so on) the note values of the motive, we create an augmentation of the motive. Mozart augments (doubles the note values of) the initial motive of Figure 15.5 after a single transposition.

Andante un poco adagio

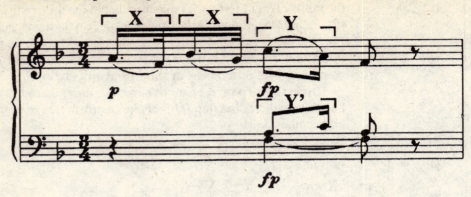

X=motive, Y=X augmented, Y'=X augmented and inverted

Figure 15.5   Mozart, Piano Sonata, K. 309; second movement

The opening dotted-sixteenth–thirty-second rhythmic motive is augmented to create a dotted-eighth–sixteenth motive. In Figure 15.6, an augmentation (Y) of the initial motive (X) provides melodic material for the last half of the tune.   Eighteenth-century performance practice requires that we perform

as if written

X = motive, Y = X augmented

Figure 15.6   Mozart, Piano Sonata, K. 331; third movement

The first three measures each contain a transposition of the basic motive (X). Mozart doubles the note values of this motive (♪ = ♩), creating the second half of his tune from the resulting augmentation, motive Y.

Diminution. If we halve (or reduce by a third, and so on) the note values of the motive we create a diminution. Let us look again at the melody of Figure 15.3, this time considering the second motive (see X in Figure 15.7).

X = motive, Y = X diminished, Z = X retrograded, diminished, and inverted

Figure 15.7   Mozart, Piano Sonata, K. 284; first movement

The figure that follows motive X of measure 2 contains two transpositions of X (marked Y). Each Y is a diminution of X. We find two retrograded *and* inverted transformations (Z) embedded in this figure as well. Even with these complex transformations, Figure 15.7 is relatively simple by comparison with the following.

X = motive, Y = X diminished

Figure 15.8   Mozart, Piano Sonata, K. 331; second movement

Here Mozart transposes motive X up a second at the beginning of each measure. In the next-to-last measure, however, he halves the values of the motive

creating a diminution (Y). Notice that the three Y motives, each a diminution of X, ascend by stepwise transposition, beginning on E, then F-natural, and then G-natural.

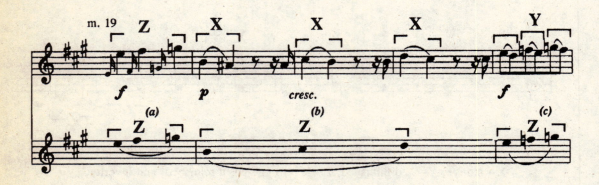

Figure 15.9   Mozart, Piano Sonata, K. 331; second movement

By adding one more measure to the excerpt (measure 19), we begin to see what Mozart is about here. Figure 15.9 begins with a new motive, Z —three ascending steps (melodic aspect) in equal note values (rhythmic aspect) (see *(a)* on the second stave of Figure 15.9). The three transpositions of X that follow (measures 20–22) create an augmented transposition of Z (see *(b)* in Figure 15.9). The three *diminished* transpositions of X that arise in the last measure (marked Y in Figure 15.9) reproduce the original Z (see *(c)* in Figure 15.9).

Motives function at many different levels of melodic organization.

Expansion and Contraction of the Motive

In more complex music, we find these techniques combined. Such combinations often create the sense that a motive expands or contracts. The first movement of Beethoven's Fifth Symphony offers the classic example. Here is the second theme of the movement.

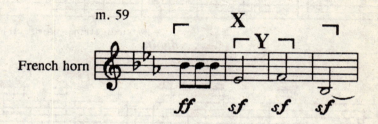

Figure 15.10   Beethoven, Symphony No. 5: first movement, measures 59–62, French horn only

In the middle of the movement, this theme returns, but with the last note left off. The motive (X) immediately shrinks to the ascending second (Y). Then it shrinks further to a single note (Z) (see Figure 15.11).

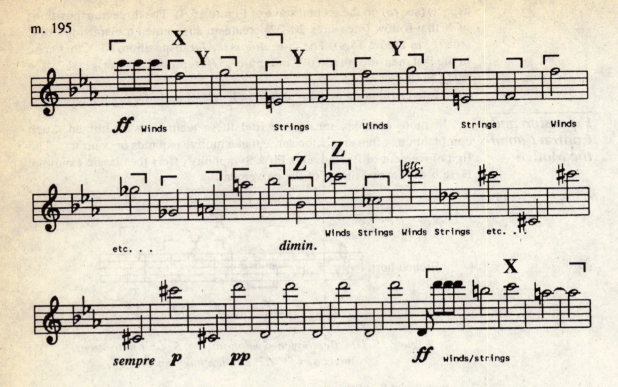

*Figure 15.11   Beethoven, Symphony No. 5: first movement,
measures 195–232*

That single note (Z) bears no resemblance to the initial motive. (It retains
neither its intervallic nor rhythmic aspect.) Yet by gradually contracting the
motives of the theme, Beethoven convinces us that these isolated pitches (Z)
are, in fact, remnants of the once-grand French horn theme of Figure 15.10,
motive X. This conviction is confirmed as motive X emerges unexpectedly
(last five measures of Figure 15.11) from a repeated D.

   Transposition, retrogression, diminution, augmentation, contraction,
and expansion combine in the following Mozart excerpt. Yet in stark contrast
to the Beethoven example above, this dense motivic web remains below the
surface. It controls and shapes the music without calling attention to itself.

Figure 15.12   Mozart, Piano Sonata, K. 282; first movement

The motive (marked with brackets) appears first in the bass (see *(a)* in Figure 15.12). The top voice of the bass staff then presents a retrograded and inverted version of the bass at *(b)*. Mozart then repeats *(a)* an octave higher in the soprano *(c)* with its rhythm diminished and changed slightly. The bass then repeats the last note of *(a)* and builds a transposition of the motive at *(d)* below the last note. In the meantime, the soprano presents a highly embellished transposition of the same motive *(e)*.

Notice that the motive of Figure 15.12 is the same filled-in descending fourth that we encountered in Figures 15.2 and 15.3. Once again, subtle changes in rhythm, accent, tempo, and articulation create from the same motivic material very different musical contexts.

PHRASE AND MELODIC TYPES

Musicians use the word *phrase* in many different ways. In what follows, a musical phrase is comparable to a clause in English. Just as a clause must contain both a subject and a predicate (verb), a musical phrase must contain both a subject (motive) and a cadence. The cadence can be strong (authentic) or weak (half), just as an English clause may be independent or dependent.

A phrase, then, has both a motivic and a harmonic aspect. When we combine phrases into a larger, complete, and self-sufficient unit, melody results. When this melody is the basis for an even larger musical structure, it is a *theme*. A theme on which an especially complex or extended musical structure is based is called a *subject*.

For discussion, we will distinguish between two melodic or thematic types: the *period* and the *sentence*. Each type represents a common manner of combining phrases.

Period

The period has two symmetrical phrases that relate to each other as *antecedent* to *consequent*. As a rule, the antecedent ends with a half cadence or tonicized V. The consequent begins like the antecedent. It ends with an authentic cadence. Antecedent and consequent are of the same length and contain the same motivic materials.

THE ANTECEDENT

The antecedent opens the period. It introduces the main motive called the *head motive*. As a rule, the antecedent is an even number of measures in length. As the opening phrase of the period, the antecedent begins on I. It ends with a half cadence or an authentic cadence to tonicized V. The cadence to V both signals the end of a phrase *and* demands completion. (The goal of the consequent is to complete the antecedent.) Less frequently, the antecedent ends on I. When it does, the cadence is often imperfect or to an inversion of the tonic.

THE CONSEQUENT

The consequent closes the period by completing the harmonic motion begun in the antecedent. It ends with an authentic cadence. The consequent is of the same length as the antecedent. As a rule, it begins with the same head motive.

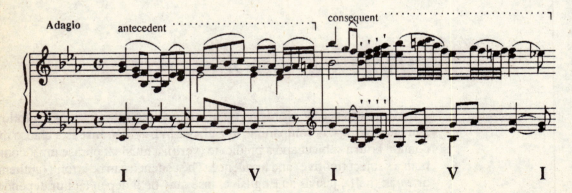

Figure 15.13   Mozart, Piano Sonata, K. 570: second movement

Here the antecedent moves to a half cadence; the consequent completes the motion from V to I with an authentic cadence. Notice that the consequent provides an embellished transformation of the antecedent melody. The consequent must alter its second half in order to transform the antecedent's half cadence to an authentic cadence.

The following example is considerably more complex.

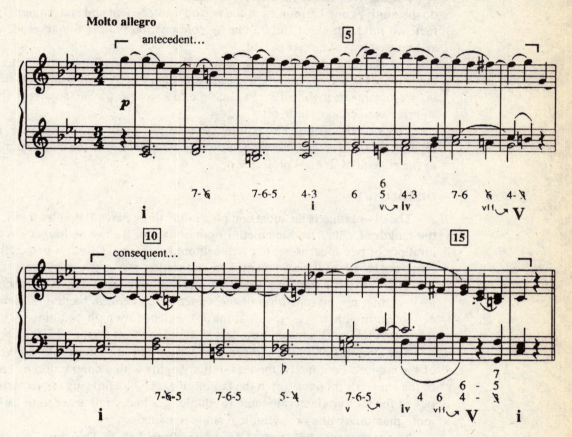

Figure 15.14   Mozart, Piano Sonata, K. 457; third movement

Despite its greater length and harmonic complexity, notice that the basic motion is the same. The antecedent's motion from i to V♯ (measure 8) completes itself in the perfect authentic cadence that closes the consequent (measures 15–16). Notice that the head motive of the antecedent (measures 1–4) repeats itself in the consequent (measures 9–12). Once again, the consequent must transform its second half in order to create an authentic cadence from the antecedent's half cadence.

Sentence

A *sentence* has three parts: the *statement*, the *continuation*, and the *dissolution*. As a rule, the dissolution is the length of the statement and continuation combined.

STATEMENT AND CONTINUATION

The motives and harmonies of the statement and continuation relate as do the motives and harmonies of the period's antecedent and consequent. In fact, we might think of the statement–continuation pair as the antecedent and consequent of a brief period.

The Statement. Usually, the statement is one, two, or four measures long. It begins on I. The statement ends on either I or V. Two motives make up the statement: the *head motive* and the *tail motive*. Most statements are so brief as to contain little else.

The Continuation. The continuation begins on V or I. As a rule, it repeats, transposes, or otherwise varies the statement. It is the same length as the statement. It ends on I or V.

DISSOLUTION

The dissolution is the most complex of the three parts. It is at least twice the length of either the statement or continuation. It may be longer (by a multiple of two measures), but will seldom be shorter. Often, it is exactly twice the length of the statement. The dissolution serves two purposes.

The Dramatic Prolongation of V. As a rule, the dissolution cadences to V, setting up the repetition of the sentence or the introduction of some new idea. In either case, the dissolution's extended length combined with its motion toward V creates a modest sense of musical drama.

The Dissolution of the Motive. The dissolution "dissolves" the motives of the subject. Frequently, the dissolution begins with a contraction of one of the subject's motives (often the tail motive). The identifying characteristics of the motive (intervallic and rhythmic) gradually fall away until little more than intervallic or rhythmic residue remains.

The statement of Figure 15.15 moves from I to V. The continuation, using the same pair of motives, completes the motion from V to I. The dissolution begins a long half cadence (I–V) with the head motive. (The rhythm remains the same while the intervallic content is transformed.) Only the first three notes of the tail motive follow (measure 5, beat 1). The simple neighbor note figure is now transformed into a descending sixth. In measure 7, this tail motive is dissolved of all its rhythmic *and* intervallic aspects. As we reach the half cadence of measure 8, only the new descending sixth remains.

Figure 15.15   Mozart, Piano Sonata, K. 311; third movement

The following sentence is simpler.

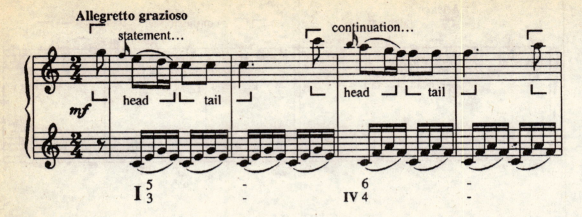

Figure 15.16   Mozart, Piano Sonata, K. 309; third movement

Statement and continuation each encompass but a single chord. (Notice, though, how the succession of those two chords points toward the cadential V of the dissolution.) This dissolution retains the head motive intact, but the repeated notes of the tail motive seem to reemerge only with the staccatissimo notes of the next-to-last measure.

Combined Types

Composers mix and combine such phrase types in many ways. We see two such combinations frequently.

THE DOUBLE PERIOD

Often two periods are paired together. The motivic structure of the resulting *double period* differs from that of the period proper. In the period proper, antecedent and consequent parallel each other motivically. The consequent sounds like both a repetition and a completion of the antecedent.

In the double period, however, the consequent functions more directly as the second half of the antecedent.

Figure 15.17   Mozart, Piano Sonata, K. 311; second movement

In Figure 15.17, the antecedent's head motive appears again only in the second antecedent. Thus the first full period serves as "antecedent" and the second full period as "consequent" of the double period.

THE DOUBLE SENTENCE

Often, a pair of sentences functions like the period pair of the double period. Here, as in the double period, the two parts (sentences, in this case) relate as antecedent to consequent, forming a larger period. To distinguish this type from the *double period*, we call it a *double sentence*.

Figure 15.18   Mozart, Piano Sonata, K. 330; third movement

In Figure 15.18, the statement–continuation pair of each sentence is identical. Notice, however, that although the dissolution of the first sentence leads to a half cadence (measure 8), the dissolution of the second sentence leads to an authentic cadence (measure 16). As a result, the first sentence sounds like the antecedent to the second sentence. The two sentences together form a complex period.

A motive is the smallest melodic unit that still retains its identity. A motive has two aspects: the intervallic and the rhythmic. Composers transform the motive through intervallic and rhythmic transformations.

Composers transpose motives by keeping the intervals the same but beginning on other scale degrees. They retrograde motives by reversing them in time. Composers invert motives by reversing the direction of each interval, thus producing a mirror image of the original melodic contour. These are the intervallic transformations.

Composers augment motives by uniformly increasing the length of the motive's original note values. They diminish motives by uniformly decreasing the length of the motive's original note values. These are the rhythmic transformations.

Motives and harmony combine to create the phrase. There are two basic phrase types: the period and the sentence.

The period has two symmetrical phrases: the antecedent and the consequent. Each is the same length. The antecedent ends on a tonicized V or on a half cadence. The consequent makes an authentic cadence to I. Both antecedent and consequent share the same motivic structure.

The sentence has three phrases. The third is the same length as the first two combined. The statement and continuation relate as antecedent to consequent. Although short, each is a complete motivic unit and expresses a clear harmonic position. The final dissolution begins with a central motive drawn from the statement/continuation pair. In a sustained prolongation of V, the dissolution gradually "dissolves" away the motives to a generic half cadence.

Composers often combine two periods in such a way that the first period relates to the second as antecedent to consequent. In this double period, the motivic relationship between the consequent and antecedent of each period is less direct.

Composers sometimes combine two sentences in such a way that the first sentence relates to the second as antecedent to consequent. We call this structure a double sentence. In the double sentence, the second dissolution makes an authentic cadence to I.

Selected Readings

Bamberger, Jeanne Shapiro, and Howard Brofsky. *The Art of Listening: Developing Music Perception.* 5th ed. New York: Harper & Row, 1988. Chapters 6–7.

Christ, William, et al. *Materials and Structure of Music.* 3d ed. Vol. I. Englewood Cliffs, NJ: Prentice-Hall, 1980. Chapter 22.

Cooper, Paul. *Perspectives in Music Theory.* 2d ed. New York: Harper & Row, 1981. Chapters 6 and 18.

Kostka, Stefan, and Dorothy Payne. *Tonal Harmony.* 2d ed. New York: Alfred A. Knopf, 1989. Chapter 8.

Ottman, Robert W. *Elementary Harmony.* 4th ed. Englewood Cliffs, NJ: Prentice-Hall, 1989. Chapter 14.

Schoenberg, Arnold. *Fundamentals of Musical Composition.* Edited by Gerald Strang and Leonard Stein, London: Faber and Faber, 1982. Chapters 1–8.

———. *Structural Functions of Harmony.* Rev. ed. Edited by Leonard Stein, New York: Norton, 1969. Chapter 11.

Westergaard, Peter. *An Introduction to Tonal Theory.* New York: Norton, 1976. Chapter 8.

16

Diatonic Sequences

When we repeat a musical pattern transposed up or down to another scale degree, we create a sequence. Sequences built upon unaltered scale degrees are diatonic sequences. Most often, diatonic sequences serve to delay V or prolong I.

STRUCTURE AND FUNCTION OF THE SEQUENCE

Sequences serve two functions: they help create tension by delaying the arrival of an important harmony; they allow musical tension to unwind by expanding and prolonging a harmonic goal.

A sequence has two parts: the *sequential unit* and the *sequential progression*.

The Sequential Unit

The musical figure that we repeat is the *sequential unit*. As a rule, sequential units move by step or by third. They can ascend or descend.

The Sequential Progression

Each sequential unit contains a pair of chords called the *sequential progression*.

We distinguish among four basic diatonic sequences (see Figure 16.1).

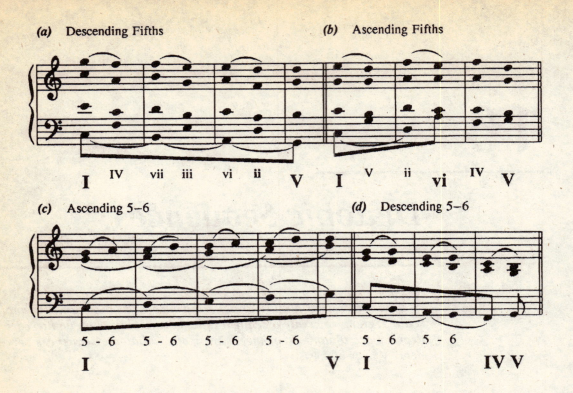

Figure 16.1   Basic Diatonic Sequences

Notice that the sequential *units* of Figures 16.1a, 16.1b, and 16.1c move up or down by step. (In the examples, the sequential units are separated by bar lines.) That is, each measure of these three examples is transposed down (or up) by step in each of the following measures. The sequential *progressions*, however, move by fifths (Figures 16.1a and 16.1b) or by a combination of thirds and fifths (Figure 16.1c). That is, the root progression of the succeeding chords is by fifth or thirds and fifths.

In contrast, the sequential unit of Figure 16.1d moves down by thirds. The sequential progression, however, moves by a combination of fifths and seconds.

As a rule, *descending sequences are more goal-oriented than ascending sequences*. Hence, most sequences descend. As a rule, *sequential motion by descending step creates the strongest voice leading*. Hence, most sequences descend by step.

TYPES OF DIATONIC SEQUENCES

Sequences that progress between scale degree triads are *diatonic sequences*. A diatonic sequence gets its name from its sequential progression. Figure 16.1a is a *descending-fifth sequence* since the root progression between chords is by descending fifth. Remember, though, the sequential unit of this descending-fifth sequence moves by descending *seconds*.

Sequential Motion by Step

DESCENDING FIFTHS

The most common diatonic sequence is by descending fifths. The voice leading of each descending fifth mimics the voice leading of a dominant–tonic progression.

> *Remember:* Only the roots of the sequential progression move by descending fifths.

Ordinarily, the bass does not move *literally* by descending fifths. It might move a fifth down and then a fourth up, still maintaining all chords in root position. Often, one or both of the chords in the sequential progression may appear in inversion.

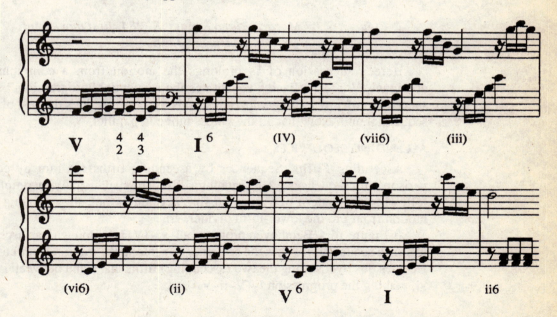

Figure 16.2   *Mozart, Piano Sonata, K. 545: first movement, measures 62–67*

The sequence in Figure 16.2 prolongs the tonic by moving from I *to* I with a cycle of descending fifths. Note that the first chord of each measure is in first inversion, providing a stepwise motion into the root of the second chord of each unit. This adds special emphasis to the root position chord on the third beat of each measure. As a result, the final I of the sequence arrives in root position—even though the sequence begins on I⁶.

DESCENDING $\frac{6}{3}$

A succession of descending $\frac{6}{3}$s can function sequentially. They form the simplest sort of diatonic sequence. In a descending $\frac{6}{3}$ sequence, both the sequential unit *and* the sequential progression move by step.

Figure 16.3   Mozart, Piano Sonata, K. 284; first movement, measures 93–96

Here a succession of $\frac{6}{3}$s prolongs the motion from a contrapuntal dominant (V⁶) to I⁶. Each $\frac{6}{3}$ constitutes the sequential "progression." The succession of 7–6 *appoggiaturas* descends by step—as does the rest of the sequential unit. Note that all the voices move in parallel.

ASCENDING SEQUENCES

Ascending Fifths. Sequences by ascending fifths are rare by comparison with sequences by descending fifths. They are usually incomplete, following the pattern of Figure 16.1b. As often as not, they prolong the motion from I to the lower-third divider, vi.

In Figure 16.4, Beethoven prolongs a I–vi–IV–I motion with an ascending-fifth sequence. He uses the sequence to prolong the motion from I to vi. He does this by inserting the two (ascending) fifths that stand between I and vi, making the progression I–(V–ii–VI♯).

Figure 16.4   Beethoven, Seven Bagatelles, Op. 33, No. 2

Why the major triad on VI? The first unit moves from I to its upper-fifth divider, V (measures 1–4). The second unit does the same (measures 5–8). If ii is the "tonic" of this unit, then vi must become a major triad in order to act as "dominant" of ii. In effect, then, VI♯ tonicizes the ii that precedes it. The ii–VI♯–IV progression, then, sounds like a i–V♯–III deceptive progression in ii, D minor. This is still a diatonic sequence—despite the altered note. Why? Because the root progression is by scale degrees. That is, the *progression* is diatonic.

Notice that Figure 16.4 has two sequential units, each occupying four measures. The second unit transposes the first *up* by a step. Each unit contains two harmonies (I–V, ii–VI♯), with the roots of each ascending by fifth to the next.

Ascending 5–6. Ascending 5–6 sequences arise even less often than ascending fifth sequences. When they do arise, they will, as a rule, follow the pattern outlined in Figure 16.1c.

m. 259

Figure 16.5   Mozart, Piano Concerto, K. 488; first movement (piano solo)

In Figure 16.5, Mozart expands a prominent IV with an ascending 5–6 sequence. He arrives on IV in the first measure shown. That IV then ascends by sequential 5–6s back to I. Once on I, it returns to the root position IV on which it began and continues where it left off. The sequential unit is a half note long. Each unit ascends by step.

Sequential Motion by Thirds

Sequences by descending thirds move from I through the lower-third divider (vi or IV⁶) to the lower-fifth divider (IV or ii⁶). Ordinarily, this motion precedes a move to the dominant.

DESCENDING $^6_3$S

We often see descending $^6_3$s paired to create a sequence of descending thirds.

Figure 16.6   Mozart, Piano Sonata, K. 283; first movement, measures 115–121

Figure 16.6 begins with a succession of $^6_3$s embellished by 7–6 suspensions (measures 1–2). An embellished version of the same progression follows immediately (measures 4–5). The sequential unit of this second sequence (X) descends by thirds to the lower-fifth divider and then to the dominant: I–vi–IV–V.

DESCENDING 5–6

The sequential progression of the descending 5–6 ascends by fifth and then descends by step. The sequential unit descends by thirds. We find a classic example of this sequence in Mozart's final opera *Die Zauberflöte* (*The Magic Flute*).

Figure 16.7   Mozart, Die Zauberflöte: *Act I, No. 5, "Drei Knäbchen"*

As the bass moves by step from $\hat{1}$ to $\hat{1}$ an octave lower, $\frac{5}{3}$s alternate with $\frac{6}{3}$s to support it. The final I$\frac{5}{3}$ moves into a half cadence on V.

Sequences in the Minor

Because of the altered pitch classes in the minor, sequences become more complex. Minor sequences can function as they would in the major, making allowances for altered notes.

Figure 16.8   Mozart, Piano Sonata, K. 310: third movement, measures 88–96

This motion from i to i through a cycle of descending fifths is almost identical to Figure 16.3, above. Notice that Mozart alters scale degrees only when necessary. That is, he avoids alterations except at the beginning and the end as V approaches i. As a result, III is momentarily tonicized.

Composers often focus a minor sequence on the relative major, III. For example, descending- and ascending-fifth sequences often outline the upper-third divider (III) in a move to V. When they do, they frequently follow the pattern shown in Figure 16.9.

(a) Ascending Fifths   **(b)** Descending Fifths

Figure 16.9   Sequences by Fifth in the Minor

Notice that in ascending-fifth sequences in the minor, the sequence *begins* on the third divider (see Figure 16.9a). The descending-fifth sequence in the minor, however, *ends* the sequence on the third divider (see Figure 16.9b). In both cases, III is momentarily tonicized.

*D*iatonic sequences move by seconds or thirds. The most common motion is downward by second.

    Descending-fifth sequences are the strongest and most common. They expand I to V. Descending 5–6 sequences, though less common, serve a similar function.

    Ascending-fifth and 5–6 sequences are rare. Ascending-fifth sequences often serve to expand the lower-third divider on its way to IV.

    In the minor, sequences often center around the relative major (III) in its role as upper-third divider between i and V.

Selected Readings

Aldwell, Edward, and Carl Schachter. *Harmony and Voice Leading*. 2d ed. 2 vols. New York: Harcourt Brace Jovanovich, 1989. Chapter 17.

Benjamin, Thomas, Michael Horvit, and Robert Nelson. *Techniques and Materials of Tonal Music*. Belmont, CA: Wadsworth, 1992. Part II, Section 16.

Ottman, Robert W. *Elementary Harmony*. 4th ed. Englewood Cliffs, NJ: Prentice-Hall, 1989. Chapter 16.

Piston, Walter. *Harmony*. 5th ed. Revised and expanded by Mark DeVoto. New York: Norton, 1987. Chapter 19.

17

Modal Mixture

T*onality recognizes two modes: major and minor. To make the minor mode work tonally, however, we must borrow scale degrees from the parallel major. This creates stronger and more coherent voice leading from $\hat{7}$ to $\hat{1}$ and, when necessary, from $\hat{6}$ to $\hat{7}$. However, certain elements of the minor mode provide even better voice leading than the major. Composers frequently borrow these elements from the minor mode to enhance voice leading in the major. This technique is called modal mixture. (Some theorists refer to the technique as borrowing—as in "borrowing from the minor.")*

When borrowing scale degrees from the parallel major or minor, be careful to spell the altered scale degree properly. In addition, treat any cross-relations that result from modal mixture with care.

MODAL MIXTURE IN THE MAJOR

Composers frequently borrow two scale degrees from the parallel minor. These borrowings enhance voice leading by providing half step (rather than whole step) upper-neighboring notes to $\hat{5}$ and $\hat{2}$.

Lowered $\hat{6}$

In the minor, $\hat{6}$ stands a half step above $\hat{5}$. It provides a much stronger neighbor to $\hat{5}$ than major $\hat{6}$. Composers frequently borrow this lowered $\hat{6}$ from the minor for use in compositions otherwise in the major mode.

Bach Chorales

Figure 17.1   Borrowed $\hat{6}$ in the Major

MINOR iv

In Figure 17.1a, Bach enhances the bass motion $\hat{6}$–$\hat{5}$ by inserting the lowered $\hat{6}$ (borrowed from the parallel minor) between diatonic $\hat{6}$ and $\hat{5}$. The iv^6 supported by this lowered $\hat{6}$ is now a minor triad. Notice two things about Figure 17.1a.

First, Bach spells the borrowed $\hat{6}$ *as* a $\hat{6}$—that is, as a kind of A, the sixth scale degree of C. Since A-flat and G-sharp are enharmonically equivalent, G-sharp would have provided the same pitch. However, G-sharp is the *wrong scale degree.* It is not the sixth scale degree of C but the fifth. Only some kind of A can function as $\hat{6}$ in C. Second, notice how Bach treats the cross-relation between diatonic $\hat{6}$ and lowered $\hat{6}$, keeping it in the same voice (see chapter 13).

DIMINISHED ii

In Figure 17.1b, Bach intensifies the $\hat{5}$–$\hat{6}$–$\hat{5}$ neighbor motion in the tenor by introducing a borrowed (or lowered) $\hat{6}$. The ii $^6_5$ that supports this borrowed $\hat{6}$ becomes a diminished triad as a result.

Notice that Bach avoids *all* cross-relations in this example. There is no diatonic $\hat{6}$ next to the borrowed $\hat{6}$ in any voice. Notice also that he spells the borrowed scale degree as D-flat, *not C-sharp.* The sixth scale degree in F must be some sort of D.

FULLY DIMINISHED vii^7

In Figure 17.1c, borrowed $\hat{6}$ once again intensifies the voice leading to $\hat{5}$. Bach supports this $\hat{5}$ with the tonic triad, however. As a result, he supports the borrowed neighbor ($\hat{6}$) with a voice leading chord to I. This makes borrowed $\hat{6}$ the diminished seventh of a fully diminished vii^7.

Major VI

We might think of the iv^6 of Figure 17.1a, the ii$^6_5$ of Figure 17.1b, and the vii^7 of Figure 17.1c as "borrowed" chords. Each duplicates the equivalent scale degree chord of the parallel minor. Another such borrowed chord functions prominently in tonal music. This is borrowed VI.

In the minor, $\hat{6}$ not only stands in a stronger voice-leading relation to $\hat{5}$ but also supports a stronger chord. In the minor, VI is a major triad. This makes of the deceptive cadence in the minor a dramatic deception indeed. The final VI is major, and it stands just a half step above the major V that precedes it. (See chapter 9 for a further discussion of VI in the minor mode.)

Composers often borrow this sixth scale degree from the minor to create an especially dramatic deceptive cadence in the major.

Bach Chorales

(a) No. 267   *(b)* No. 322   *(c)* No. 24

Figure 17.2   Borrowed $\hat{3}$ and $\hat{6}$

In Figure 17.2a, a routine authentic cadence comes to a dramatic deceptive cadence above borrowed—that is, lowered—$\hat{6}$. Notice that Bach also borrowed $\hat{3}$ (tenor A-flat) from the parallel minor to create the proper perfect fifth above lowered $\hat{6}$.

Lowered $\hat{3}$

In the minor, $\hat{3}$ stands a half step above $\hat{2}$. It provides a stronger neighbor to $\hat{2}$ than major $\hat{3}$. Occasionally, composers borrow lowered $\hat{3}$ from the minor to enhance the voice leading to $\hat{2}$.

"IV ^{7}"

In Figure 17.2b, a borrowed $\hat{3}$ (B-flat) intensifies the bass $\hat{3}$–$\hat{2}$ motion. A $^4_2$ results above that borrowed $\hat{3}$. This might be an applied V$^4_2$ of vii. It is not, however, for it fails to tonicize the vii^6 that follows. (As a diminished triad, vii^6 cannot be heard as "tonic.") Rather, it arises from borrowing and serves only to intensify a bass $\hat{3}$–$\hat{2}$–$\hat{1}$ progression. (Notice that, once again, Bach keeps the cross relation in the same voice.)

DIMINISHED vii ^{7} OF V

Borrowed $\hat{3}$ often does serve to intensify a tonicization of V, however. In Figure 17.1c, Bach uses borrowed $\hat{3}$ as the seventh of a vii^7 of V. This creates a fully diminished seventh above this applied vii.

Notice that Bach keeps the cross relation in the same voice. Note as well that he spells borrowed $\hat{3}$ as a third scale degree—that is, as a kind of F.

The Subtonic in the Major

Remember that, in the minor, we keep the lowered form of $\hat{7}$ (the subtonic) when it descends. Use the leading tone (raised $\hat{7}$) only when ascending to $\hat{1}$. We can borrow this subtonic scale degree from the parallel minor to intensify a motion *down* from $\hat{1}$. This often results in a minor triad above $\hat{5}$.

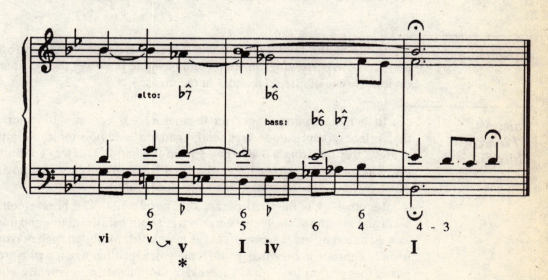

Figure 17.3   Bach, Chorale 279

This chorale ends with a grand plagal cadence below a tonic pedal (soprano B-flat). Note the V (marked with an asterisk) that precedes I. A borrowed $\hat{7}$ (alto A-flat) replaces the expected leading tone. Why? Because that $\hat{7}$ does not function as a leading tone but as the upper neighbor of $\hat{6}$. Now, the plagal iv that follows uses borrowed $\hat{6}$ (G-flat) as an intensified upper neighbor to $\hat{5}$. When $\hat{7}$ returns as a passing note to $\hat{1}$ (bass, measure 2), Bach *still* uses the borrowed form—presumably to avoid the augmented second that would otherwise result.

This cadence is tonally ambiguous. Is it a plagal cadence borrowed from B-flat minor? Or is it a half cadence (i–V♯) in E-flat minor? Perhaps the text will help.

The cadence arises above the word *büssen* ("atone" or "remedy"). Allow us to atone for the suffering and pain brought on the world by our sins, pleads the sinner. Is the hard-won tonic B-flat of the last measure an "atonement" for all the "sufferings" (borrowed from the parallel minor) in the earlier bars? Or does the tonal ambiguity point out the impossibility of such an atonement? Perhaps a study of the rest of Cantata 48, the source of this chorale setting, would help us decide, but that is beyond the scope of this text.

MODAL MIXTURE IN THE MINOR

Raised $\hat{6}$ and $\hat{7}$

In the minor, both altered $\hat{6}$ and $\hat{7}$ are, in effect, borrowings from the major. These borrowings make the minor mode possible. (See chapter 9 to review the use of altered $\hat{6}$ and $\hat{7}$ in the minor.)

Raised $\hat{3}$ ("Picardy Third")

In fact, these borrowings from the major are so common in minor works that minor compositions frequently end on a *major* tonic. Composers achieve this by using a $\hat{3}$ borrowed from the parallel major. Traditionally, musicians call a borrowed $\hat{3}$ in the final tonic of a minor composition a *Picardy third*. (The origin of this name is obscure.)

Figure 17.4 is the final phrase of Chorale 324. The phrase combines sixth and seventh scale degrees drawn from both parallel major and minor—as well as a startling borrowed $\hat{3}$ in the last chord. Although such borrowings usually enhance good voice leading, the voice leading here is awkward. The bass arpeggiation to $\hat{1}$ ((a) in the example) clashes dramatically with the raised-$\hat{7}$ neighbor in the alto. (Both $\hat{1}$ and its lower neighbor sound simultaneously!) At *(b)*, the raised $\hat{6}$ needed for the applied V^{6}_{5} of V creates a jarring cross-relation with the preceding bass diatonic $\hat{6}$. (Note that the cross-relation moves the "wrong" way—from an outer voice *to* an inner voice, from a strong voice to a weak one!) What is going on here?

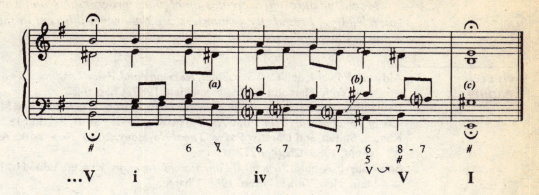

Figure 17.4   Bach, Chorale 324

Again, we must look to the text. In this last phrase, the sinner pleads, "Jesus protect me [from the storm and stress of life]." The Picardy third at *(c)* arises above the word *decken* ("protect," "guard"). Is the borrowed $\hat{3}$ intended to make up for—redeem, perhaps—the "storm and stress" of this awkward voice leading? Although the music itself raises it, this question can never really be answered.

*T*o *intensify voice leading, composers often substitute scale degrees from the parallel mode. The result is modal mixture. The scale degrees most often borrowed—in major and minor—are $\hat{3}$, $\hat{6}$, and $\hat{7}$.*

In the major, a $\hat{6}$ borrowed from the parallel minor functions as an intensified upper neighbor to $\hat{5}$. It is often supported by a minor iv or diminished ii as voice-leading chords to V. Less frequently, borrowed $\hat{6}$ serves as the seventh above a vii^7 voice-leading motion to I.

In the major, borrowed $\hat{3}$ serves as an intensified upper neighbor to $\hat{2}$—often as the seventh above an applied vii of V. It serves as well as the fifth of a sixth-scale-degree triad borrowed from the minor. Built on borrowed $\hat{6}$, borrowed VI functions most often in deceptive cadences.

Composers occasionally borrow the subtonic from the parallel minor. This lowered $\hat{7}$ intensifies the voice leading to $\hat{6}$. Sometimes this results in a minor triad above $\hat{5}$. We should not confuse this minor v with the major V that serves as upper-fifth divider. Minor v serves merely to enhance local voice leading.

In the minor, composers regularly use borrowed $\hat{6}$ and $\hat{7}$ from the major. The tendency of the minor to move to the major finds expression in the so-called Picardy third as well. A $\hat{3}$ borrowed from the parallel major provides a major I at the final cadence of a composition otherwise in the minor mode.

Modal mixture often creates ambiguous progressions and chromatic voice leading. Frequently, composers use the drama inherent in this technique to illustrate texts.

Selected Readings

Aldwell, Edward, and Carl Schachter. *Harmony and Voice Leading*. 2d ed. 2 vols. New York: Harcourt Brace Jovanovich, 1989. Chapter 22.

Benjamin, Thomas, Michael Horvit, and Robert Nelson. *Techniques and Materials of Tonal Music*. Belmont, CA: Wadsworth, 1992. Part II, Section 15.

Kostka, Stefan, and Dorothy Payne. *Tonal Harmony*. 2d ed. New York: Alfred A. Knopf, 1989. Chapter 21.

Schoenberg, Arnold. *Structural Functions of Harmony*. Rev. ed. Edited by Leonard Stein. New York: Norton, 1969. Chapter 7.

18

Chromatic Voice Leading to V

Composers often embellish a motion to the dominant with chromatic voice-leading harmonies. These harmonies arise when standard approaches to V transform themselves with chromatic passing notes. Such harmonies both delay and reinforce the arrival on the dominant by making the approach longer and the voice leading stronger. This chapter discusses two such chromatic approaches to the dominant: the augmented sixth chord and the Neapolitan $\frac{6}{3}$.

AUGMENTED SIXTH CHORDS

In Figure 18.1, root-position VI moves directly to root-position V. Bach embellishes the repeated alto D with a chromatic lower neighbor (marked by the asterisk). This 7–6 motion turns the root-position VI into what looks like an altered iv^6. The unaltered iv^6 commonly serves as a neighboring chord to V in the minor since the bass of iv^6 ($\hat{6}$) is a half step upper neighbor to the root of V ($\hat{5}$).

Figure 18.1   Bach, Chorale 19

But this new chord is not *really* a iv. When that 7 "resolves" to 6 it does not resolve to the diatonic $\hat{4}$, but to ♯$\hat{4}$ instead. The root, C, has been raised to C-sharp. An augmented sixth results (E-flat–C-sharp). This augmented sixth provides both a lower and an upper half-step neighbor to $\hat{5}$.

The augmented sixth between lowered $\hat{6}$ and raised $\hat{4}$ arises in several different harmonic guises. However, *the basic voice leading is the same in each*: the augmented sixth itself is usually formed above the bass. The augmented sixth resolves outwards, lowered $\hat{6}$ resolving *down* to $\hat{5}$ and raised $\hat{4}$ resolving *up* to $\hat{5}$.

The Italian $\frac{6}{3}$

Traditionally, musicians call the augmented sixth chord that arises as an altered "iv⁶" the *Italian $\frac{6}{3}$* or *Italian sixth*. (The augmented sixth chord of Figure 18.1 is an Italian sixth.) In addition to the augmented sixth, the Italian $\frac{6}{3}$ contains $\hat{1}$—the third above the bass. Never double the notes of the augmented sixth itself in *any* augmented-sixth chord. In the Italian $\frac{6}{3}$, double the third above the bass instead. As a rule, then, the Italian sixth arises from a chromatic passing motion above iv⁶ (see Figure 18.2).

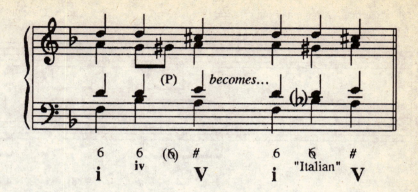

Figure 18.2   Origin of Figure 18.3

In Figure 18.3, Mozart contracts this chromatic motion, dropping $\hat{4}$ and retaining only the raised $\hat{4}$ (marked in the example with a left-pointing arrow).

Figure 18.3   Mozart, Piano Sonata, K. 280: third movement, measures 99–104

The augmented sixth (between bass B-flat and treble G-sharp) obliterates the harmonic identity of the iv^6. In fact, the Italian $^6_3$ that results is no longer even a triad, being neither a diminished, minor, major, or augmented triad. The Italian $^6_3$ *and all augmented sixth chords* are pure voice-leading chords; they result entirely from linear embellishments.

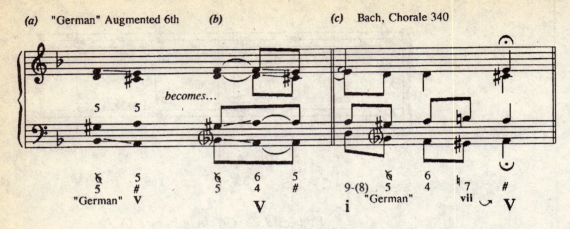

Figure 18.4   German $\frac{6}{5}$

The German $\frac{6}{5}$

To intensify further the voice leading to V, composers frequently build an augmented sixth chord from the iv$\frac{6}{5}$. The so-called *German $\frac{6}{5}$* or *German sixth* results. The German $\frac{6}{5}$ adds a lowered $\hat{3}$ to the Italian $\frac{6}{3}$. This lowered $\hat{3}$ stands a perfect fifth above the lowered $\hat{6}$ bass. The augmented sixth of the German $\frac{6}{5}$ resolves outward to $\hat{5}$ in both voices—as it does in the Italian sixth. However, resolving lowered $\hat{3}$ to $\hat{2}$ at the same time creates parallel perfect fifths (see Figure 18.4a).

For this reason, the German sixth usually resolves first to a cadential $\frac{6}{4}$ and *then* to the V $\frac{5}{3}$ (see Figure 18.4b). In Figure 18.4c, Bach resolves the German $\frac{6}{5}$ to the expected $\frac{6}{4}$. However, he intensifies the resolution of the $\frac{6}{4}$ to V $\frac{5}{3}$ with an applied vii[7] of V.

In free composition, the resolution of the German $\frac{6}{5}$ is more flexible. In Figure 18.5, Mozart simply sidesteps the parallel-fifth problem. He moves from the four-voice texture above the German $\frac{6}{5}$ to a three-voice texture at its resolution.

*Figure 18.5   Mozart, Piano Sonata, K. 284: first movement,
measures 105–107*

By leaving out the fifth of V (E) in the last measure, Mozart eliminates the parallel fifths that would result from its presence. The major mode requires that Mozart lower diatonic $\hat{6}$ (B becomes B-flat) to create the augmented sixth of Figure 18.5. (Notice that Mozart must also lower $\hat{3}$ to F-natural to obtain the perfect fifth above lowered $\hat{6}$ (B-flat) as well as the half-step upper neighbor to $\hat{2}$.)

At the resolution, Mozart moves to three voices. This allows the bass of the augmented sixth (B-flat–G-sharp) to resolve to octave $\hat{5}$s (A) in the left hand. The third above the bass ($\hat{1}$, D) resolves down to the leading tone ($\hat{7}$, C-sharp) in the right hand. Since Mozart does not resolve the fifth above the bass (lowered $\hat{3}$, F-natural) directly, there are no parallel fifths! Naturally, this solution is only available in free style, where the number of voices varies with the context. *In chorale style, the German* $^6_5$ *should resolve to a* $^6_4$ *above* $\hat{5}$.

> *Remember:* The German $^6_5$—like the other augmented sixth chords—is *not* an altered iv $^6_5$. It is not a triad at all, but a pure voice-leading harmony. (We will discuss the German $^6_5$ further in chapter 19.)

The French $^4_3$

The least common augmented sixth type, the so-called *French* $^4_3$ adds $\hat{2}$ itself to the Italian $^6_3$. This creates an apparent $^4_3$ above the bass. Though the result looks like an altered ii $^4_3$, it is not. Once again, this is no triad at all, but a pure voice-leading harmony. The French $^4_3$ adds an augmented fourth ($\hat{2}$) above the lowered $\hat{6}$ bass. This $\hat{2}$ remains as a common note in the resolution to V. As a result, the French $^4_3$—like the Italian $^6_3$—may resolve directly to V.

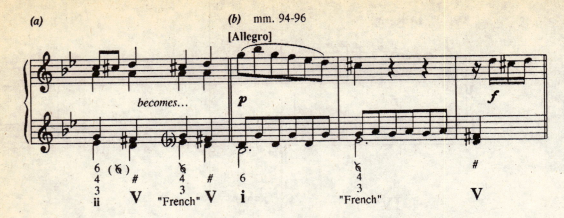

Figure 18.6   Mozart, Piano Sonata, K. 570; first movement

In Figure 18.6a, we can see how a French $\frac{4}{3}$ arises from a diatonic ii $\frac{4}{3}$ by way of the chromatic passing note between soprano $\hat{4}$ and $\hat{5}$. In Figure 18.6b, an Italian $\frac{6}{3}$ becomes a French $\frac{4}{3}$ with the added upper-neighbor note (A) in the left hand. The augmented sixth (bass E-flat–soprano C-sharp) resolves to $\hat{5}$ (D) in both voices. The third above the bass, $\hat{1}$ (G), resolves down to $\hat{7}$ (F-sharp). (The fourth above the bass, A, would remain as a common note if Mozart had not left the fifth out of the V triad to which it resolves.)

We have a much more complex situation in Figure 18.7. Here the bass descends chromatically to $\hat{5}$. Bach supports the final bass motion (lowered $\hat{6}$–$\hat{5}$) with a French $\frac{4}{3}$.

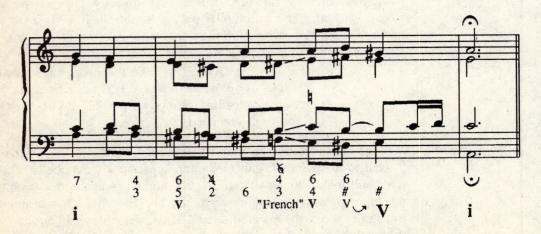

Figure 18.7   Bach, Chorale 146

But Bach delays the V. The French $\frac{4}{3}$ moves first to the cadential $\frac{6}{4}$. It then moves to an applied V^6 of V before finally resolving to V itself. (This is similar to Bach's treatment of the German sixth in Figure 18.4c.)

THE NEAPOLITAN SIXTH (PHRYGIAN II)

Another common chromatic embellishment of V arises from an altered ii^6. Compare the progressions in Figures 18.8a and 18.8b.

Figure 18.8   Bach, Chorale 262

We can see how Bach contracts two chromatic passing notes (Figure 18.8a, tenor and alto) into an altered "ii^6". In fact the new harmony (called a *Neapolitan* $\frac{6}{3}$ or *Phrygian II*) is a major triad built on lowered $\hat{2}$. Two powerful upper neighbors result, to $\hat{1}$ (lowered $\hat{2}$) and $\hat{5}$ (lowered $\hat{6}$).

We see this Neapolitan $\frac{6}{3}$ again in Figure 18.9. The flatted $\hat{2}$ in the soprano (measure 2, first beat) resolves down to $\hat{1}$ in a $\frac{6}{4}$ above $\hat{5}$ (measure 3, first beat).

Figure 18.9   Mozart, Variations on a Minuet by Duport, K. 573;
Variation VI

However, the Neapolitan $^6_3$ of Figure 18.10 moves directly to V. Flatted $\hat{2}$ moves directly to the leading tone ($\hat{7}$). A melodic diminished third (soprano, B-flat–G-sharp) results. This linear dissonance eventually resolves both the B-flat and the G-sharp to $\hat{1}$ (A).

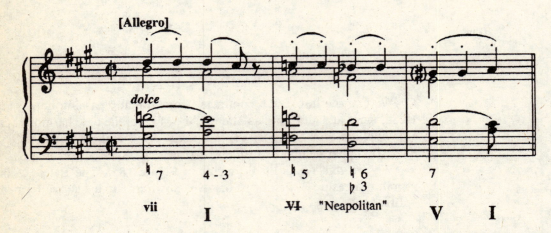

Figure 18.10   Mozart, Six Variations on an Allegretto, K. 137;
Variation VI

To avoid this diminished third, *Neapolitan $^6_3$s usually resolve to a cadential $^6_4$* (as in Figures 18.8 and 18.9).

An augmented sixth arises between a lowered $\hat{6}$ bass and a raised $\hat{4}$ in an upper voice. It serves as a chromatic voice-leading approach to $\hat{5}$. In the augmented sixth, both the lowered $\hat{6}$ and the raised $\hat{4}$ resolve to $\hat{5}$. Three types of augmented sixth chords appear: Italian, French, and German. All three share the augmented sixth as well as that note a third above the bass.

An Italian $^6_3$ arises from an altered iv^6. It resolves directly to V. The third above the bass ($\hat{1}$) resolves to $\hat{7}$ as both notes of the augmented sixth resolve outward to $\hat{5}$.

The German $^6_5$ adds a perfect fifth above the bass to the Italian $^6_3$. This altered "iv$^6_5$" usually resolves to a cadential $^6_4$. This avoids the parallel fifths that would result from a direct resolution to V.

The French $^4_3$ arises from an altered ii$^4_3$. It adds an augmented fourth above the bass to an Italian $^6_3$. The French $^4_3$ resolves directly to V; the added fourth ($\hat{2}$) remains as a common note between the French $^4_3$ and V.

The Neapolitan $^6_3$ arises from the major triad built on lowered $\hat{2}$. Placed in first inversion, it functions as a chromatic voice-leading chord to V. Because lowered $\hat{2}$ moves naturally to $\hat{1}$, the Neapolitan $^6_3$ ordinarily moves first to the cadential $^6_4$ before resolving to V $^5_3$.

Selected Readings

Aldwell, Edward, and Carl Schachter. *Harmony and Voice Leading.* 2d ed. 2 vols. New York: Harcourt Brace Jovanovich, 1989. Chapters 28–29.

Benjamin, Thomas, Michael Horvit, and Robert Nelson. *Techniques and Materials of Tonal Music.* Belmont, CA: Wadsworth, 1992. Part III, Sections 4 and 5.

Christ, William, et al. *Materials and Structure of Music.* 3d ed. Vol. II. Englewood Cliffs, NJ: Prentice-Hall, 1980. Chapter 5.

Cooper, Paul. *Perspectives in Music Theory.* 2d ed. New York: Harper & Row, 1980. Chapters 20 and 21.

Kostka, Stefan, and Dorothy Payne. *Tonal Harmony.* 2d ed. New York: Alfred A. Knopf, 1989. Chapters 22 and 23.

Piston, Walter. *Harmony.* 5th ed. Revised and expanded by Mark DeVoto. New York: Norton & Company, 1987. Chapters 26 and 27.

19

Other Chromatic Voice-Leading Chords

Chromatic voice leading serves mainly to prolong or intensify diatonic harmonies. Many chromatic voice-leading harmonies prolong a scale-degree triad by providing chromatic neighbors above a pedal point bass. They intensify a diatonic chord by delaying that chord's arrival or by providing dissonant chromatic alterations that require further resolution. Although the individual chords may appear complex, their functions are, for the most part, straightforward.

ALTERED DIATONIC HARMONIES

Occasionally, we see diatonic triads altered chromatically to intensify their voice-leading function.

Augmented Triads

When the fifth of a major triad rises by step to a chord tone of the next chord, we can intensify that step with a chromatic passing note.

Figure 19.1   Voice-Leading Origin of the Augmented Triad

In the second measure of Figure 19.1a, a tonic triad moves to a vii[7]. The upper voice rises by step. To intensify this motion, Mozart inserts a chromatic passing tone (D-sharp). A transient augmented triad (the asterisk) results. In Figure 19.1b, a I[6] moves to IV. The soprano intensifies its stepwise ascent with a chromatic passing note (C-sharp). For a moment that I[6] becomes an augmented triad (at the asterisk). Notice that in both these cases, *the augmented fifth created by the chromatic passing note resolves up by step*. Mozart decorates the resolution of the C-sharp (Figure 19.1b) with an upper neighbor (E) to the note of resolution (D).

In Figure 19.2, the augmented triads (marked with asterisks) take on a more independent character. Notice that, when the augmented triad is an independent harmony, the fifth still resolves up by step. Notice also that the voice leading of Figure 19.2 is the same as in Figure 19.1, though more prolonged. The augmented fifth ($\sharp\hat{2}$) arises from an unsupported diatonic $\hat{2}$ on its way to $\hat{3}$.

Translation: "A fairy tale. . ."

Figure 19.2   Liszt, "Die Lorelei"

Altered Dominants

Composers sometimes contract such a progression, omitting the diatonic fifth and retaining only the chromatic (augmented) fifth. Frequently, the dominant receives an augmented fifth in this way.

AUGMENTED V AND V⁷

Figure 19.3 presents such a case. Wolf raises $\hat{2}$ (C) to intensify the neighbor note motion around $\hat{3}$ (D). A root-position augmented triad above each V results.

Wolf places the passing augmented V of Figure 19.1 in an accented position here, omitting the diatonic V altogether. In the augmented V$^6_5$ that begins the Figure 19.3, we have *two* dissonant voice-leading motions to $\hat{3}$—from the augmented fifth (#$\hat{2}$–$\hat{3}$) and from the seventh ($\hat{4}$–$\hat{3}$). (See measure 2, beat 4 of Figure 19.4 as well for an augmented V⁷—this one in root position.)

Translation: "O receive me"

Figure 19.3   Wolf, "Mühvoll komm'ich und beladen"
("Troubled I come, and heavy laden")

DIMINISHED V [7]

Occasionally, we may see a diminished triad on V. The lowered fifth (lowered $\hat{2}$) functions as a chromatic upper neighbor to $\hat{1}$. More often than not, such diminished dominants arise in $\frac{4}{3}$ position, the lowered $\hat{2}$–$\hat{1}$ motion in the bass. In this position, they function purely as voice-leading chords, not as altered dominants. (We will discuss these diminished $\frac{4}{3}$s below, in "Augmented Sixths to Degrees Other than V.")

CHROMATIC VOICE-LEADING HARMONIES

Chromatic voice leading flourished in the nineteenth century. When dealing with such music (and the techniques abstracted from it), we must constantly keep in mind the linear origin of these harmonies.

Apparent Seventh Chords

In Figure 19.4a, consider the chord on the first beat of measure 3 (the question mark).

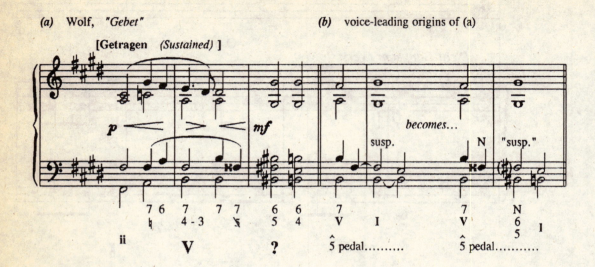

Figure 19.4   *Apparent Seventh Chords*

Taken in isolation, this chord appears to be a G-sharp dominant seventh in first inversion. But does it make any sense to consider this a dominant built on G-sharp? In context, no. Such an artificial dominant would arise to tonicize a C-sharp triad, vi in E major. It does not; it resolves instead to a $^6_4$ above $\hat5$, B. What is this G-sharp dominant seventh, then? Is it an applied dominant gone bad?

A simpler solution suggests itself. In Figure 19.4a, a V^7 (measure 2) resolves to I (measure 3, third beat) above a dominant ($\hat5$, bass B) pedal (see the voice-leading reduction of Figure 19.4a in 19.4b). The apparent G-sharp dominant seventh chord results from chromatic voice leading between the V^7 that precedes it and the I that follows. Wolf chromatically alters a simple suspension and dominant pedal point by providing each with a chromatic upper neighbor.

That a chord might look like one thing but be another seems a paradox. But it is not, really. It merely reminds us once again that tonal music does not arise from chords strung one after the other like beads on a string. Rather, it arises from linear progressions that unfold the tonic triad. In understanding this music, we will find it more useful to decipher the *function* of a particularly chord than to worry about how to name or label it.

Special Uses of the Augmented Sixth

Augmented sixth chords are a perfect example of the ambiguity of labels. We have seen how such chords intensify the approach to V by providing $\hat{5}$ with both its chromatic neighbors. Eventually, composers began to use the augmented sixth chord to intensify the approach to other scale degrees as well. In identifying a chord as "augmented sixth chord," we have done little until we determine in what way that particular chord *functions* as an augmented sixth chord—that is, how the chromatic alterations arise from voice leading.

AUGMENTED SIXTHS TO DEGREES OTHER THAN $\hat{5}$

The simplest and most direct application of the augmented sixth is to intensify a degree other than V. The most common application is to $\hat{1}$ itself.

Figure 19.5   Schubert, Quintet, Op. 163, D. 956; fourth movement

Here Schubert supplies both chromatic neighbors (bass D-flat, soprano B-natural) in a final motion to $\hat{1}$, the tonic. This $\frac{4}{3}$ above D-flat resolves like an augmented sixth—but here, it moves to the tonic rather than the dominant. We know that augmented sixths usually precede V. How can an augmented sixth resolve to $\hat{1}$? Why does it not make the tonic sound like a dominant?

The expected chord in measure 3 is, of course, V^7. In fact, we might consider this next-to-last chord an altered V—one with a diminished fifth (D-flat). All the voice leadings of the upper voices function as if supported by $\hat{5}$ in the bass. (The leading tones resolve up to $\hat{1}$; the "seventh," F, resolves down to $\hat{3}$.) So what should we call this chord? An "altered V $\frac{4}{3}$" or an "augmented sixth to $\hat{1}$"? Does it really matter?

Not if we understand the function. This harmony (whatever we call it) serves to prolong the tonic harmony that surrounds it. It provides half-step neighbors to its root and third. However, to call this a "V" might be misleading. The harmony seems to arise from chromatic linear motions, not from a root progression by fifth. For that reason, we might prefer to think of it as a French augmented sixth chord—that is, a *pure* voice-leading chord rather than a scale-degree triad.

AUGMENTED SIXTHS ABOVE A TONIC PEDAL

Augmented sixths intensify a prolongation of I in other ways as well. In Figure 19.6 we have an augmented sixth to $\hat{5}$—that is, the usual type of augmented sixth chord. And although the augmented sixth itself (A-flat–F-sharp) does resolve to $\hat{5}$, that $\hat{5}$ is supported by the tonic triad. As a result, this augmented sixth serves as a chromatic embellishment of the tonic triad. (Some theorists call this common chromatic embellishment a *common-note augmented sixth.*)

Schubert, *"Am Meer"*
[**Sehr Langsam** *(Very slow)*]

Figure 19.6   Augmented Sixths above a Tonic Pedal

We see this type of augmented sixth chord once again in Figure 19.7. Here, however, the embellishing augmented sixth arises only gradually from the tonic.

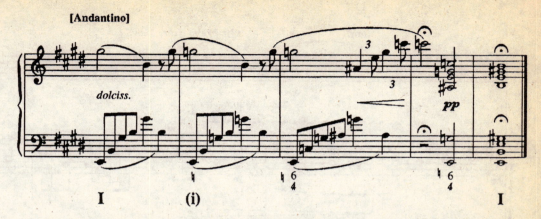

Figure 19.7   Liszt, "Freudvoll und Leidvoll" *("Joyful and woeful")*

First Liszt lowers 3̂ (soprano, measure 2), creating a minor i. Retaining lowered 3̂, Liszt then substitutes both chromatic neighbors of 5̂ for 5̂ itself (measures 3–4). By the fermata, the augmented sixth (A-sharp–C-natural) is completely formed. In the final two chords, Liszt resolves the augmented sixth back into I.

Note that the "augmented sixth" has become a diminished third; that is, it has been inverted. The resolution remains the same, however. Both notes of the diminished third—just like those of the augmented sixth—resolve to 5̂—here, C-natural–B and A-sharp–B. All this happens above a tonic (E) pedal as an intensification of the final, cadential I of the composition.

GERMAN SIXTH AND DOMINANT SEVENTH

A German augmented sixth, if respelled, becomes a dominant seventh. (Recall that an augmented sixth is enharmonically equivalent to a minor seventh. See Figure 19.10, page 233.) Composers have found this fact very useful, as we will soon see. The student, however, may find that it creates a certain amount of confusion, as well.

German Sixth as Apparent Dominant Seventh. Figure 19.8 is one of the boldest and most striking uses of the German augmented sixth in the literature.

Translation: ["I have now kissed] your mouth."

Figure 19.8   Richard Strauss, Salome; *final scene (piano reduction)*

As the upper line unfolds a glittering C-sharp major tonic, the lower voices move to a startlingly dissonant dominant seventh on A. This sonority makes no sense as a "dominant seventh," however. (Where is the D triad that it would tonicize?) We must look elsewhere for a voice-leading explanation.

Figure 19.9   Enharmonic spelling of Figure 19.8

By comparing Figure 19.9 with 19.8, we can see that, in fact, this dominant seventh on A is simply an enharmonic spelling of the same common-note augmented sixth that we have just discussed. (The G-natural is "really" an F-double sharp that resolves to G-sharp.) Even the bass motion from C-sharp to A-natural and back does not obscure the augmented-sixth-like voice leading of this progression.

This striking effect arises from the drama. Salome, having received John the Baptist's severed head on a silver platter, kisses the bloodied lips. The moment is *both* voluptuous and repulsive. A more vivid musical representation is difficult to imagine. (The squeamish may be relieved to learn that immediately after this moment of high drama, Herod orders Salome crushed beneath his soldiers' shields and the opera ends.)

German Sixth as Enharmonic Dominant Seventh. Composers frequently use the enharmonic identity of the German augmented sixth and dominant seventh as a means of modulation. For example, a chord that arises as an augmented sixth can—through respelling—become a dominant seventh in a new key area. Or, conversely, a dominant seventh can—through respelling—become a German augmented sixth to a dominant in a new key area.

Translation: ["...drops of purple] become thee: but child-like dost thou..."

Figure 19.10 Wolf, "Auf eine Christblume" ("To a Christmas Flower")

In measure 1 of Figure 19.10, a chromatic progression in G-flat leads to a dominant seventh in that key. In the last eighth of measure 1, Wolf respells the seventh (C-flat) as B-natural. This pitch is no longer a minor seventh above D-flat, but an augmented sixth. Thus, instead of resolving like a V^7 to I in G-flat, it resolves like a German augmented sixth. As spelled, this German sixth points to V in F major. In measure 2, it resolves to the dominant of F major effecting a sudden modulation to F.

Diminished Sevenths above a Tonic Pedal

Frequently, the diminished seventh functions purely as a chromatic voice-leading chord. This use is similar to the augmented sixth above a tonic pedal discussed above.

COMMON-NOTE DIMINISHED SEVENTHS

The so-called *common-note diminished seventh* arises from a neighbor note motion around the tonic.

(a)   Mahler, *"Oft denk' ich"*
Ruhig bewegt, ohne zu eilen
(Tranquil, unhurried)

(b)   Schubert, Quintet, Op. 163, I (piano reduction)

Allegro ma non troppo

Figure 19.11   Diminished Seventh above a Tonic Pedal

In Figure 19.11a, we see a diminished $\frac{4}{2}$ above the bass $\hat{1}$. This diminished seventh arises from a pair of chromatic neighbor notes (F-sharp and A-natural) in the upper voice. In Figure 19.11b, a diminished $\frac{4}{3}$ arises from the same neighbor note motion around the tonic triad. The F-sharp (measure 3) arises and resolves as a chromatic lower neighbor to $\hat{5}$ (G). The E-flat (measure 3) arises and resolves as a chromatic lower neighbor to $\hat{3}$ (E-natural). Although the spelling of the common-note diminished triad is different in the two figures (the first, $\frac{4}{2}$; the second, $\frac{4}{3}$), the function of both is the same: a chromatic neighbor embellishment of the tonic.

LEADING-TONE DIMINISHED SEVENTH ABOVE TONIC PEDAL

In Figure 19.12a, we see a similar technique. Here, the chromatic neighbors around the tonic triad form a fully-diminished seventh on the leading tone. This harmony arises, however, above a tonic pedal.

(a) Schubert, *"Der greise Kopf"*   *(b)* Liszt, *"Mignons Lied"*

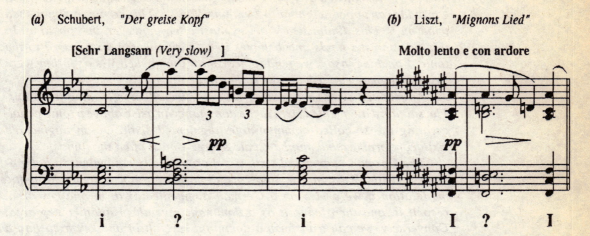

Figure 19.12   Leading-Tone Seventh Above a Tonic Pedal

In both excerpts, the fully diminished vii^7 arises from neighbor-note motion around the chord tones of a tonic triad (see Figure 19.13).

(a) Voice-leading analysis of Ex. 19-12a   *(b)* Voice-leading analysis of Ex. 19-12b

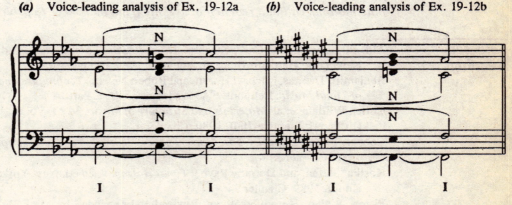

Figure 19.13   Voice-Leading Origin of Figure 19.12

If the fifth of a major triad ascends by step to the next chord, we can intensify that motion with a chromatic passing note. This chromatic passing note creates an augmented triad.

On occasion, V or V^7 arises with an augmented fifth. The augmented fifth (♯$\hat{2}$) intensifies a $\hat{2}$–$\hat{3}$ voice leading motion. Less frequently, a lowered $\hat{2}$ provides an upper neighbor to $\hat{1}$ within a V or V^7. This creates a diminished triad on $\hat{5}$. This diminished V arises most often, however, in $\frac{4}{3}$ position. In this position it sounds and behaves like an augmented sixth chord to the tonic. For this reason, we tend to hear most diminished V^{7}s as if they were French augmented sixth chords rather than altered Vs.

Augmented sixth chords serve several special voice-leading functions. The standard augmented sixth to the dominant can arise above a tonic pedal, creating the so-called common-note augmented sixth. Or an augmented sixth can form around another scale degree—most often the tonic.

The German augmented sixth is enharmonically equivalent to a dominant seventh. We can use this special property to create a chromatic modulation if we arrive on a German augmented sixth in one key area, respell it, and then leave it as a dominant seventh in another key area. Conversely, we can transform a dominant seventh in one key area into a German augmented sixth in another key area merely by respelling it.

Simultaneous neighbor note motions around the tonic triad occasionally produce apparent seventh chords. These apparent fully diminished sevenths arise above a tonic pedal. There are two common types. The common-tone diminished seventh creates a fully diminished seventh chord that incorporates the $\hat{1}$ pedal as a chord tone. The apparent vii^7 superimposes a fully-diminished vii^7 above the tonic pedal. Both types arise from neighbor-note motions within a rearticulated tonic triad and serve to prolong I.

Selected Readings

Aldwell, Edward, and Carl Schachter. *Harmony and Voice Leading.* 2d ed. 2 vols. New York: Harcourt Brace Jovanovich, 1989. Chapter 30.

Benjamin, Thomas, Michael Horvit, and Robert Nelson. *Techniques and Materials of Tonal Music.* Belmont, CA: Wadsworth, 1992. Part III.

Christ, William, et al. *Materials and Structure of Music.* 3d ed. Vol. II. Englewood Cliffs, NJ: Prentice-Hall, 1980. Chapter 4.

Cooper, Paul. *Perspectives in Music Theory.* 2d ed. New York: Harper & Row, 1980. Chapter 21.

Kostka, Stefan, and Dorothy Payne. *Tonal Harmony.* 2d ed. New York: Alfred A. Knopf, 1989. Chapter 24.

Piston, Walter. *Harmony.* 5th ed. Revised and expanded by Mark DeVoto. New York: Norton, 1987. Chapter 28.

Appendix A

PITCH CLASS NAMES AND OCTAVE DESIGNATIONS

Pitch Class Names

English	C	D	E	F	G	A	B
German	C	D	E	F	G	A	H
French	ut	ré	mi	fa	sol	la	si
Italian	do	re	mi	fa	sol	la	si
Spanish	do	re	mi	fa	sol	la	si

English	C-sharp	C-flat
German	cis	ces[1]
French	ut dièse	ut bémol
Italian	do diesis	do bemolle
Spanish	do sostenido	do bemol

[1] In German, B-flat is irregular. Instead of the expected **Hes**, it is **B** (pronounced "Hä"). The German **B**, therefore, translates into English as "B-flat."

English	C-double-sharp	C-double-flat
German	cisis	ceses
French	ut double-dièse	ut double-bémol
Italian	do doppio diesis	do doppio bemolle
Spanish	do doble sostenido	do doble bemol

Octave Designations

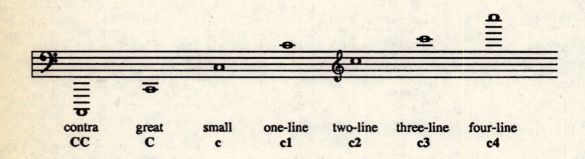

contra	great	small	one-line	two-line	three-line	four-line
CC	C	c	c1	c2	c3	c4

Appendix B

NOTE NAMES

American	Whole Note	Half Note	Quarter Note	Eighth Note[1]
English	semi-breve	minim	crotchet	quaver
German	Ganze Note	Halbe Note	Viertel Note	Achtel Note[2]
French	ronde [pause]	blanche [demi-pause]	noire [soupir]	croche[3] [demi-soupir]
Italian	semibreve	minima, or bianca	semiminima, or nera	croma[4]
Spanish	redonda	blanca	negra	corchea[5]

American	Sixteenth Note	Thirty-second Note	Sixty-fourth Note
English	semiquaver	demisemiquaver	hemidemisemiquaver
German	Sechzehntel	Zweiunddreissigstel	Vierundsechzigstel
French	double-croche [quart de soupir]	triple-croche [huitième de soupir]	quadruple-croche [seizième de soupir]
Italian	semicroma	biscroma	semibiscroma
Spanish	semicorchea	fusa	semifusa

[1] English speakers indicate the rest by substituting the word "rest" for "note" (that is, whole rest, half rest, and so on).

[2] To indicate a rest, German speakers replace *Note* with *Pause* (*Ganze Pause, Halbe Pause,* and so on).

[3] The French terms in brackets refer to the corresponding rest.

[4] In Italian, rests are indicated by the formulation *pausa di...* (*pausa de semibreve, pausa di minima,* and so on).

[5] In Spanish, rests are indicated by the formation *silencio de...* (*silencio de redonda, silencio de blanca,* and so on).

Appendix C

COMMON DYNAMIC AND ARTICULATION MARKINGS

Dynamic Markings

BASIC DYNAMICS

These are relative terms, ranged here from the softest to the loudest.

ppp (pianississimo)
pp (pianissimo)
p (piano)
mp (mezzo piano)
mf (mezzo forte)
f (forte)
ff (fortissimo)
fff (fortississimo)

VARIATIONS IN DYNAMICS

cresc. (crescendo) Gradually louder.
decresc. (decrescendo) Gradually softer.
dim. (diminuendo) Gradually softer.
fp (forte–piano) *Forte*, then suddenly *piano*

Basic Articulation Markings

= (staccato) short, brief	= short, hard accent
= (staccatissimo) very short	= (tenuto) broad, full value
= (accent) sharp attack, louder than current dynamic	= (marcato) accented and sustained
sfz or *sf* or *fz*	= (sforzando, sforzato; lit., forced) sudden, strong accent

Appendix D

TEMPO MARKINGS

Basic Tempo Markings

These are relative terms, ranged here from the slowest to the fastest. Each suggests a mode of performance as well as a relative speed.

Largo   Stately
Largamente   Broadly
Larghetto   The diminutive of *largo* and a bit faster
Grave   Serious, solemn
Lento   Slowly (often used as a temporary marking)
Adagio   Expressive (lit., "at ease")
Andante   Tranquil, quiet, flowing
Andantino   Slightly faster than *andante*
Moderato   Moderately (no affective character)
Allegretto   Animated (the diminutive of *allegro*)
Allegro   Lively, animated (lit., "cheerful")
Vivace   Vivacious, rapid
Presto   Quick, rapid
Prestissimo   The superlative of *presto*: as fast as possible

VARIATIONS IN TEMPO

Rubato Slight, expressive accelerations and retardations (lit., "robbed")

Accelerations

Accelerando   Gradual increase in speed
Affrettando   Hurriedly; temporary increase in speed
Doppio movimento   Twice as fast
Incalzando   With growing fervor
Più   More
Piú mosso, piú moto   More motion: suddenly faster
Poco a poco   Little by little
Veloce   Greatly increased speed
Velocissimo   Very fast

Retardations

Allargando   Broadening
Calando   Gradually slower and more subdued
Mancando   Slower and softer
Meno   Less
Meno mosso or *meno moto*   Less motion: suddenly slower
Morendo   Dying away
Rallentando, ritardando   Gradually slower
Ritenuto   Slower, temporarily
Smorzando   Smothering: slower, softer, gradually subdued

Appendix E

INTERVAL NAMES AND SIZES

**Interval Size
And Quality**

INTERVAL		QUALITY	HALF STEPS
UNISON	C-C	perfect	0
	C-C♯	augmented	1
SECOND	C-D♭♭	diminished	0
	C-D♭	minor	1
	C-D	major	2
	C-D♯	augmented	3
THIRD	C-E♭♭	diminished	2
	C-E♭	minor	3
	C-E	major	4
	C-E♯	augmented	5
FOURTH	C-F♭	diminished	4
	C-F	perfect	5
	C-F♯	augmented	6

INTERVAL		QUALITY	HALF STEPS
FIFTH	C-G♭	diminished	6
	C-G	perfect	7
	C-G♯	augmented	8
SIXTH	C-A♭♭	diminished	7
	C-A♭	minor	8
	C-A	major	9
	C-A♯	augmented	10
SEVENTH	C-B♭♭	diminished	9
	C-B♭	minor	10
	C-B	major	11
	C-B♯	augmented	12
OCTAVE	C-C♭′	diminished	11
	C-C′	perfect	12
	C-C♯′	augmented	13

Foreign Equivalents

LANGUAGE

	English	German	French	Italian	Spanish	Latin
C-C	unison	Prime	uni(sson)	prima	unísono	unisonus
C-D	second	Sekunde	seconde	seconda	segunda	tonus
C-E	third	Terz	tierce	terza	tercera	ditonus
C-F	fourth	Quarte	quarte	quarta	cuarta	diatesaron
C-G	fifth	Quinte	quinte	quinta	quinta	diapente
C-A	sixth	Sexte	sixte	sesta	sexta	tonus cum diapente
C-B	seventh	Septime	septième	settima	séptima	ditonus cum diapente
C-C′	octave	Oktave	octave	ottava	octava	diapason

Appendix F

INTERVAL INVERSIONS

This interval	. . .		inverts into	. . .		this interval.
UNISON	perfect	0	←→	12	perfect	**OCTAVE**
	augmented	1	←→	11	diminished	
SECOND	diminished	0	←→	12	augmented	**SEVENTH**
	minor	1	←→	11	major	
	major	2	←→	10	minor	
	augmented	3	←→	9	diminished	
THIRD	diminished	2	←→	10	augmented	**SIXTH**
	minor	3	←→	9	major	
	major	4	←→	8	minor	
	augmented	5	←→	7	diminished	
FOURTH	diminished	4	←→	8	augmented	**FIFTH**
	perfect	5	←→	7	perfect	
	augmented	6	←→	6	diminished	

Appendix G

TRIADS AND SEVENTH CHORDS

Triad Quality	Bottom Third	Top Third	Fifth
MAJOR	MAJOR	minor	perfect
Minor	minor	MAJOR	perfect
Diminished	minor	minor	diminished
AUGMENTED	MAJOR	MAJOR	AUGMENTED

Name of Seventh Chord (Less common name in parentheses)	Quality of Triad	Quality of Seventh
Dominant Seventh (MAJOR-minor)	MAJOR	minor
Major Seventh (MAJOR-MAJOR)	MAJOR	MAJOR
Minor Seventh (minor-minor)	minor	minor
Minor-major	minor	MAJOR
Half-diminished (diminished-minor)	diminished	minor
Full-diminished (diminished-diminished)	diminished	diminished

Appendix H

KEY SIGNATURES

Rule: Given a major key with a key signature in sharps, *the pitch a minor second above the last sharp is the tonic.*

Rule: Given a major key with a key signature in flats, *the second-to-last flat in the key signature is the tonic.* (Exception: F major, one flat.)

MAJOR KEYS

MINOR KEYS

Appendix I

THE QUALITY OF SCALE-DEGREE TRIADS

		I	II	III	IV	V	VI	VII
MAJOR		M	m	m	M	M	m	d
MINOR	"natural"	m	d	M	m	m	M	M
	"harmonic"	m	d	A	m	M	M	d
	"melodic"	m	m	A	M	M	d	d

M = major, **m** = minor, **d** = diminished, **A** = augmented

Appendix J

RULES FOR FIGURED BASS REALIZATION

1. The pitch classes generated by figures depend on the key signature.

2. A sharp before a figure *raises* the pitch class that it represents by a half step. A flat before a figure *lowers* the pitch class that it represents by a half step. A natural before a figure represents the unaltered form of the pitch class that distance from the bass.

3. An accidental standing alone (without a figure) applies to the *third* above the bass.

4. A slash through any part of a number requires that the pitch class represented by that number be raised by a half step.

5. Figures do not specify the disposition of the upper voices. In a $\frac{6}{4}$, say, the pitch class specified by the 4 can be above or below that specified by the 6 in any octave above the bass.

6. Abbreviated figures are as follows:

[no figure], 3, or 5 = $\frac{5}{3}$

$7 = \begin{smallmatrix} 7 \\ 5 \\ 3 \end{smallmatrix}$

$6 = \frac{6}{3}$

$\frac{6}{5} = \begin{smallmatrix} 6 \\ 5 \\ 3 \end{smallmatrix}$

$\frac{4}{3} = \begin{smallmatrix} 6 \\ 4 \\ 3 \end{smallmatrix}$

2 or $\frac{4}{2}$ = $\begin{smallmatrix} 6 \\ 4 \\ 2 \end{smallmatrix}$

7. A dash or dashes following a figure or a vertical group of figures indicate that the upper voices remain on the same notes and do not move as the bass moves to another note.

8. Frequently, two or more successive figures do not indicate different triads but only nonharmonic notes. For example, the 4–3 of *8.*, below, shows the suspension in the alto voice.

Appendix K

SCALES AND THE
DIATONIC COLLECTION

**Scales and
Collections**

We can visualize the distinction between scale and collection by thinking of the C major and A minor scales.

How do C major and A minor differ? They are ordered differently. In C major, C is the first scale degree, D is the second scale degree, and so forth. In A minor, however, *A* is the first scale degree and *B* is the second. In making this distinction we consider each an *ordered collection* of pitch classes: we give pitch classes in A minor different ordinal positions than we give the same pitch classes in C major.

Now, *what do C major and A minor have in common?* Both contain the same seven pitch classes—in this specific case, the "white notes." So one could say that C major and A minor represent different ordering of the same *un*-ordered collection of pitch classes, the "white notes." To put it another way, C major and A minor share the same unordered collection of pitch classes, but their orderings differ.

The unordered collection that these two scales share—and that every major scale shares with its relative minor—is the *diatonic collection*. Each major–relative minor key pair comprises a different diatonic collection.

We can construct a diatonic collection simply by constructing a major or pure minor scale. However, the diatonic collection (often referred to simply as "the diatonic") has a much more fundamental structure.

THE CYCLE OF PERFECT FOURTHS AND FIFTHS

If we begin on any pitch class, say F, and ascend or descend from this pitch class uniformly by perfect fourths or fifths (that is by units of five or seven half steps), after twelve steps we will pass through each of the twelve pitch classes (without repeating any) and, on the thirteenth try, return once again to our starting point (here, F).

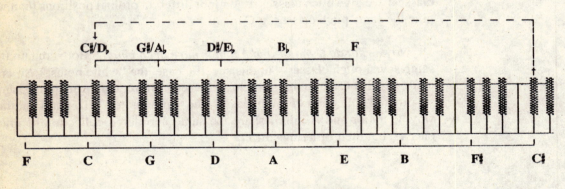

Cycle of Fifths

This cycle can be represented more clearly with a clock face in which we replace the twelve hours with the twelve pitch classes, ascending by fifths when read clockwise, by fourths when read counterclockwise.

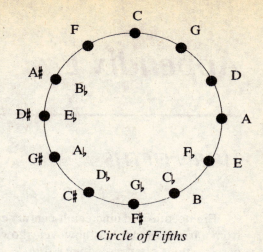

Circle of Fifths

Music students recognize this figure as the "circle of fifths" (although we might just as well call it the "circle of fourths"). The musical significance of this figure is not nearly as abstract as it might now seem.

Examine the pitch classes on the circle. Put one finger on F and another on B; now, look at the series of pitch classes that connect (clockwise) F to B. This is the white note collection, our prototypical diatonic collection. If you move both fingers one pitch class clockwise (or counterclockwise) you will find once again that the intervening pitch classes form another diatonic collection. In fact, *any group of seven adjacent positions on this circle will yield a unique diatonic collection.*

If you take the seven pitch classes from F clockwise to B (the "white note" diatonic) and then move one step clockwise, what happens? The F at one end is replaced by an F-sharp at the other: the C major/A minor diatonic has been replaced (going clockwise from C to F-sharp) by the G major/E minor diatonic—the first sharp key.

Now, if you had moved counterclockwise from the F to B diatonic, rather than replacing F with F-sharp, you would have replaced B with B-flat, thus replacing the C major/A minor diatonic with the F major/D minor diatonic— the first flat key.

Notice that the sharps progress in key signature sequence clockwise around the circle, and the flats progress counterclockwise. Thus, the circle of fifths is a convenient tool for learning and remembering key signatures, major/minor scales, and the concept of "closely related keys."

Appendix L

HORN FIFTHS

Eighteenth- and nineteenth-century composers seldom exclude the third from a triad. Figure L.1, however, shows an example of a significant class of exceptions often called *horn fifths*.

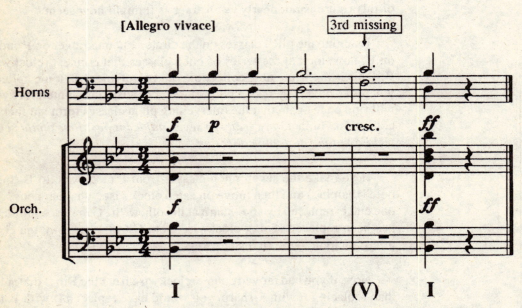

Figure L.1   Beethoven, Symphony No. 4, Op. 60; third movement

Composers occasionally support the soprano motion $\hat{2}$–$\hat{1}$ with a $\hat{5}$–$\hat{1}$ bass. The open fifth above the $\hat{5}$ suggests a dominant harmony with the third missing. The missing third imitates the natural (valveless) horn which is unable to produce the leading tone (the third of V). Whenever the leading tone is omitted in supporting $\overset{\wedge}{2}$, even by some other instrument, natural horns come to mind, and the technique takes on a certain pastoral character.

Such omitted thirds do not occur in chorale style but are frequent in instrumental works. The two Mozart excerpts that follow are characteristic.

Figure L.2   Mozart, Sonata, K. 570; second movement

Figure L.3   Mozart, Eight Variations, K. 352; *Variation VI*

Appendix M

FOUR BACH HARMONIZATIONS OF WERDE MUNTER, MEINE GEMÜTE

(Original in B-flat)

Figure M

Glossary

Terms defined elsewhere in the glossary are set in *italics*.

See Appendix C for a comparative glossary of common dynamic markings. See Appendix D for a comparative listing of common tempo markings.

Accent To stress one note in relation to another. An accent can be tonic, resulting from implicit harmonic or metrical emphasis; dynamic, resulting from an increase in relative loudness; agogic, resulting from greater relative length. The accent mark ( ) shows a dynamic accent.

Accidental A symbol used to alter the pitch of a note. There are five: *flat, sharp, double-flat, double-sharp*, and *natural*.

Alla breve Indicates that the half note represents the pulse. Associated today with $\frac{2}{2}$ time and often represented ₵ . See *cut time*.

Alto The second-highest voice in a four-voice texture, written on the treble staff with stems pointing down. *Alto* is also French for viola—the alto member of the violin family.

Alto clef The *clef* that locates middle C on the middle of the five lines.

Antecedent First phrase of a *period*. It ends with an authentic or half cadence.

Anticipation A rhythmic figuration in which the first of two notes a step apart moves to the second note early.

Applied chord Also called secondary chord. A chromatically altered triad or seventh chord that serves to tonicize a scale degree triad. It creates an artificial V, V^7, vii, or vii^7 that resolves to the tonicized degree or its substitute.

Appoggiatura A melodic figuration created when a voice leaps to an accented dissonance that then resolves by step. See *escape note*, *passing note*, *neighbor note*.

Arpeggiation Also called *chordal skip*. The motion of one voice between harmonic notes of the same triad.

Articulation The manner in which a pitch is initiated. Articulation marks indicate how a note is to be begun, sustained, and ended (see Appendix C).

Augmentation In traditional composition, to increase uniformly the durations of a motive. ♩ ♩ ♩ ♩ is an augmentation of ♪♪♪♩

Bar See *measure*.

Bass In general, the lowest-sounding voice of a texture. In chorale style, the lowest of the four voices, notated on the bass staff with stems descending.

Bass clef The *clef* that places the F below middle C on the second line from the top of the staff.

Beat See *pulse*.

Brio Italian for "spirit" or "dash," as in the performance direction *con brio*, suggesting a bright, rapid mode of performance.

Cadence The harmonic formula that completes a phrase. There are three basic types of cadences: authentic (V–I), plagal (IV–I), and half (I–V).

Cantabile Songlike.

Chorale Four-voice setting of a simple melody. In general, the four voices of a chorale move in rhythmic unison. The chorale style arose during the Reformation in settings of evangelical hymns. Bach's collected chorales (the so-called 371 Chorales) form one of the great monuments of Western musical art.

Chord The simultaneous presentation of three or more notes. See *interval, simultaneity*.

Chordal skip A type of melodic figuration in which one voice leaps between notes of the same chord. See *arpeggiation*.

Clef A symbol used to determine the name and pitch of the notes on the staff to which it is prefixed. Four clefs are used today: *treble, bass, alto*, and *tenor*.

Collection An unordered group of *pitch classes*. The white keys of the piano form the *diatonic collection*. See *mode, scale*.

Common time Another name for $\frac{4}{4}$ time, indicated

Composing out The process that extends and embellishes the tonic triad in time. Composing out is accomplished through the techniques of *unfolding* and *prolongation*.

Compound meter   A *meter* in which the pulse divides into three equal parts.

con   "With" in Italian, used in phrases such as *con fuoco* ("with fire"), *con brio* ("with dash"), *con moto* ("with motion"), and so on.

Conjunct motion   Melodic motion by step. See *disjunct motion*.

Consequent   Second *phrase* of a *period*. Usually, a consequent ends with an authentic cadence. See *antecedent, period, double period*.

Consonance   A relatively stable *note, interval,* or *chord*. In particular, there are two kinds of consonances: imperfect (thirds and sixths) and perfect (unisons, fourths, fifths, and octaves). This designation is not absolute, however. For example, harmonic consonances (unisons, thirds, fifths, sixths, and octaves) are distinct from linear consonances (major and minor seconds, thirds, and sixths; perfect fourths, fifths, and octaves). No diminished or augmented intervals are consonant.

Continuation   Second part of a *sentence*. It represents a motivic variant of the first part, the *statement*. See *period*.

Contrary motion   Motion in opposite directions. Given two voices, if the first moves in one direction while the second moves in the other direction, *contrary motion* results. See *parallel motion, similar motion, oblique motion*.

Cut time   *Alla breve*. Another name for $\frac{2}{2}$ time and indicated ¢

Diminution   In traditional compositional practice, to decrease uniformly the durations of a *motive*. ♪♪♪ ♩ is a diminution of 𝄽 ♩ ♩ ♩ ♩

Disjunct motion   Melodic motion between notes more than a *step* apart. See *conjunct motion*.

Dissolution   Third part of the *sentence*. It follows the *statement* and *continuation* and is as long as both combined. As a rule, the dissolution takes the main motives of the statement and continuation and strips them of their characteristic features.

Dissonance   Any *note, interval* or *chord* that is relatively unstable and impelled to motion. Seconds, sevenths, and all augmented and diminished intervals are traditionally dissonant. This designation is not absolute, however. A fourth, for example, is dissonant when formed with the *bass*, but otherwise consonant. Sevenths and augmented and diminished intervals remain dissonant in a linear context, whereas major and minor seconds are linear consonances.

Dolce   Sweetly, softly.

Dolcissimo   Superlative of *dolce*.

Dominant   The fifth scale degree ($\hat{5}$). The triad built on the fifth scale degree (V) is the dominant triad.

Doppio movimento "Twice as fast." Often associated with *cut time* or *alla breve*.

Dotted note A note value created by placing a dot after a basic note value. The dot increases the value of the basic note value by one half. ♩. equals ♩ ♪

Double flat An *accidental* that lowers the pitch of a note by a whole step.

Double period Two *periods* combined to form a larger phrase. The two periods relate to each other as *antecedent* to *consequent*.

Double sharp An *accidental* that raises the pitch of a note by a whole step.

Doubling Occurs when the same pitch class appears in more than one voice of a chord.

Escape note A type of melodic figuration in which a voice leaps away from an unaccented dissonance that has been approached by step.

Espressivo, con espressione Expressively.

Fifth The distance between two notes standing five lines and spaces (counted inclusively) apart. Also, that member of a *triad* that stands a fifth above the *root*.

First inversion See *harmonic inversion*.

Flat An *accidental* that lowers the pitch of a note by a half step.

Frequency The rate of vibration of a uniformly resonating body.

Fundamental See *harmonic*.

Grazioso Gracefully.

Half step The smallest interval, a minor second.

Harmonic Both a general acoustic phenomenon and a specific application of this phenomenon to stringed instruments. A vibrating body creates many pitches. Generally, the pitch of the lowest frequency is the pitch that we perceive. It is the first harmonic and is called the *fundamental*. Other pitches are present in the sound as well. The frequency of each is a whole-number multiple of the fundamental frequency. Each of these is a harmonic. The first harmonic is the fundamental; the second harmonic has a frequency twice that of the fundamental; the third harmonic has a frequency three times that of the fundamental and so on. Stringed instrument players can produce thin, flutelike sounds by artificially creating these subdivisions of the string. These sounds are called harmonics. See *overtone*.

Harmonic inversion Placing some other pitch class than the root as the lowest note of a triad or seventh chord creates an inversion of that triad or seventh chord. First inversion has the third in the bass; second inversion has the fifth in the bass; third inversion has the seventh in the bass. See *inversion, intervallic inversion, melodic inversion*.

Interval The distance between two notes. We may measure the diatonic interval (that is, the distance measured in terms of lines and spaces) or the absolute interval (the distance measured in number of half steps). In tonal music, both measurements are necessary to specify an interval fully.

Intervallic inversion Placing the bottom pitch class of an interval on top. See Appendix F.

Inversion There are three types of inversion: *harmonic inversion, intervallic inversion*, and *melodic inversion*.

Isometric A type of rhythm in which every duration is a multiple or fraction of a *pulse* and in which pulses are organized into *measures* of equal length. As a rule, the *rhythm* of tonal music is isometric.

Key The major or minor scale on which a tonal composition is based.

Key signature The collection of sharps or flats placed on the staff after the clef that tells us the basic collection of pitch classes on which a tonal composition is based.

Keyboard style A variant of chorale style designed for keyboard performance. Soprano, alto, and tenor are all notated on the treble staff, while only the bass is notated on the bass staff. In keyboard style, the tenor range is extended and the restriction on voice overlaps is loosened.

Leading tone The seventh scale degree ($\hat{7}$) in the major; the raised seventh scale degree in the minor. The triad built upon the leading tone (or raised seventh scale degree in the minor) is the leading tone triad (vii).

Ledger lines Horizontal lines placed above or below the staff used to extend the staff, sometimes spelled leger.

Ma "But," as in *ma non troppo*, "but not too much."

Measure Sometimes *bar*. A metrical unit made up of a collection of pulses.

Mediant The third scale degree ($\hat{3}$) on which the mediant triad (iii or III) is built.

Melodic inversion The creation of a mirror image of a motive or melody by reversing the direction of its intervals.

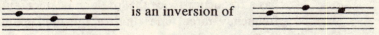 is an inversion of

Meter The organization of pulses into units of equal duration. There are two kinds of meter: *simple meter* and *compound meter*.

Meter signature Also *time signature*. A fraction placed after the key signature at the beginning of a composition that designates the nature of the pulse and the number of beats in a measure.

Middle C   That C found in the middle of the piano keyboard, usually beneath the pianomaker's name.

Mode   A collection of pitch classes ordered from low to high. The same collection of pitch classes can generate several modes simply by changing the beginning note.

Motive   The smallest melodic unit that still retains its identity. As a rule, we may identify a motive by either its rhythmic or intervallic structure.

Neighboring note   A melodic figuration that embellishes a repeated harmonic note by inserting the note a step above or a step a below between the repeated notes.

Non   "Not," as in *non troppo*, "not too much."

Note   A symbol that represents a relative duration and, when placed on a staff, a particular pitch.

Note name   See *pitch class*.

Oblique motion   Occurs when one voice moves while another stays in the same place. See *parallel motion, similar motion, contrary motion*.

Octave   The *interval* formed when two notes stand eight lines and spaces apart (counted inclusively).

Overtone   Any *harmonic* above the fundamental. Thus, the first overtone is the second harmonic.

Parallel motion   Occurs when voices move in the same direction by the same interval. See *similar motion, oblique motion, contrary motion*.

Partial   See *harmonic*.

Passing note   A melodic figuration that fills in the gap between the two notes of an arpeggiation with the intervening note (or notes).

Period   A basic phrase structure that consists of two phrases of equal length: the *antecedent* and the *consequent*.

Phrase   A dependent division of a melody, like a clause in prose.

Pickup   Colloquial name given to the incomplete beat (or measure) that begins a phrase or composition.

Pitch   The auditory sensation of relative highness or lowness created by a sound of discrete frequency.

Pitch class   Any one of the twelve different pitches that divide the octave, as well as their octave duplications. When we talk about all C's, in general, we are discussing a pitch class. When we talk about, say, middle C, we are discussing a pitch.

Progression   Can be either harmonic or melodic. A harmonic progression is a directed succession of harmonies. A melodic progression is one that fills in a melodic interval in the process of *composing out* that interval.

Prolongation   Extending the arpeggiation of a triad through techniques of melodic and harmonic figuration.

Pulse   Also called *beat*. The beat or regular subdivision that we sense beneath most tonal music. That to which we tap our feet.

Quality   The characteristic size of an *interval* or *triad*, as indicated by the terms *diminished*, *minor*, *major*, and *augmented*.

Realization   Fleshing out, as in realizing a figured bass—that is, completing it in four voices.

Rearticulation   The repetition of a note or chord, usually in preparation for some form of embellishment.

Register   The relative range of an instrument, voice, or composition. The register of the flute is high relative to the register of the tuba.

Resolution   When a relatively dissonant *note, chord,* or *interval* moves to a relatively consonant note, chord or interval.

Retrograde   To reverse a motive.

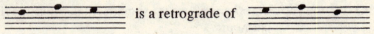

Rhythm   A succession of durations. See *meter, pulse, tempo.*

Root   The *pitch class* on which a triad is built. If we arrange the pitch classes of a triad such that they stand a third and a fifth above the lowest note, the lowest note is the root of that triad. Do not confuse *root* with *bass*.

Root position   When the notes of a triad are so disposed that the root is the lowest-sounding pitch, that triad is in root position. See *harmonic inversion.*

Scale   A *collection* of pitch classes so ordered that each pitch class has a functionally different position within that ordering.

Secondary Dominant   See *applied chords.*

Second inversion   See *harmonic inversion.*

Semitone   Half step.

Semplice   Simply, without affectation.

Sentence   A basic phrase structure with three parts: *statement, continuation,* and *dissolution*. The last part is as long as the first two combined.

Sharp   An *accidental* that raises the pitch of a note by a half step. ♯

Similar motion Voices moving in the same direction but by different intervals. See *parallel motion, oblique motion, contrary motion*.

Simple meter A meter in which the pulse is divided into two equal parts.

Skip Motion by an interval greater than a *step*.

Soprano In a four-voice texture, the highest voice. Written on the *treble staff* with stems ascending.

Sound An auditory sensation created by changes in atmospheric pressure made by a vibrating body. In the West, a musical sound has three components: pitch, timbre, and duration.

Spirito Spirit, verve, as in *con spirito* ("with spirit").

Staff Also, *stave* (pl., staves). The five horizontal lines on which we notate music.

Statement The first phrase of a *sentence*.

Stave See *staff*.

Step The distance from a line to an adjoining space or from a space to an adjoining line.

Subdominant The fourth scale degree ($\hat{4}$) upon which the subdominant triad (IV or iv) is built.

Subject The melodic theme of a complex musical form such as a fugue.

Submediant The sixth scale degree ($\hat{6}$), on which the submediant triad (vi or VI) is built.

Supertonic The second scale degree ($\hat{2}$) upon which the supertonic triad (ii) is built.

Suspension A type of rhythmic figuration in which the first of two notes a step apart delays the arrival of the second note.

Syncopation In a regular pattern of strong and weak beats, the displacement of a strong beat to where a weak beat should be.

Tempo The relative speed of the *pulse* of a musical work. See Appendix D.

Tenor In a four-voice texture, the next-to-lowest voice. Notated on the bass staff with stems ascending.

Tenor clef The *clef* that places middle C on the second line from the top of the staff.

Theme The main or primary melody or *motive* of a musical work. A musical work may have several themes.

Third The interval between two notes that are on either adjacent lines or spaces. Also, that member of a *triad* that stands a third above the *root*.

Tie The curved line that connects two note heads of the same pitch and joins their durations together.

Timbre The quality of sound that distinguishes one instrument from another.

Time signature   See *meter signature*.

Tonality   The *key* of a musical work, as well as the complex harmonic and melodic system that supports it.

Tone color   See *timbre*.

Tonic   The first scale degree ($\hat{1}$) and the note upon which the tonic triad (I or i) is built.

Tonicization   The treatment of a scale degree other than the tonic as if it were the tonic. Two types of tonicization are possible: melodic and harmonic. A melodic tonicization might tonicize a scale degree by providing it with an artificial leading tone. On the other hand, a harmonic tonicization tonicizes a scale degree by approaching it from an *applied chord*.

Treble clef   The *clef* that places G above middle C on the second line from the bottom of the staff.

Triad   The basic harmonic unit of tonal music. The triad has three pitch classes: the *root, the third*, and the *fifth*. The third stands a third above the root; the fifth stands a fifth above the root. See Appendix G.

Tritone   The interval of six half steps.

Troppo   "Too much," as in *non troppo* ("not too much").

Unfolding   Prolonging a harmony over time by arpeggiating it.

Unison   The interval between two notes written on the same line or space.

Voice leading   The art of controlling the relationship between voices in a multivoice texture.

Whole step   The interval of two half steps.

Index